Changing on the Fly

Critical Issues in Sport and Society

Michael A. Messner, Douglas Hartmann, and Jeffrey Montez de Oca, Series Editors

Critical Issues in Sport and Society features scholarly books that help expand our understanding of the new and myriad ways in which sport is intertwined with social life in the contemporary world. Using the tools of various scholarly disciplines, including sociology, anthropology, history, media studies and others, books in this series investigate the growing impact of sport and sports-related activities on various aspects of social life as well as key developments and changes in the sporting world and emerging sporting practices. Series authors produce groundbreaking research that brings empirical and applied work together with cultural critique and historical perspectives written in an engaging, accessible format.

Rachel Allison, *Kicking Center: Gender and the Selling of Women's Professional Soccer*

Jules Boykoff, *Activism and the Olympics: Dissent at the Games in Vancouver and London*

Diana Tracy Cohen, *Iron Dads: Managing Family, Work, and Endurance Sport Identities*

Cheryl Cooky and Michael A. Messner, *No Slam Dunk: Gender, Sport, and the Unevenness of Social Change*

Jennifer Guiliano, *Indian Spectacle: College Mascots and the Anxiety of Modern America*

Kathryn E. Henne, *Testing for Athlete Citizenship: Regulating Doping and Sex in Sport*

Jeffrey L. Kidder, *Parkour and the City: Risk, Masculinity, and Meaning in a Postmodern Sport*

Alan Klein, *Lakota Hoops: Life and Basketball on Pine Ridge Indian Reservation*

Michael A. Messner and Michela Musto, eds., *Child's Play: Sport in Kids' Worlds*

Jeffrey Montez de Oca, *Discipline and Indulgence: College Football, Media, and the American Way of Life during the Cold War*

Joshua I. Newman, Holly Thorpe, and David L. Andrews, eds., *Sport, Physical Culture, and the Moving Body: Materialisms, Technologies, Ecologies*

Stephen C. Poulson, *Why Would Anyone Do That?: Lifestyle Sport in the Twenty-First Century*

Courtney Szto, *Changing on the Fly: Hockey through the Voices of South Asian Canadians*

Nicole Willms, *When Women Rule the Court: Gender, Race, and Japanese American Basketball*

Changing on the Fly

Hockey through the Voices of South Asian Canadians

COURTNEY SZTO

Rutgers University Press

New Brunswick, Camden, and Newark, New Jersey, and London

Library of Congress Cataloging-in-Publication Data

Names: Szto, Courtney, author.
Title: Changing on the fly : hockey through the voices of South Asian Canadians /
    Courtney Szto.
Description: New Brunswick, New Jersey : Rutgers University Press, 2020. | Series: Critical
    issues in sport and society | Includes bibliographical references and index.
Identifiers: LCCN 2020004892 | ISBN 9781978807938 (paperback) |
    ISBN 9781978807945 (cloth) | ISBN 9781978807952 (epub) | ISBN 9781978807969 (mobi) |
    ISBN 9781978807976 (pdf)
Subjects: LCSH: Hockey—Social aspects—Canada. | South Asians—Canada—Social
    conditions. | South Asians—Cultural assimilation—Canada. | National characteristics,
    Canadian.
Classification: LCC GV848.4.C2 S97 2020 | DDC 796.9620971—dc23
LC record available at https://lccn.loc.gov/2020004892

A British Cataloging-in-Publication record for this book is available from the British Library.

♾ The paper used in this publication meets the requirements of the American National
Standard for Information Sciences—Permanence of Paper for Printed Library Materials,
ANSI Z39.48-1992.

www.rutgersuniversitypress.org

Manufactured in the United States of America

This book is dedicated to the late Patti Hillman, the first teacher who encouraged me to challenge my assumptions about the way the world works (by telling me, "I don't care where you sit!") and for letting the writer in me flourish. And, to my late mother, Lynn Szto, the greatest cheerleader a daughter could have. I miss you every day.

Contents

Acronyms

AHL	American Hockey League
ASHL	Adult Safe Hockey League
BCHL	British Columbia Hockey League
CBC	Canadian Broadcasting Corporation
CHL	Canadian Hockey League
CIS	Canadian Interuniversity Sport
CRTC	Canadian Radio-Television and Communications
CSSHL	Canadian Sport School Hockey League
CWHL	Canadian Women's Hockey League
DIY	do-it-yourself
EBM	evidence-based medicine
ECHL	East Coast Hockey League
ESPN	Entertainment and Sports Programming Network
FARE	Football Against Racism in Europe
HHOF	Hockey Hall of Fame
HIFE	Hockey is for Everyone
HNIC	Hockey Night in Canada
MLB	Major League Baseball
MVP	Most Valuable Player
NBA	National Basketball Association
NCAA	National Collegiate Athletic Association
NFL	National Football League
NHL	National Hockey League
NSWC	North Shore Winter Club
NWHL	National Women's Hockey League
OHL	Ontario Hockey League
QMJHL	Quebec Major Junior Hockey League

Title IX	Title IX of the Education Amendments Act of 1972
TSN	The Sports Network
UHL	United Hockey League
USHL	United States Hockey League
USTA	United States Tennis Association
WHL	Western Hockey League
WNBA	Women's National Basketball Association
WPHL	Western Professional Hockey League

Changing on the Fly

Introduction

The first thing I wanted to be as a child was a National Hockey League (NHL) goaltender. It never occurred to me that none of the NHL players looked like me, either in race or gender. I am unsure as to whether naivety, precociousness, or poor observational skills made such a dream possible. Alternatively, my dream could have stemmed from a national mythology that told me I could be anything that I wanted to be and that hockey was a game for Canadians, the only identity I really knew at the time. It would take many years for me to really engage with the idea that hockey is not yet for everyone, despite the NHL's attempt to literally sell the idea that "Hockey is for Everyone."

This point was driven home by an incident that occurred years later while I was working as a part-time sales associate at the national sporting goods chain, Sport Chek. I helped many Canadian children participate in the hallowed national tradition of ice hockey through the fundamental step of buying hockey equipment, but one particular customer's experience made apparent the hidden ways that hockey is in fact *not* for everyone. One day a young Sikh boy entered the store with his mother looking to buy the appropriate gear to play ice hockey. We started with the skates and from there found him shin pads, pants, a chest protector, and so on. At no time did cost seem an issue for the family. The mother stood quietly by in an engaged, yet passive manner. Once he was suited up from skates to neck guard it was time to fit him for a helmet. He wore a patka (a small head covering worn by many young Sikh boys), which posed an uncommon problem. He took his patka down, releasing the braids from their cloth. Still, no helmet seemed to fit properly. I asked his mother if he could take his braids out in order to play hockey. She replied with a calm, "No." After trying all the helmets in the store and struggling with adjustments, unable to find a helmet that would both fit and protect his head, the boy and his mother had a quiet conversation in Punjabi. The boy then placed all of the gear in a pile and left the store with his mother.

We were often told as sales associates that we were not selling equipment; we were selling a lifestyle. My own faded professional hockey dreams had led me to realize that the opportunities for people to consume certain lifestyles are not equal. But the incident described above made the point in a different way. I do not know if that boy ever got the opportunity to play ice hockey, but what I do know is that the conversation he had with his mother is not one that most children have had in the sporting goods store: a conversation about how religion and ethnicity pose challenges to participation in one of the most iconic activities in the national culture.

In the last decade or so, there has been increasing scholarly interest in the lack of color that exists in both Canada's sporting history and contemporary sporting landscape. Robert Pitter (2006) points out that "the larger story of hockey in Canada is told as if Aboriginal Canadians, black Canadians, and Asian Canadians were simply not here" (p. 128), which gives the impression that either these people do not play hockey or they are not considered Canadian. As a result, the few accounts of Indigenous (e.g., Bennett, 2018; Robidoux, 2018; Tootoo, 2014; Valentine, 2012) and Black experiences (e.g., Carnegie, 1997; Fosty & Fosty, 2008; Harris, 2007) in hockey provide necessary counter-narratives to the dominant discourse of the sport's history.[1] For example, the Mi'kmaq Indigenous Peoples of the Dartmouth region of Nova Scotia[2] are believed to have played *Oochamkunutk*, a "[precursor] to modern ice hockey" (p. 48) and were known to make the best hockey sticks at that time (Bennett, 2018); however, these contributions are often downplayed, erased, and/or white-washed.

The Indigenous relationship with hockey is also complicated by the fact that hockey was used in residential schools to assimilate Indigenous children into a settler vision of a nation-state (in the United States they were known as Native American boarding schools) (Forsyth & Giles, 2013). Residential schools were federally authorized Christian schools that separated Indigenous youth from their families and culture in an attempt to "kill the Indian" to "save the child." In the Truth and Reconciliation Commission of Canada, published in 2015, residential school survivors reflected on how sports like hockey offered an escape from their living trauma; yet, at the same time, they were also reminders of that violence. Here is an excerpt from one survivor's statement to the commission: "And this hockey stick—his broken hockey stick that everybody knew—he called it Hector. And he'd hit me and made me stand up. And I remember clearly because I wasn't able to straighten out my head" (Truth and Reconciliation Commission of Canada, 2015a, p. 192).

Sport was used at residential schools to assimilate Indigenous youth into a patriarchal and gendered society, thus breaking them from their traditionally matriarchal social structures (Forsyth & Giles, 2013). As an example, Bev Beaver, a Mohawk player from Ontario's Six Nations Reserve, pretended to be a boy so that she could play hockey and, even when she was exposed as a girl, was one of the best players at her school (Paraschak, 1990). Many believe that she was an Olympic-caliber athlete, had it been an option when she was playing during the 1950s and 1960s.

Similarly, Black Canadian contributions to the modern game of hockey, such as the slapshot and "butterfly" style of goaltending, are often ignored in the broader history of hockey's re-telling as a "white man's game." In concluding their book, *Black Ice: The Lost History of the Colored Hockey League of the Maritimes, 1895–1925*, Fosty and Fosty (2008) offer the following reflection:

> Today there are no monuments to the Colored Hockey League of the Maritimes and few hockey books even recognize the league. . . . There is no mention in the Hockey Hall of Fame of the impact that Blacks had in the development of the modern game of hockey. . . . It is as if the league had never existed. . . . In Canadian history, as it is in winter, the landscape is that of bleached white. It is a white world of seeming beauty, yet one without color. It is a sterile landscape, deadened by cold and time, blinding to all who are lost within its blanketed form. (pp. 221–222)

Thus, historical accounts that fail to acknowledge various experiences, such as the Canadian Library and Archives' "Backcheck: A hockey retrospective," offer Canadians an incomplete narrative by erasing influential contributions that came from racialized Canadians and Indigenous Peoples (Library and Archives Canada, 2014). By exposing these erasures, we gain a better understanding of the inequities and complexities that have long been part of Canada's history and culture. Fosty and Fosty's (2008) description of a white-blanketed conventional view of Canadian history is largely correct. But, Canada itself is more complex. Canada *is* a northern white settler nation with an oppressive colonial past, but it is also an immense, geographically, culturally, and racially varied country, with significant Indigenous and immigrant histories that differ from province to province. The notion that hockey is a white man's game is, in fact, a well told lie.

Therefore, I seek to recover some of the diversity missing from the national winter pastime narrative by analyzing South Asian experiences in and around the game. The creation of the *Hockey Night in Canada Punjabi* broadcast (herein referred to as *Hockey Night Punjabi*) in 2008 and the 2011 hockey film *Breakaway*, about a young Sikh Canadian man's navigation of family, religion, and hockey in Canada, point to growing interest in voices that have been missing from the hockey landscape—voices that are proudly Canadian, yet are often faced with questions of belonging and value. It is with these voices in mind that this project examines the growth of both South Asian hockey fandom and community hockey participation in Canada as a form of cultural citizenship. More specifically, I explore the intriguing relationship to hockey that has developed in South Asian communities in Canada, and particularly on Canada's west coast, since the 1960s. I shall also discuss challenges that South Asian Canadians face in hockey and how these challenges may be connected to broader racial discrimination in early twenty-first century Canada.

In 1993, Gruneau and Whitson published *Hockey Night in Canada: Sports, Identities, and Cultural Politics*, a book now widely regarded as a seminal work in Canadian cultural studies (e.g., see Mookerjea, Szeman, & Faurschou, 2009). Issues such as national identity, power, commercialism, class, gender, and masculinity that Gruneau and Whitson brought to the fore still resonate more than 20 years later. However, while acknowledging the enduring strength of hockey's powerful grip on imaginations and collective memories, Gruneau and Whitson conclude: "Since the 1960s, a significant fracturing of older hierarchies of identity and the proliferation of new points of cultural attachment have opened up spaces for re-imagining the role that hockey might play in Canadian life ... [including] a re-imagining of our own Canadian self-understanding" (p. 279).

These tendencies have arguably been exacerbated in recent years by a continued influx of immigrants from countries whose majority populations are not secular, Christian, or white. Significant tensions and debates around citizenship, multiculturalism, and the tolerance of difference have accompanied this influx, often influenced by significant fears of international terrorism and a resurgence of nativist/nationalist discourses in many parts of the world.

In this regard, I hope to expand and update Gruneau and Whitson's (1993) work on the cultural politics of hockey, with specific reference to issues of race, ethnicity, and citizenship that were not developed systematically in their analysis. More than ever, in my view, questions of *who* is Canadian, *who is present or underrepresented*, and *who is enabled or discouraged* in Canadian culture are negotiated on the ice, within the confines of Canada's national pastime. I contend popular cultural practices, such as hockey, are sites where personal and group identities as well as claims to equality of citizenship can be exercised and contested. Hockey has particular relevance because of the widely acknowledged iconic place it occupies in Canada's national culture.

Complicating Canadian Culture

Culture and citizenship can be positioned as both synonymous and incompatible. In its broadest sense, the word *culture* simply refers to "a whole way of life" (R. Williams, 1958/2011). From this perspective, to speak of hockey as an iconic aspect of Canadian culture is simply to reference the game's longstanding importance in the everyday worlds of Canadian players, fans, businesses, community centers, and volunteers. In this usage, the concepts of culture and citizenship tend to implicitly align. Yet, the word culture can also be made plural to reference a diversity of sensibilities, identities, and opportunities—*cultures*, differing ways of living, rather than a single national culture.

As Renato Rosaldo (1993) explains, in North American society the analysis of culture requires that we "seek out its differences" (p. 198); in other words, to reference culture has become synonymous with difference itself. For example, Surrey, British Columbia, hosts annual "Culture Days" and the list of performances for the 2017 event were limited to: "The Wild Moccasins Dancers," "African Stages," "Immigrant Lessons" (which includes elements of Afro, House, and Hip Hop), and "The Re-Enactors" (City of Surrey, n.d.). These performances help to conflate popular conceptions about diversity and "cultural" experiences as stemming from immigrants and racialized bodies. For Rosaldo, "full citizenship and cultural visibility" are often "inversely related." In his words: "full citizens" can appear to "lack culture, and those most culturally endowed" can "lack full citizenship" (p. 198). He is not arguing that a dominant population of full citizens has no culture; rather, he means to say that a dominant culture has a taken-for-granted character, something that seems neutral or universal. In this regard, to speak of Canadian culture can too easily submerge recognition of the constituent cultural differences within that culture in favor of imagined cultural singularity of homogeneity.

If we look at the history of writing about the Canadian national (winter) pastime, this cultural submersion becomes evident. When Canadian journalist Peter Gzowski (2014) referred to hockey as "The Game of Our Lives," or the poet Al Purdy identified hockey as "The Canadian Specific" (as cited in Gruneau & Whitson, 1993, p. 3), they were tacitly equating Canadian culture with the experiences of primarily white, heterosexual, cis-gendered males. Consequently, the dominant culture has tended to recognize, confirm, and naturalize some identities over others in the national narrative. In contrast, I will argue that the end goal of full cultural citizenship requires a national narrative that is not based on naturalized and misleading abstractions constructed from an imagined singular history. In this respect, I am particularly interested in the ways that hockey can facilitate, inhibit, and complicate the ability of some racialized groups and individuals more than others to contribute to the national culture. This study prioritizes the ability to create and produce spaces of meaning, instead of the ability to participate in predetermined opportunities.

Citizenship and race in Canada have complicated histories. Notably, along with other intersections such as gender, race has traditionally been used as a factor in determining who is considered worthy of full rights of citizenship. Discussions about race have become increasingly pertinent in the twenty-first century and have perhaps, been exacerbated by Canada's self-proclaimed identity as a multicultural nation. Black residents in colonial Canada were largely enslaved from the 1600s through to the late eighteenth century and were often subjected to continued discrimination in electoral politics, even after the abolition of slavery in Canada in 1834. Women in Canada were not given the right to vote in federal elections until 1918, and in Quebec elections until 1940. Indigenous Peoples did not achieve full political rights of citizenship until 1960 (Chunn, Menzies, & Adamoski, 2002). Growing numbers of non-white immigrants from Caribbean, African, Middle Eastern, and South and East Asian countries since the 1960s have posed newer challenges for Canadian culture, especially for Canada's self-proclaimed late twentieth century identity as a multicultural nation.

Sunera Thobani (2007) claims that race poses a significant challenge to Canada's self-identification as a multicultural society because "the racialized marking of the body cannot be overcome, no matter the sophistication of one's deportment, the undetectability of one's accent, the depth of one's longing to belong" (p. 172). In this context, even in an environment featuring public political commitments to recognize equality and to value difference, racism and racist struggles are largely experienced informally in everyday life (Sue, 2010). Critical race scholars suggest it is not in the extreme cases of hatred where we learn about racism, but in the routine interactions of both public and private life (e.g., Knowles, 2010; Sue, 2010). In any case, in Thobani's view, there is little public space available for the discussion and debate over the changing contours of racism in the Canadian ethnoscape.

Nowhere is this more evident than in mainstream discussions of Canadian sport. As Joseph, Darnell, and Nakamura (2012) argue, Canadian sport tends to be treated as "race-less" further "[perpetuating] myths [about] Canada's egalitarian racial past and present" (p. 3). Hockey does not escape this general critique. Race and ethnicity have always been at play in hockey; yet, their meanings and significance have shifted depending on the historical conjuncture. Abdel-Shehid (2000) points to the lack of hockey narratives that speak to Black, Indigenous, and other non-whites, accordingly there is an urgent need to "[write] hockey thru race" (p. 76).

The exploration of South Asian voices presented in this book expand our understanding of hockey both as a vehicle for cultural assimilation and for ethnic self-expression and emancipation (Robidoux, 2012). The intersection of South Asians and hockey presents a uniquely Canadian conundrum because, even though only three players of South Asian heritage have skated in the NHL, South Asians have taken up hockey, both as players and fans, in a remarkable fashion.[3] The Vancouver Canucks 2011 Stanley Cup run has been credited for much of the South Asian fervor around the game. This excitement was expressed through "bhangra tributes posted on YouTube, mass prayer vigils for the team's success and spontaneous parades in the heavily Punjabi suburb Surrey" (Sax, 2013, para. 50). However, South Asian fandom is, perhaps, best exemplified by the *Hockey Night Punjabi* broadcast, which was created in 2008 by the Canadian Broadcasting Corporation (CBC) but found a more legitimate home in 2014 on the multicultural channel Omni Television. Thanks to the popularity and marketability of *Hockey Night Punjabi* broadcasts, for Punjabi Canadians, *"Mahriaa shot, keeta goal"* has replaced the patented "he shoots, he scores" call from the broadcast booth. David Sax (2013), of the *New York Times*, explains that the Punjabi broadcast "marries Canada's national pastime with the sounds of the Indian subcontinent, providing a glimpse of the changing face of ice hockey" (para. 5). In areas with a large South Asian presence, some hockey leagues, such as in Brampton, Ontario, reported a 20% increase in South Asian participation between 2011 and 2013, with many participants citing *Hockey Night Punjabi* as an encouraging factor. In 2014, the Calgary Flames became the first NHL team to offer online segments in Punjabi (Sportak, 2014), and, between 2012–2014, the Abbotsford Heat of the American Hockey League (AHL) instituted annual Punjabi Night celebrations (Sidhu, 2012). Indigenous hockey leagues and the Colored League of the Maritimes remain important parts of hockey's history in Canada, but neither of these stories has received the same kind of mainstream attention and market space that South Asian fandom has created.

Despite Canada's identity as a multicultural country, the intersection of sport and South Asian communities takes place against a backdrop of tumultuous post-9/11 racism. For example, since September 11, 2001, media constructions of the turban have been conflated with Muslims, terrorism, and Osama Bin Laden (Ahluwalia & Pelletiere, 2010). Consequently, in both the United States and Canada, Punjabi Sikhs received significant backlash after the 9/11 attacks, with record rates of hate crimes, and religious profiling (Ahluwalia & Zaman, 2009; United Sikhs, n.d.). Ahmad (2011) explains racial hierarchy as a "citizenship exchange market in which the relative belonging of any one racial or ethnic community fluctuates in accordance with prevailing social and political pressures" (p. 342). After 9/11, Muslim-looking became a racial category transcending all racial configurations as the global Other (Ahmad, 2011). Indians, Pakistanis, Sikhs, Hindus, Arabs, Christians, and even Latinos have been categorized as Muslim-looking or "Middle-Eastern looking," but Sikh men have borne a disproportionate amount of racial profiling based on racialized conflation.

To illustrate, when television anchors Gurdeep Ahluwalia and Nabil Karim of The Sports Network's (TSN) main show, *SportsCentre*, hosted together for the first time, they received comments such as, "When did TSN move to the middle east? #WTF" and "Couple of terrorists working the night shift on #TSN #Sportscentre #lolol" via the social media platform Twitter

(CBC, 2013). Additionally, a view of *Hockey Night Punjabi* as emblematic of Canadian multiculturalism is challenged by online comments such as "punjabi people dont [sic] even know hockey" (Szto, 2016, p. 214). Such reactions reflect a view where hockey's white as ice reality conflicts with Canada's equally problematic mythology of multiculturalism.

Unfortunately, much of the academic literature on South Asian immigrant experiences comes from American (e.g., Dhingra, 2016; Pandya, 2013; Shankar, 2016; Thangaraj, 2013, 2015) and British scholars (e.g., Burdsey, 2007, Ratna, 2011, 2014, 2018; Samie, 2013), with little Canadian contribution despite the long history of Punjabi Sikhs in this nation. South Asians in Britain have described their existence as "a community apart" or living "parallel lives" (Fletcher, 2014) in relation to their English counterparts. Stories about race can sometimes parallel stories about ethnicity and religion in different societies, with the experiences of exclusion and oppression of Jews being an obvious example. The ethnic tensions that were more prevalent in the postwar period between Anglo Canadians and Irish Catholics (Andrew-Gee, 2015) or Russian Doukhobors in western Canada (Friesen, 1995) have lessened somewhat with white passing ethnicities merging to become the dominant vision of Canada (although not necessarily in equal measure). Still, visible markers of racial difference are more easily recognized and, historically, have provided greater opportunities for marginalized white ethnic groups to accrue advantages by leveraging whiteness in ways that are not available to groups whose non-white status is more visibly obvious.

Research Methods

The data that inform this study are the result of a review of literature conducted in combination with participant observation and qualitative interviews, undertaken over a period of 15 months, from January 2016 to April 2017. This included three visits to the OMNI studio where I observed rehearsals and taped pieces for the *Hockey Night Punjabi* broadcast. I also took notes at 10 local hockey games and 4 hockey events held in the Vancouver area. A total of 26 semi-structured interviews (6 women, 20 men) were conducted with South Asian hockey players (current and former), parents, coaches, and *Hockey Night Punjabi* representatives. Research participants ranged in age from 16 years old to their mid-50s, and their level of hockey participation spanned recreational house league hockey to the elite levels (i.e., university, semi-pro, professional). Pseudonyms have been provided for everyone except *Hockey Night Punjabi* representatives; however, if representatives were speaking more generally about their experiences and not directly about the show, they have been given a collective identification to provide some confidentiality. Recruitment was limited to the Lower Mainland of British Columbia, a culturally defined area that comes with a variety of constitutions because there is no defined geographical boundary for the Lower Mainland. For the purposes of this study, the Lower Mainland includes Metro Vancouver and the surrounding suburbs, the Fraser Valley, and as far north as the municipality of Squamish (Boei, 2009). The demographics of the area will be further discussed in the next chapter.

Readers should also be aware of certain language choices that have been made:

Racialized: The term denotes the act of being raced. It is an active descriptor that implies a relation of power between those who are marked as "people of color" by those who are privileged enough to remain colorless. Largely attributed to Toni Morrison (1993), the term attempts to highlight the social construction of race by expressing it as an act that is imposed upon people.

Marginalized: Marginalization usually connotes a spatial relationship where people, concepts, and/or places are forced to the periphery of what is socially normal/significant. These groups are excluded from decision-making processes and oftentimes their own representation. As Pitts and Smith (2007) point out, "marginalization is not necessarily an objective fact but a relation of power in particular circumstances"; these are imaginative zones (Abraham & Shryock, 2000). Spivak (1988) further elucidates that the margins are not so much about difference as they are about a silence at the center that governs "who can speak, how, when, and where, and, just as importantly, who listens and how. It does not mean there are no utterances" (Hurley, 2007, p. 182). Still, who we label as marginalized does not necessarily reflect who feels marginalized in real life. For example, the participants in this study rarely spoke of anything that equated to marginalization. On a sports team, even though many of these participants felt alone because of their racialized difference, or underrepresented, they did not articulate marginality in relation to their teams or the broader hockey community.

Minoritized: Minoritized replaces the term *visible minorities* because, much like the term *racialized*, it highlights the power relations involved. To speak of visible minorities connotes a minority/majority dichotomy "reducing the problem of power relations to one of numbers" (Brah, 1996, p. 187). The term *minorities* does a disservice to immigrant groups by giving the illusion that their lack of social, political, and economic power is associated with their lack of population size.

My positioning in this study was interesting at times because of the racial mismatch with my participants. As a Chinese woman, the obvious question should be: Why not study Chinese/East Asian experiences in hockey? (One participant did ask me this question before our interview.) The practical answer is that the *Hockey Night Punjabi* broadcast offers a unique entry point to examine issues of citizenship, race, multiculturalism, and mythology—an entry point that does not exist for Chinese Canadians at this point in time. However, religion did play an important role in the imagination of this project because, in the Lower Mainland especially, the Sikh religion creates an additional point of tension that does not exist with Chinese Canadians because many have adopted Christianity, are atheist, or their beliefs are not as visibly identifiable in public spaces. Ultimately, this specific tension was observed to be less crucial than imagined; it is a tension that is essentially externally imposed and (re)produced.

I do believe that a study of East Asian experiences is necessary and would likely result in unique data; but, on a more personal level, growing up in North Delta, British Columbia, I had more South Asian friends through grade school than I did Chinese/East Asian friends. My Asian-ness never really resonated with me until my undergraduate studies at the University of British Columbia, pejoratively referred to as "UBC: University of a Billion Chinese." And, working at Sport Chek in Strawberry Hill meant I had many interactions with South Asian customers centered around hockey participation. Therefore, even though I am not a member of the South Asian community, the South Asian community has been an integral part of my upbringing and experience as a Canadian.

Furthermore, there is an assumption that ethnic matching encourages a richer understanding of the research data along with an assumed interest in the welfare of the community (Ashworth as cited in Gunaratnam, 2003), but this assumption presumes that empathy across racial lines is somehow incompatible or disingenuous, or that sameness is required for understanding. Carrington (2008) notes that, generally, literature has focused on dilemmas that exist for white social scientists in researching so-called non-white cultures, groups, and communities, thus presuming race to be a defining marker of difference instead of class, gender, and/or region. Carrington contends that racialized researchers may, in fact, be able to produce "more complex accounts of how racism intersects with class, gender, and sexuality" (p. 428). I found that during interviews participants and I often bonded over similar experiences such as challenges to our belonging, lamenting over having not learned our mother tongue better as children, the inability of white Canadians to pronounce our names, or discussing immigrant frugality and the emphasis on education. Hence, even though our experiences as racialized Canadians were not identical, they were similar enough to situate a common understanding of hockey and Canada.

I did, however, perceive that my unknown place in hockey culture created a (small) barrier for many participants. Almost everyone asked at some point during interviews if I play, or have ever played, hockey. Alternatively, if I mentioned in passing where I play women's hockey they would often respond with, "Oh, so you know." This was a telling statement because it signaled an additional level of comfort and honesty in our discussions. Participants would suddenly use more hockey lingo and get into the specifics of the game knowing that they did not have to explain these things to me. There was, ironically, an underlying assumption that a Chinese woman would not have participated in ice hockey. Consequently, we must acknowledge that in this context, the identity of "hockey player" counts for a lot in the web of intersectionality. As a unique subculture, the norms set by hockey culture work to police who can and cannot access insider knowledge, and if I were marked as an outsider with nothing but inquisitiveness about racism in hockey, there may have been suspicions about the intent behind my research. Yet, as a fellow hockey player, tensions seemed to have been eased with an assumption that there is a shared understanding of the value that the game offers.

Overview of the Book

This study represents a culmination of life experience and media developments that have occurred in a Canada full of contradictions. As a Canadian-born, middle-class Chinese woman who grew up in a suburb of Vancouver with very few East Asian classmates but many South Asian and white classmates, the narratives that follow are not about my life, but they are about the community that I consider home and its tensions. I should also note that this study, while critical of hockey and Canada, is a project of love. Often the voices critical of sport are labeled as those attempting to destroy or eliminate the game, when the reality is that those who rail against the very foundations of the game are usually those who love it the most, understand its value, and know that we can (and must) do better. Likewise, patriotism should not be defined by unconditional loyalty but instead by holding one's country accountable for its espoused values.

The narrative arc that follows is, in a general sense, a sequence of understanding who we are talking about, why this group's experiences are important and unique, how racism presents itself in hockey culture, and what the implications are of its existence. Chapter 1 lays the groundwork for this intersectional analysis by unpacking the dominant national myths that undergird the manuscript. The first myth is that hockey *is* Canada, and the second is that, as a multicultural nation, Canada inherently values racialized and ethnic differences. I also contextualize the South Asian demographic in Canada and, more specifically, racial tensions in the Lower Mainland of British Columbia.

Chapter 2 uses media narratives and interview data conducted with members of the *Hockey Night Punjabi* broadcast to discuss cultural citizenship as the main theoretical framework. I use a specific understanding of cultural citizenship that moves beyond looking at opportunities for participation and instead privileges co-authorship as a way to assess one's value as a citizen. *Hockey Night Punjabi* is used as a case study to illustrate the importance of alternative interpretations of Canada's storied pastime. It creates space for additional narratives and encourages us to ask what co-authored citizenship might look like for racialized Canadians if viewed through the lens of Canadian hockey.

Chapter 3 explores how the hockey rink polices membership in the hockey community and is symbolic of broader issues related to citizenship and national belonging. Because racialized bodies are constantly being policed, both externally and internally, I contend that racialized participants are forced into a state of perpetual unease or lack of certainty about their claims to space in hockey culture. Additionally, research participants unpack their own self-identifications, contributing to the articulation of difference and what it is like being the only South Asian in a hockey space.

Chapter 4 focuses on discursive (re)productions of racism and its dismissals. Participants reflect on some of the hateful comments they received on the ice, and I identify a conflation between racism and gamesmanship. I argue that the dismissal of racism and the reluctance to refer to these instances *as* racism helps propagate the idea that hockey is an equitable and meritocratic space. This reluctance is also indicative of a system that offers little recourse for racist behavior and may mark those who complain about racism as troublemakers. The chapter concludes with a theoretical reflection on the concept of evidence. What is the point of providing evidence of racism if those who provide it are dismissed as unreliable witnesses? What counts as evidence and who gets to determine these terms? And what do we do when no one cares how much evidence has been gathered? The ease with which evidence of racism can be dismissed and/or ignored is, arguably, indicative of second-class citizenship.

Chapter 5 focuses on gendered experiences and distinctions in the game. The chapter begins by unpacking the specificity of hockey performativity and explains how whiteness informs and enables particular gendered performances. In turn, other racialized performances that take place at the rink are often constrained. I then move into discussing the intersection of racism and masculinity. If masculinity is predicated on freedom and entitlement to space, place, and work, then challenges to one's racialized identity are equally challenges to one's manliness. The latter half of the chapter historicizes South Asian femininities and challenges the notion of Canada's game through the lens of women's hockey as gendered inequality within the broader whiteness of the nation. I contend that institutional racism benefits from the sound proofing that racialized players provide when they downplay the racism they encounter. That is to say that racialized participants help insulate racism within the hockey community through their individualized responses.

Chapter 6 considers the institutional nature of discrimination by using Pierre Bourdieu's forms of capital to explain how racialized players have been historically disadvantaged in a supposedly meritocratic system. Economic capital is often marked as the most consequential factor for access and opportunity in hockey, but I assert that cultural and social capital are equally as important, if not more important, for gaining a foothold into the higher (and more exclusive) levels of the game. Furthermore, because racialized hockey players face racism and seem resigned to that fact, they are forced to become resilient citizens; yet, this resilience is also what sustains an inequitable system. I critique resilience as a concept built on and as a manifestation of neoliberal injustice.

Building on the ideas of capital and all its facets, chapter 7 focuses on class mobility as one cause of racial tension in hockey culture. Because many South Asian hockey families have economic capital but lack the cultural and social capital required to truly impact their children's hockey careers, some South Asians are starting to create South Asian–specific hockey spaces. From the outside, these programs look like self-segregation; however, they are the result of persistent discrimination combined with increased wealth. White fragility is used to theorize the perceived resentment that some South Asians have faced as a result of their ability to "throw money" at the game. This is the only chapter where research participants describe an active and collective response to racism and discrimination.

Chapter 8 brings the discussion full circle back to the role of the media as arbiters in the politics of public memory. I challenge institutions of public memory, such as the Hockey Hall of Fame, and its influence in the erasure of racialized contributions and experiences from the larger story of hockey in Canada. I call for a more inclusive and collective retelling of the history of hockey and Canada as one method to exercise cultural citizenship and achieve anti-racism. If hockey *is* Canada then its history should reflect the various multicultural contributions that have made the game what it is today.

1

Myth Busting

Hockey, Multiculturalism, and Canada

> I don't choose to address racism, but
> racism exists so I have no choice.
> —Walter Beach, 1964 Cleveland Browns

W.E.B. Du Bois famously claimed in *The Souls of Black Folk* (2007) that the key problem of the twentieth century would be "the problem of the color-line" (p. 15). The poignancy of this prediction, unfortunately, was not that it was true of the twentieth century but that it has continued to be a pivotal issue well into the twenty-first century. The experience of being Canadian in birth, loyalty, sport, and home, but still never being Canadian enough—the sense of being in a place but not of a place—are anxieties that every racialized Canadian is made to feel at one point or another. Consequently, this project examines the state of the color line in one of the most hallowed, lucrative, and conservative Canadian spaces: the ice rink. But, first, it is important to unpack the two myths that are fundamental to this analysis: the idea hockey *is* Canada, and that Canada values multiculturalism.

Myth #1: Hockey Is Canada

> Developing as a hockey fan becomes akin to developing as a Canadian for many, and participation in the rituals and discourses of fandom plays a significant role in developing national identity, for individual and country alike.
> —Zuurbier, 2016, p. 252

Canada has long perpetuated the idea that hockey is highly significant for the relevance and identification of the nation, but how do racialized Canadians interpret this mythology? Who really benefits from hockey as a tool of integration? Who is changed by these interactions, if anyone? How important is hockey mythology in an increasingly globalized world?

There is no doubt that hockey continues to provide an anchor point for a young white settler nation that has historically defined itself through negative associations—we are neither the United States nor Britain. Despite all of the racist comments, gatekeeping hurdles, marked difference, and resentment described in the chapters that follow, the research participants in this study spoke fondly about the game as well as the friends and memories that were made along the way. None of these participants regret getting involved in hockey, but their love of the game should not overshadow the fact that both the sport and the nation can and must be better. We also have to acknowledge that many have exited the game because of the abuse suffered, yet we tend to elevate narratives of perseverance. The mythological belief that participation in hockey signals (unconditional) entrance and acceptance into the broader Canadian polity remains a dubious propagation.

Mythology is intimately connected in the production of "national character" (Slotkin, 1973, p. 3). National myths provide direction and coherence to those who choose to believe in them (Slotkin, 1973). Myth, according to Roland Barthes (1972), serves two communication functions: "It points out and it notifies, it makes us understand something, and it imposes it on us" (p. 226); it denotes something fictional while referencing concepts that are positioned as timeless and universally accepted truths. According to Slotkin (1973), myths are exercises of the mind. Perhaps most importantly, myth impoverishes meaning, thus making it appear "neutral and innocent" (Barthes, 1972, p. 235). A significant part of Canada's love of hockey stems from the mythological relationship between hockey and the physical environment in Canada (Holman, 2018). Barthes (2007) proclaimed, "To play hockey is constantly to repeat that men have transformed motionless winter, the hard earth, and suspended life and that precisely out of all this they have made a swift, vigorous, passionate sport" (p. 47). It is a particular kind of Canadian man who makes this myth possible.

Canadian mythology suggests it is in this relationship between sport and the physical elements that a national pastime was born. Certainly, many Canadians appear to be nostalgic for this seemingly natural memory; yet, the idea of Canadian children honing their hockey skills on frozen ponds, while picturesque, is a distant reality for urban/suburban Canadians. This is due, in part, to the effects of climate change (J. Johnson & Ali, 2016) but also a divide (whether psychological or geographical) between metropolitan centers such as Montreal, Toronto, and Vancouver and the rest of Canada. Case in point, one of the respondents, Sunny, a 20-year-old elite player, reflected on the importance of hockey and being Canadian: "Like the stereotypical Canadian kid, I think it's, I don't think it's . . . in our area . . . we're from the Vancouver area, I mean, I don't think it's that big of a deal. I feel like there's kids playing a lot more other sports but playing with guys from Alberta, Saskatchewan, further out east, I feel like that's the way they grow up—it was just hockey" (Personal communication, July 21, 2016).

Sunny talked about backyard rinks being a different reality from how he grew up and participated in hockey culture. A former elite player, Raj, echoed a similar geographical separation, "I think it's pretty . . . well it depends. If you go three hours North of Vancouver, or East of Vancouver four hours, you're in cold weather and in the snow. Only Vancouver gets [temperate] weather like this all year around, right" (Personal communication, June 21, 2016). To both Raj's and Sunny's points, Vancouver was home to the first artificial ice rink in Canada, Denman Arena, because of its temperate weather (Ludwig, 2016). The nostalgia for a time once lived by some Canadians perpetuates an idyllic game that emerged from the ice and snow of the Great White North. We often forget (or are made to forget) that hockey was not actually born out of nature but is a social and cultural production. As Canada continues to welcome immigrants into the country, the mythology of hockey finds itself constantly challenged by new and fluid interpretations of national identity.

These mythologies are also upheld by the belief that hockey is a defining feature of our Canadian-ness; it *makes* us Canadian. Yet, Kevin, a 46-year-old hockey parent, offered an interesting delineation about his identity. When I asked him how important he thought hockey is to *being* Canadian there was a long pause before he answered: "It's a very good question. I'll answer in two ways. As a hockey fan, as a Canadian who loves hockey and enjoys hockey I think it's great. . . . As a son of immigrants, as an immigrant myself, in the scheme of things—no. . . . Hockey is, I think, a default because Canadians, generally speaking, are so good at it. We recognize that it's Canada's sport even though it's not. I relate myself as Canadian differently" (Personal communication, November 21, 2016).

Kevin felt that hockey was very important as a school of life for his son, but as an immigrant he went on to describe the importance of hockey as "meh, it's there." He was the only participant to draw such a distinct line between hockey culture and his identity as a racialized Canadian. Kevin's point about hockey being Canada's default because we are good at it raises the question: Would hockey still be as important to our national identity if we were not as dominant on the international stage? Where then would we find our identity?

Some participants in this study, such as elite players Suki, 21, and Billy, 20, felt that Canada's love of hockey is part of the national vocabulary. In other words, people may not have to play hockey themselves, but understanding the game opens up a multitude of other opportunities for social connection. Conversely, Gurp, a 25-year-old recreational player, felt that Canadians overplay the connection to hockey, stating: "I think hockey is a big part of being Canadian but there's so many people that are not fans of hockey that how can you say that really? . . . I was friends with [people] in high school that were not fans of hockey at all, how can you say they're not Canadian? They're born here, they're raised here, they've lived their entire lives—they're not Canadian?" (Personal communication, May 10, 2016).

Sara, a relatively new hockey parent, answered that the national narrative about hockey was "pretty accurate" until I asked her if she felt that her participation in the sport made her "feel any more Canadian," to which she responded, "I don't think it makes me any more Canadian" (Personal communication, October 10, 2016). Amit, a 24-year-old recreational player, explained that one does not necessarily need to be a hockey fan to be Canadian because "that's not going to make you less Canadian or less accepted in society" (Personal communication, May 16, 2016). Hockey parent Greg, 47, stated very bluntly, "I don't think it's got anything to do with being Canadian—Canadian is who you are. You live in Canada and that's the only Canadian we are" (Personal communication, November 21, 2016).

Therefore, as much as the myth wants us to believe that the motive for playing hockey is *to be* Canadian, the reality is that being Canadian precedes any participation in hockey. Slotkin (1973) asserts, "myths reach out of the past to cripple, incapacitate, or strike down the living" (p. 5); hence, the mythology of hockey blinds us to the consequences of a collective memory rooted in colonial, gender, race, and class exclusions. Inversely, the relationship between hockey and Canadians appears natural, symbiotic, and reinforcing. Nonetheless, Slotkin (1973) contends that once a myth loses its religious devotion "[it] ceases to function as a myth" (p. 8). Could these interpretations of hockey's mythology, as experienced by racialized Canadians, indicate deterioration of the myth? Would white Canadians necessarily answer this question any differently?

Who or What Are We Integrating?

In Aihwa Ong's (1999) analysis of "flexible citizenship" she explained how wealthy Asian immigrants would often register for modeling classes to "learn how to dress, walk, and generally comport themselves in a way that would make them 'more acceptable to the Americans'" (p. 88). This notion of being palatable to the host society is precisely what is intended by promoting hockey as something that *integrates* new and racialized Canadians into mainstream culture. Hockey supposedly gives Canadians a universal talking point, educates racialized Canadians about national values, and generally helps folks blend in, but to what extent is this true? Is being a hockey player, coach, or parent enough to become acceptable and overcome one's Otherness?

Frisby, Thibault, and Cureton (2014) highlight that despite Canada's fascination with multiculturalism and its associated policies, "there are no policies tying it directly to sport at the federal level" (p. 106). Yet, organizations such as the Institute for Canadian Citizenship (2014) promote the notion that sports are a way to "build respect, tolerance and foster intercultural awareness and relationships, assist in the integration of newcomers, and provide opportunities for youth at risk" (p. 14). The assumption from this plural ideal is that a unity will be derived where "man is born, works, laughs, and dies in the same fashion everywhere" (Barthes, 1972, p. 196)—hockey supposedly performs an erasure of cross-cultural difference. Unfortunately, hockey is not that powerful.

The majority of my research participants were born in Canada and by extension did not feel the need to be integrated. If anything, my participants gave examples of how their white teammates often had questions about South Asian culture and traditions:

CS: Do you find that kind of opens the door for some discussion? Do guys ask you questions about your culture?

BILLY: Oh definitely. I've gotten asked tons of questions. I always get asked where are your parents from? Can you speak East Indian, Punjabi? They ask me if I speak Punjabi, lots of times they want me to teach them words. But yeah, they ask if I understand it. Food. A lot of them, actually when my mom comes down they are obsessed with her cooking, so my mom will make some extra food and bring it down and the guys come over and eat butter chicken and stuff like that.... I think if we didn't show, if I didn't show that it's okay to be comfortable around me about my culture and be respectful about it, I don't think some of these relationships would be there. (Personal communication, July 20, 2016)

Kiran, a 22-year-old elite player, would have to explain cultural, ethnic, and/or geographic differences to some of her teammates ("There's different types of Indians") who perceived Indian as a uniform identity (Personal communication, April 28, 2016). Likewise, Prav, a 20-year-old recreational player, used these discussions as educational opportunities: "They'll know all about the food but then some will want to know in depth about the culture like where it started or our temples and stuff like that. Some people do take interest in that. I guess it gives us a platform, in a way, to educate people about who we are so they don't have that stereotype that we're all generalized as 'brown people.' They can learn the variation between a Sikh, Hindu, and a Muslim" (Personal communication, September 1, 2016).

When we speak of integration and assimilation, we often envision the margins being folded/incorporated into the center—that difference becomes diluted when added into the core. This relationship is Orientalist in nature in that the center—the Occidental—may grow in size but remains largely static in nature, the rest of the world acquiescing to its existence (Said, 1978). But I contend that the language of integration and assimilation hides the fact that change must also occur at the core/center/mainstream of society.

Whether discursively (re)producing hockey as a common denominator (Dimanno, 2010), a cultural language, and/or as a tool of integration, these conceptions share the underlying presumption that hockey does not change. Former Canadian Prime Minister Stephen Harper told *Sports Illustrated*, "One of the first things you see [is] immigrants start to belong to Canadian society when their kids start to come to the hockey rink. Then the parents start to integrate with the other parents. . . . So it's a great common denominator" (Farber, 2010). *They* integrate and so do *their* kids; in other words, Canada and its people may change, but hockey does not. Ergo, if the nation *must* change, the pastime cannot. This, of course, is a myth that offers false comfort because the institution of hockey changes constantly. Rule changes, league expansions, new stadiums, and shifting global markets all exemplify a dynamic cultural artifact. The key to mythology, however, is the illusion of stability. Billy, Parm, and Kiran are all Canadian-born citizens, which means their integration into Canada (in a literal sense) is implicit. Their white teammates, on the other hand, are the ones who have something to learn about in an ever-globalizing Canadian society and are the ones who, arguably, gain something from being in the locker room with racialized teammates. So, who, in these interactions, are the ones being "integrated?

Myths serve to naturalize discursive practices by distorting, rather than erasing, history (Barthes, 1972). The distortion here is the projection of integration as a unidirectional activity, whereas the participant narratives above elucidate how diversity in hockey may alter the directionality by tinkering with the center. By positioning racialized hockey players as abnormal in Canadian society they become "objects of our experience instead of . . . subjects of experience with whom we might identify" (Wendell, 1996, p. 60). For example, in Parm's realization that hockey offers him a platform to educate his teammates about his heritage and culture, Parm is the one facilitating integration. Parm remains unchanged in this specific relationship, and it is his white teammates who are incorporated into a new normal—a new Canada. Likewise,

FIG. 1.1 2017 Hometown Hockey event in Vancouver, British Columbia.

Shane, a 20-year-old competitive player, explained, "Some players, they are from a different culture too, they're not always Canadians, maybe from Europe. Those players tend to be more interested in learning about our culture" (Personal communication, September 1, 2016). Again, Shane's experience and expertise serve as the center in these interactions—he is integrating non-Canadians into Canadian society; yet, from a broad view Shane would be the "non-Canadian," the one who needs to be folded into the mix. The notion of integration mistakenly centralizes power, but here we witness some of the oscillations that take place between the center and the margins (Hurley, 2007). These are some of the nuances that are overshadowed when we uphold whiteness as the default experience.

We can discursively challenge the assumption that hockey is used to Canadianize (P. Kim, 2014) racialized citizens by re-writing the mainstream into this equation: Hockey used to globalize Canadians. Oftentimes, we are so preoccupied with highlighting those who are marginalized that we forget another way to combat white supremacy is to *write in* the oppression—make the invisible, visible—by making the racism apparent. DiAngelo (2016) uses the example of headlines meant to celebrate baseball icon Jackie Robinson to illustrate how power can be made both visible and invisible: "Robinson is often celebrated as 'the first African American to break the color line and play in major league baseball' . . . this story line depicts Robinson as racially special; a black man who finally had what it took to play with whites, as if no black athlete before him was qualified enough to compete with whites. Imagine if instead, the story went something like this: 'Jackie Robinson, the first black man whites allowed to play major league baseball'" (p. 149).

Similarly, I believe that reproducing the idea that hockey serves as a common denominator and tool of integration performs an erasure of white supremacy and colonialism in Canada. White Canadians are written out of this equation because white Canadian has become synonymous with "hockey and Canada" (just as the term *African* has become synonymous with Black people despite, as an example, the existence of white South Africans [Coombes, 2003]). Through the mythological positioning of hockey and nation, white Canadians are made to appear "neutral and innocent" (Barthes, 1972, p. 235). Hockey is cleansed of any historical or political tensions, and the myth forces us to look backwards for exclusion, because as Whitson and Gruneau (2006) propose, "at the moment of its greatest strength a mythology thus insulates itself from criticism" (p. 4). That is to say, if the institution of hockey is never the "bad guy," then there is little impetus for systemic change.

Myth #2: Canada Is a Multicultural Haven

The other dominant myth in operation here is that racism cannot exist in Canada because multiculturalism is one of the nation's central values. Race and racism are tricky topics to research. In her most recent book, Sara Ahmed (2017) articulates race as "a complicated address" (p. 118). I interpret this statement to mean that we *live* race in our bodies as strangers, as residents, as citizens; as people who can be dislodged from our place of residence; that we can be made to feel uncomfortable in our homes; that the space we inhabit or reside in can be either forever questioned or never questioned. Moreover, class position is often marked by one's address further complicating the perceived social location of race. Race is a complicated location to inhabit because it so often requires explanation ("What are you?"). It is a location not easily found because it is never a permanent address—it is complicated in its fluidity. To speak of race unfortunately reifies a social construction, but we must still acknowledge that this imagined difference has very real consequences; hence, "we find ourselves in a classic Nietzschean double bind: 'race' has been the history of an untruth, or an untruth that is unfortunately our history" (Radhadkrishnan as cited in Gunaratnam, 2003, p. 31). As African American scholar Imani Perry (2011) contends, "strange days" (p. 2) of trying to assess race and racism continue.

Categorizing people by race has been used to solidify class distinctions (e.g., American slavery [S. Hall, 1996], South African apartheid [Wolpe, 1972], India's caste system [Dumont, 1980]), for religious persecution (e.g., the Holocaust, Irish Catholic oppression, ethnic cleansing of Myanmar's Rohingya Muslims), and to rationalize colonial expansion (e.g., the dispossession of Indigenous Peoples in the Americas). In each of these examples, race became a distinctive feature for the purpose of imposing hierarchies; yet, *how* race is/ was manipulated and animated is key to understanding how groups of people become racialized into a complicated existence. In this way, race shifts when necessary and lines of difference are limited only by the historical period in which they exist.

For the purposes of this study, race is defined as a relation of power that is anchored to a historical period, political context, or group(s) of people, and broadly encompasses notions of ethnicity, skin color, religion, language, customs, indigeneity, and cultural habits (Joseph et al., 2012). For example, in the U.S. Census, Indian migrants were labeled as Hindus between 1930 and 1940 despite the majority of migrants identifying as Sikhs (Koshy, 1998). Because the term Indian had already been assigned to Native Americans, a new category had to be created for people from India. From 1950–1970, Indian migrants were categorized as Other/white based on the belief that Indians were descendants of Aryans; however, this interpretation has since been widely discredited (Koshy, 1998). In 1980, in an attempt to benefit from affirmative action programming, Indian migrants lobbied to be included in the Asian American category (Koshy, 1998). Somewhat similarly, Canada's *Indian Act* legally determines one's Indigenous status based on marriage, birth, and gender, further demonstrating the fluidity of racial constructions and how they are used to serve those in power (Thompson, 2009).

On the one hand, racialized groups are generally conceptualized as fitting in a vertical hierarchy that positions whites at the top and Blacks at the bottom, with every other group falling somewhere in between (e.g., Al-Solaylee, 2016; Matsuda, 1993; Okihiro, 1994). On the other hand, C. J. Kim (1999) suggests that we consider race as a field of positions in which each race is relational to the others because each group has "been racialized relative to and through interaction with whites and blacks" (p. 105). Specifically referencing the racial positioning of South Asians in Britain during the 1990s, Carrington (2010) observed: "While South Asians may have had the wrong religion, being seen largely as Sikh, Hindu, or Muslim, they at least had, so the argument went, a strong value system and a set of traditional beliefs that was helping to integrate South Asians into 'mainstream' British society, in contrast to the inherently dysfunctional black families and their lawless black youth" (p. 149).

As a result, the privileging of South Asians in this particular political climate assisted in the oppression of Blacks in Britain. South Asians are often represented as model minorities, a group that has been constructed as capable of picking themselves up by the proverbial bootstraps to establish themselves in their new homeland (to be discussed further in chapter 7). However, scholars such as Prashad (2000) are quick to point out that this positive stereotype of hard work and academic intelligence is born out of the subjugation and disposability of groups such as African Americans, Latinx, and Indigenous Peoples.[1]

Racialized brown skin (to be further unpacked in chapter 3) must also be understood in relation to the newly formed Muslim-looking group that was mentioned in the Introduction. Some scholars argue that Muslim-looking people have become the primary Other in contemporary Western society with a debatable reduction and/or reconfiguration in the differences between Blacks and whites (Ahmad, 2011). The development of Muslim-looking as a new racial category illuminates the fluid and contested nature of race. Due to the fact that the Sikh turban and beard have been confused with images of Muslim terrorists, Sikh men have reported record high rates of discrimination and hate crimes since 9/11 in the United States and Canada (Ahluwalia & Pellettiere, 2010; Bahdi, 2003). We must then juxtapose the fear-inducing and suspicious Muslim-looking group against Bollywood festivals and South Asian cultural nights characterized by color and fun, further proving the constructed existence that South Asians must learn to navigate (Ghosh, 2013). The precarious social position of South Asian communities signals an important shift in the racialized exclusion of the "racial middle" (O'Brien, 2008) and bolsters the need for further scholarly examination. As Edward Said has observed, "Each age and society re-creates its 'others'" (as cited in Ghosh, 2013, p. 42).

Furthermore, we should think of race and ethnicity (defined here as the shared social aspects of life such as culture, language, and religion) as provisional identities that are strategically necessary to locate individuals in a world in constant flux. For Hall (1996), identities mark *difference and exclusion* more than they do a traditional notion of an identity, and, even though there may be very distinct and historically defined South Asian experiences, just as there are for other racialized groups, it is "'the diversity, not the homogeneity, of [South Asian] experience" that demands and deserves our attention" (as cited in St. Louis, 2011, p. 110). Therefore, the purpose of this project attempts to inject multiplicity into our understandings of South Asian.

Ethnicity and religion are inextricably connected in many of today's current events and Canada's history of citizenship (Bramadat & Seljak, 2009). After World War II, the notion of Canadian citizenship was used to help manage the existing ethnic tensions between majority and minority groups, and dissipate individual attachment to racial, religious, linguistic, and/or other cultural identifiers (Bohaker & Iacovetta, 2009). Christianity has historically played an integral role in the disempowerment of many living within Canadian borders and, even with Islamophobia on the rise, the most reported hate crime today continues to be anti-Semitic in nature (Minsky, 2017). Still, it would be misleading to think that racialized differences usurp ethnic tensions in contemporary Canada because, as examples, there is friction between Chinese Canadians from Hong Kong and Chinese Canadians from Mainland China (Todd, 2014) as well as between first- and second-generation South Asians (Bramadat & Seljak, 2009). Nayar (2012) elucidates that there is even a complicated relationship between the Punjabi culture, which has been in existence for over two millennia, and the Sikh religion that developed in the sixteenth century to contrast pan-Indian and Punjabi cultural values and practices that promoted the subjugation of women and the caste system.

In the era of new racism, it is no longer socially acceptable to talk about race as a potentially limiting factor. To recognize race is often deemed racist in societies that have declared themselves color-blind. Color-blind rhetoric holds that if we treat everyone as equals, regardless of their racialized appearance, these actions will be enough to create an equitable society (Bonilla-Silva, 2017). Unfortunately, treating a systemic issue such as racism on an individual basis does little to alter white supremacy at an institutional level. In a self-identified multicultural nation, to speak of racial discrimination becomes an act of treason enabling racist acts to be dismissed as aberrations and/or isolated incidents. But S. Johal (2002) contends, when everyday experiences are aggregated into a "substantial body of isolated bits of evidence" (p. 231) the issue grows from one of individual concern into one that should be highlighted as a problem of society. This adapted racism is (re)produced as a fear of cultural difference instead of skin color (Goldberg, 2009). Whether it is a fear of terrorists living next door or wealthy Asians "taking over" Canadian cities, each stereotype constructs the "white nation" as something that must be protected from racialized Others (Grace et al., 1998, p. 10). Cultural uniformity has usurped the need for racial supremacy by "parading under the politics of nationalism and patriotism" (Hill Collins & Solomos, 2010, p. 7). By extension, cultural arenas such as hockey become vital sites of exploration because they are supposed to represent a point of connection yet too often become an additional space for exclusion.

Racism is predominantly assumed to be an issue of the past, with culture representing the new dividing line. Some contend that multicultural policies premised upon adding people of color and "stirring" have officially failed because it conceives of culture as "ethnic property to be owned and held under copyright" (Gilroy, 2006, p. 43); that is, cultures can be combined only because they are presumed to be static entities. It is a colonial arrangement that does not require a reconstituted identity based in equality (Gilroy, 2006). Gilroy's (2006) suggested way forward is for an open-source co-production of multiple cultures, a perspective that will be extended through the framework of cultural citizenship in chapter 2.

It is imperative that studies of new racism in Canada are differentiated from the British and American contexts precisely because of Canada's official privileging of multiculturalism juxtaposed to a history of subjugating people of color and Indigenous communities (Mackey, 2002). S. Hall (2000) has posed the multicultural question to the British state, asking if and how it can create a more inclusive and egalitarian society that respects difference rather than trying to obliterate it. Canada has quietly grappled with the same conundrum.

Canadians must question how all cultures can be equally valued if its very history is based on a conflictual, and grossly inequitable, partnership between Anglo settlers, Quebecois, and Indigenous groups (Denis, 1997, p. 26). Stein (2007) argues that Canada tends to celebrate a "shallow multiculturalism" (p. 19) that publicly celebrates difference, usually through festivals and food, but simultaneously protects white supremacy. Bissoondath (1994) believes that Canadian multiculturalism emphasizes difference by making racialized Canadians "museums of exoticism . . . [because] multiculturalism as we know it indulges in stereotype, depends on it for a dash of colour and a flash of dance" (p. 111). In other words, difference is allowed in the public sphere primarily when it is officially sanctioned or can be commodified, otherwise it should remain hidden in private spheres (Boyer, Cardinal, & Headon, 2004).

Designating a special month where *Hockey is for Everyone* (HIFE) or organizing multicultural nights at sporting events epitomizes well-meaning but shallow multiculturalism. For example, HIFE month seeks to foster inclusion for all types of marginalized groups stating: "We believe all hockey programs—from professionals to youth organizations—should provide a safe, positive and inclusive environment for players and families regardless of race, color, religion, national origin, gender, disability, sexual orientation and socio-economic status. Simply put, Hockey is for Everyone" (NHL, 2017).

HIFE coincides with Black History Month, and, much like Black history, is necessary because every other month inherently leaves white supremacy unmarked. It is the one month where pointing out difference is acceptable, so long as there is a positive story attached. What is often lost in these displays of shallow multiculturalism is that the celebration of culture and difference simultaneously protects the white privilege that takes place on the ice. Because, even though Canadians of all colors connect through ethnic food and music, more often than not, there are only white male faces participating in the actual hockey game—the centerpiece around which a celebration of multiculturalism is made possible. Such multicultural events confirm Anglo Canadian culture as normative.

Whiteness in Canadian Hockey

Although this project attempts to centralize South Asian voices and experiences, it is equally an examination of whiteness in Canada. Whiteness can be understood as an unearned package of privileges (Long & Hylton, 2002), but it is not necessarily directly connected with white skin (O'Connell, 2010). Its position is fundamentally dominant, and therefore the normalized reference point for all (Frankenburg, 1993). White people and white culture are (re) produced as race-less, and by extension everyone else becomes raced (Dyer, 1997). Whiteness supports white supremacy by situating white experiences and interests as universal. Conversely, issues of racism become discursively reproduced as special interests. Still, even in its dominance, whiteness is not static and is also hierarchical in structure. It has the ability to include and exclude groups, communities, and ethnicities depending on the political, geographical, cultural, and historical context. Crucially, one does not need to be white to receive some of the privileges associated with whiteness. For example, despite the presence of indelible markers of difference, an advantaged class position, speaking without an accent, and having an Anglicized name are privileges from which racialized Canadians can benefit. Moreover, racialized Canadians can (and do) help reproduce whiteness by privileging white culture and/or norms. To illustrate, in the next chapter, some research participants will discursively reproduce *Hockey Night in Canada* as the standard for hockey broadcasting but, at the same time, that cultural norm has never been challenged in any meaningful way until the *Hockey Night Punjabi* broadcast came along.

For this project, whiteness and the notion of white norms must be understood within very specific confines. For one thing, it is hard to separate the intersections of race, class, and masculinity in Canada from the role that sport plays as a national identifier; therefore, to speak of whiteness in the context of hockey refers to a privileging of middle and working class, Christian (Protestant), heterosexual, Anglo Canadian, male heritage. According to Robidoux (2002), this Canadian interpretation of masculinity is an amalgamation of European sensibilities (Victorian and French) with the First Nations' "alternative model of masculinity ... one where physicality, stoicism, and bravado were valued and celebrated, not repressed" (p. 214). It is through the national pastimes of lacrosse (originally known as baggataway) and hockey that Canadian nationalism has fostered a white identity separate from British authority (Robidoux, 2018). Arguably, these cultural influences explain how Canadians are able to present themselves as polite and peace-loving people but also physically capable and potentially violent when "necessary." The developments of lacrosse and hockey enabled a specific ensemble of constitutive elements of whiteness to emerge as uniquely Canadian.

Don Cherry, host of *Hockey Night in Canada's Coach's Corner*, is a prime arbiter of this specific construction of white masculinity. Kristi Allain's (2015) analysis of *Coach's Corner* observed that Cherry's weekly rhetoric produces a consistent suspicion of academics, reporters, and other intellectuals who Cherry positions as "disconnected from the 'real' concerns and passions associated with the everyday lives of hardworking men, particularly those from small-town Canada" (p. 126). Small-town Canada is also presented as the heart of authentic Canada because, "regardless of where hockey is actually played, mythologically, it is located in small-town Canada" (p. 124). Cherry refers to men who are able to balance roughneck ruggedness with a gentleman's aptitude for respectful deference and duty as "good ol' Canadian boys"

(Allain, 2015); it is this imagined group of white men that I refer to when I write about the construct of whiteness and/or white norms.

Claude Denis (1997) refers to the intersection of whiteness, masculinity, and the liberal-capitalist ethos privileged by the Canadian nation-state as the "whitestream." The analogy of movement proposes that even those marked as Other can be swept up by this normative force, in turn contributing to the dominance of the whitestream. Speaking about hockey specifically, Krebs (2012) posits that because normative Canadian masculinity is intimately constructed through white male hockey players, racialized Canadians "emulate [white bodies] as we swim with the current of the whitestream" (p. 86). In other words, there is little attempt to subvert, challenge, or offer alternative interpretations of racialized masculinities because racialized citizens are so often absorbed into a whitestream that capitalizes on racialized desires to integrate into Canada. The power of the whitestream masks the concept of integration as a fundamentally colonial project and this is particularly evident in hockey because, while racialized hockey participants may question their place in the sport, very rarely is hockey challenged as part of a broader colonial project and history. In other words, if hockey *is* Canada and the Canadian nation-state is inherently racist, then by extension the institution of hockey is also inherently racist. This is why attempts at diversifying the sport have had little impact on the game as a whole, because the culture has yet to address inequalities of power, privilege, and access. Or as Black sports historian and former elite hockey player Bob Dawson asserts, changing the face of the sport will not change the culture, but changing the culture will change the face of hockey (Szto, 2019).

Consequently, ethnic/masculine hierarchy remains central to the maintenance of hockey as a "white man's sport" (Poniatowski & Whiteside, 2012). For example, Russian superstar Alex Ovechkin is discursively produced as a "dirty" player who supposedly lacks the civility found in Canadian players (Allain, 2016). Cherry has referred to Europeans as "goofy" (Allain, 2015, p. 120) and generally creates distance by framing them as effeminate men who feminize the game of hockey. Even Canadian icon Sidney Crosby has been pejoratively called "Cindy Crosby" (ecozens, 2013) or a "whiner" because his playing style contradicts "the requisite masculine character required by those men and boys who play the game" (Allain, 2010, p. 4). Crosby's outstanding skill, skin color, and citizenship cannot fully absolve him of his "effeminate" playing style; this is the narrow field upon which the dominant form of Canadian white masculinity exists.[2]

Rightly or wrongly, hockey has become synonymous with whiteness in Canada. In early 2019, white nationalist posters were shared around the University of Toronto's downtown campus (Takagi, 2019). The poster depicts an illustrated white man wearing a red and black toque, black winter jacket, red and black mittens (seemingly inspired by Hudson Bay's Olympic mittens), gazing off into the distance while holding a hockey stick. The bottom third of the poster reads, "If everyone is Canadian then to be Canadian means nothing," and the website www.studentsforwesterncivilisation.com is listed at the bottom. According to the Students for Western Civilisation webpage, the poster is part of its 2019 campaign against multiculturalism because "multiculturalism and Canadian National Identity are mutually exclusive." While this white nationalist rhetoric may not speak to the Canada that many want it to be in 2019, it does invoke a very real history that informs how race continues to operate within the national boundaries and how hockey can be perceived as a conservative space that promotes and privileges white supremacy.

Citizenship

> For white man's land we fight.
> To Oriental grasp and greed
> We'll surrender, no, never.
> Our watchword be "God Save the King"
> White Canada Forever
> —Popular Canadian song cited in Grace, Strong-Boag,
> Anderson, & Eisenberg, 1998, p. 9

Simms asserts, "Citizenship is not only a legal definition; it is a testimony to how one is treated in a given society. When the concept of racism clashes with that of citizenship, racism, not citizenship emerges victorious" (as cited in W. Kaplan 1993, p. 339). Thobani (2007) argues in settler nations, such as Canada, the state and its natural-born citizens exist as "exalted subjects" against immigrants and Indigenous Peoples. Canadian citizenship has been made possible through the dispossession of Indigenous communities and the reproduction of white supremacy. Therefore, despite Canada's projected image as a haven for immigrants and refugees, "citizenship emerged as integral to the very processes that transformed insiders (Aboriginal peoples) into aliens in their own territories, while simultaneously transforming outsiders (colonizers, settlers, migrants) into exalted insiders (Canadian citizens)" (Thobani, 2007, p. 74). Moreover, through Canada's official policy of multiculturalism, "race became configured as culture and cultural identity became crystallized as political identity, with the core of the nation continuing to be defined as bilingual and bicultural (that is white)" (Thobani, 2007, p. 145). In this dialectical relationship of multiculturalism and citizenship, each group is forced to define themselves in relation to an opposing group; as immigrants fight for their own inclusion in their adopted homeland, they inherently contribute to the ongoing oppression of Indigenous communities.

When the citizenship and immigration guide was revamped from the long-running *A Look at Canada* to *Discover Canada* in 2009, the guide became significantly longer, included noticeable imagery of war and Canadian sports triumphs (both of which were absent from *A Look at Canada*), and had eliminated any mention of unionized labor, universal health care, environmentalism, and human rights (some of which now exists briefly in the current version, last updated in 2012). *Discover Canada* also reduced the number of practice test questions from 113–197 in *A Look at Canada* to just 50. All of these changes resulted in increased citizenship test failures in the following years, particularly from those applying in the family class to join other landed members (Beeby, 2010; McKie, 2013).

Hockey plays a prominent role in *Discover Canada*. The guide includes color images of Wayne Gretzky hoisting the Stanley Cup, Paul Henderson celebrating his game-winning goal against the Soviets in the 1972 Summit Series, two boys (who appear white) playing street hockey, some of the 1978 Montreal Canadiens with Stanley Cup in hand, and one of the last images in the guide is a half-page image of the 2010 Men's Olympic hockey team celebrating with their gold medals. The guide informs new Canadians about the NHL, the Clarkson Cup for women's hockey, and about the national penchant for collecting hockey cards (Citizenship & Immigration Canada, 2012). This is a drastic departure from *A Look at Canada*, which made no mention of hockey or competitive sports and only briefly mentioned recreation. Additionally, in recent years, citizenship ceremonies have become incorporated as part of hockey events such as the World Cup of Hockey (Garrioch, 2016) and Ottawa Senators games (Government of Canada, 2019). It would seem that as diversity increases in Canada, the role of hockey as a cultural artifact becomes more central and entwined with notions of citizenship.

Then-minister for Immigration and Multiculturalism, the conservative politician Jason Kenney, explained that *Discover Canada* was a response to a "growing demand for a deeper sense of citizenship" (Friesen & Curry, 2009, para. 8) and that he hoped it would be "a useful resource for all Canadians, particularly young Canadians to better know their country. I'm frankly more concerned about historical amnesia and civic literacy amongst native-born young Canadians than I am about immigrants who become Canadians" (para. 9). Still, it is imperative that we acknowledge that certain forms of literacy are more "dominant, visible and influential than others" (Barton, Hamilton, & Ivanic, 2005, p. 12), with reading and writing in English versus French in Canada serving as a prime example of how literacies can exist in conflict. C. Reid and Nash (2004) argue that because forms of literacy come into conflict with each other, literacy represents a discursive struggle of regulation, containment, and coherence: "Literacies change; they evolve and reconfigure themselves. The stakes are high in this contest given that the capacity to contain and to fix individual literacy practices coincides with the capacity to establish and maintain social identities, not to mention the power and privilege that such identities entail" (pp. 36–37).

Understanding this more nuanced interpretation to literacy, civic literacy then extends far beyond knowledge *about* Canadian politics to understanding what is involved in the social practices of *being* Canadian. With the volatility of Canadian citizenship under the microscope and the role that hockey plays as a form of literacy, or cultural capital (see chapter 6) in Canada, the study that follows highlights the very tensions that Reid and Nash (2004) describe as struggles over identity, power, privilege, and stability as they exist around hockey rinks for some South Asian Canadians.

South Asians in Canada

The Canadian government identifies South Asians as a racialized group inclusive of people from (or with heritage from) India, Pakistan, Bangladesh, Sri Lanka, and Nepal (Statistics Canada, 2016b). They represent the largest demographic of "visible minorities" in Canada.[3] Academically, the term South Asian comes with various interpretations, usually with India, Pakistan, Sri Lanka, and Bangladesh as main actors, whereas "Afghanistan, Nepal, Bhutan and Myanmar are arbitrarily included and excluded" (Ghosh, 2013, p. 36) from this group depending on who has the power to write in and write out. Other scholars include British India in its entirety, meaning that the West Indies, Fiji, and East Africa are added into the South Asian population (Ghosh, 2013). As Ghosh (2013) asserts, "'South Asia' as a region is in fact a political project of others—to map, categorize and denote ex-colonial non-white bodies" (p. 39).

This study casts a wide net including those who identify under the Statistics Canada definition as well as those who identify with British Indian heritage. Therefore, it is imperative to acknowledge outright that this geographically determined group boasts a wealth of diversity with regard to culture, history, language, religion, and customs; in fact, "it is a myth that there is *a* 'South Asian' culture" (Ghosh, 2013, p. 38). To lump these nationalized groups together also erases conflicts that exist between them. This heterogeneity means the term South Asian has very little meaning to individuals (Ghosh, 2013) but will be used in this study to refer to the entire group of participants, including multiple communities. Conversely, individuals will be referenced by their chosen self-identification (see Appendix B) and hopefully the diversity of perspectives and voices present will demonstrate the imagined nature of any sense of South Asian-ness.

The first South Asians who migrated to Canada were Sikhs from the Punjab province of India traveling with the British army during the late 1800s and early 1900s. Punjab is a small area in the northwestern region of India that borders Pakistan. Upon Indian independence in 1947, the Punjab region was divided, with the majority of Hindus and Sikhs moving inside the Indian border and Muslims leaving India to reside within Pakistan's newly formed border (Nayar, 2012). Due to the level of military, communications, and economic infrastructure in the region, Punjab has been referred to as the heartland or breadbasket of India (Helweg, 1987). Its geopolitical location has made those living in the Punjab region necessarily resilient and self-reliant under the constant threat of warfare and invasion (Nayar, 2012). The British referred to Sikhs as a martial race, and Punjabi soldiers made up the core of the Indian army (Basran & Bolaria, 2003). Despite its significance and location, Punjab is a small region and Punjabi Sikhs are a minority population in India. While 60% of those in Punjab practice the Sikh religion, Sikhism is practiced by only 2% of all Indians.

The first Sikhs who settled in Canada were met with discrimination on multiple levels. In 1908, British Columbia took away their right to vote; this move followed the disenfranchisement of the Chinese in 1874 and the Japanese in 1895 (Nayar, 2012). They were forced into dangerous and exploitative labor positions and prohibited from employment in fields such as law and pharmacy (Basran & Bolaria, 2003). The notorious Continuous Passage Act was legislated in 1908, barring any immigrants who were unable to arrive on Canadian soil via a direct route from their homeland. At the time, travel from India to British Columbia was impossible without stopping on the way; hence, the Continuous Passage Act stemmed fears of a "Hindu Invasion" without overtly discriminating against any particular group. There was an accepted sentiment in Canada and America at the time that "the Indian" was "the most undesirable immigrant in the state. His lack of personal cleanliness, his low morals and his blind adherence to theories and teachings, so entirely repugnant to American principles, make him unfit for association with American people" (Prashad, 2000, pp. 42–43). This construction of racialized difference made policies such as the Continuous Passage Act (enacted from 1908–1947) possible. Today, India is the second-largest immigrant source country after China (Agrawal & Lovell, 2010). Estimates predict the South Asian population in Canada will reach approximately 2.1 million around 2031 (Gee, 2011). Sikhs make up 80% of the South Asians in Vancouver (40% in Toronto), but there is increasing South Asian diversity as more immigrants arrive from Sri Lanka, Bangladesh, and Pakistan (Gee, 2011).

Few scholars have studied South Asian Canadians as high-income earners (Agrawal & Lovell, 2010, p. 144). Walton-Roberts and Pratt (2005) write, "The stereotypical idea of the Indian immigrant is often predicated on that of absence—absence of wealth, opportunity and quality of life—but for middle- and upper-class Indians their lifestyle is often marked by incredible luxury and wealth" (p. 177). Still, we cannot ignore the fact that Indian-born families are disproportionately represented below the poverty line at 19%, compared to 9% of all Canadian families, and also experience higher rates of unemployment

(Agrawal & Lovell, 2010). The image of the impoverished South Asian immigrant continues today, generally fueled by a representation void of history and the effects of colonization. This study offers a counternarrative to these stereotypes of absence because my interview participants represent a growing number of South Asian Canadians occupying the middle and upper classes of Canadian society.

There are two distinct South Asian groups represented in this study. The first group are descendants of some of the first Sikh sojourners to arrive on Canadian soil. The longevity of Punjabi Sikhs in Canada provides generational histories that some racialized groups do not have. In the early 1900s, South Asian men (along with other Asians and Indigenous Peoples) embodied cheap labor for British Columbia's growing forestry, agricultural, and fishing industries (Nayar, 2012). Soon after their arrival, Punjabi men would often form cooperative sawmills. The presence of Punjabi-run mills facilitated increased employment for other Punjabi men as well as slightly higher wages and the ability to advance beyond manual labor (Nayar, 2012). In the 1940s and 1950s, Punjabi-operated sawmills were at their peak in British Columbia, and despite technological changes in the 1950s that decreased the need for human labor, "the success of these industrialists reflected the Punjabi entrepreneurship in an environment where skilled and managerial positions were given primarily to Anglo-Canadians" (Nayar, 2012, p. 30). Therefore, the interconnected histories of British Columbia's resource industries and the need for manual labor offer some insight into the complex socioeconomic position of many Punjabi Canadians today. On the one hand, Punjabi men and women continue to be found as low-paid seasonal workers in agriculture (overrepresented at 21% of British Columbia's immigrant farm population in 2006, compared to 11% Indian representation in the province generally [Statistics Canada, 2006]) (Weiler, Dennis, & Wittman, 2014). However, on the other hand, the ability to accumulate wealth and property, and become self-enterprising families, all while undergoing the assimilation process means that a significant number of South Asian families have moved into the suburban middle-class and, as a result, are able to participate in hockey culture in a way that other racialized families may find difficult.

The second group tends to represent the influx of family class and skilled labor immigration during the late 1960s and early 1970s, which was conversely framed as a brain drain upon the Indian state (Ghosh, 2014). The economic cycles and needs of the host countries "determine immigration policies, thereby dictating who from the periphery gets in, where and when" (Ghosh, 2014, p. 218); in Canada's case, the state suddenly saw a people-to-people relationship with India as extremely beneficial, a drastic change from the days of the Continuous Passage Act (Walton-Roberts, 2003). The demographics of a nation at any given time are a manifestation of what the federal government deems beneficial to the national economy.

The location of this study is significant in the interpretation of the data for two reasons. First, the demographics of the Lower Mainland of British Columbia offer access to a large South Asian population. According to the 2016 census, the Lower Mainland is home to 92% of the province's Punjabi speakers, 94% of its Hindi speakers, and almost 91% of all South Asians in British Columbia (Statistics Canada, 2016a). In 2013, the City of Surrey was home to over 70,000 self-identified Indian households (Statistics Canada, 2013) and almost 94,000 Punjabi speakers (Statistics Canada, 2012). Second, the racialization of Surrey as a space within the Lower Mainland contributes to a specific perception about South Asians. As the fastest growing city in the Lower Mainland, the development of Surrey "has fueled intense resentment and hostility among those white residents who claim that the landscape belongs to them" (G. S. Johal, 2007, p. 179). Johal (2007) explains: "The symbolic and material borders that map the landscapes of Surrey into zones of respectability and degeneracy are constantly being negotiated, adhered to, and contested by those who live in Surrey. Residents of Surrey who have immigrated from, or who are descendants of those who have immigrated from regions outside Europe are constantly faced with the hegemony of a "bourgeois subjectivity" as a mechanism for gaining respectability. They also face the challenge of claiming space for their own purposes" (p. 182).

The Sikh community in the Lower Mainland is the largest non-Christian religious group (Nayar, 2012), and Surrey/North Delta was home to the first Sikh temple (gurdwara) in the area. With approximately 200 Sikh families living in the Surrey-Delta area during the 1970s, an old house was converted into a gurdwara in 1975. Two years later a fire demolished the temple in North Delta and local residents forced the temple to be rebuilt in what was then an undeveloped part of Surrey known as Strawberry Hill (Nayar, 2012). Thus, the perceived ethnic enclave in the current Strawberry Hill and Newton areas of Surrey "was not voluntary but was rather a result of societal pressures to live apart from the mainstream" (Nayar, 2012, p. 224). Surrey has been produced in Vancouver's white imagination as a working-class suburb; hence, the fight over how Surrey develops offers a microcosm of broader racial tensions.

The way that both North Delta and Surrey relegated the gurdwara to a space deemed undesirable is telling: "The space of the Gurdwara was often depicted as a congregation point for bodies that were incapable of the self-discipline necessary to gain the respect of Canadians. Whether the vision was of parading crowds or of a vice den, the space was deemed incompatible with the normal functions of the city" (G. S. Johal, 2007, p. 200).

The area of Strawberry Hill used to be home to early Japanese settlers who used the land to farm fruit and raise poultry. They chose to live on the outskirts of Vancouver where they could avoid discrimination and establish their own farms. This land was seized from these Japanese families during

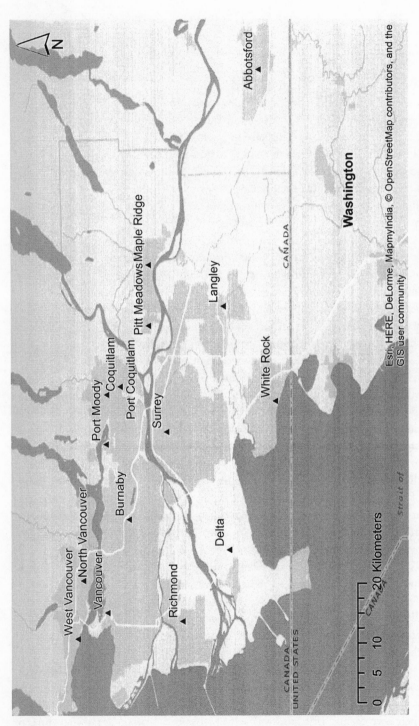

FIG. 1.2 Map of the Lower Mainland of British Columbia (Queen's University, Kingston, ON: Francine Berish, October 2019).

FIG. 1.3 Map of Canada (Queen's University, Kingston, ON: Francine Berish).

the Second World War. Consequently, when we look at the history of racial discrimination in Surrey/Vancouver, we witness a pattern of dismissal that results in entrepreneurial endeavors and what appear to be self-segregated spaces.

Moreover, as Thobani (2007) impresses upon on us the role that racialized Canadians play in the subjugation of the Indigenous peoples, the area of Surrey sits on Indigenous land belonging to the Kwantlen and Semiahmoo First Nations. As a result, the fight to create a "respectable" Surrey devoid of color ignores "the fact that bodies of colour existed when the history of Surrey began," which "helps disrupt the myth that the migration of bodies of colour to Surrey is something new" (G. S. Johal, 2007, p. 186). The utopic vision of Vancouver as "multiculturalism done right" is perhaps most useful in elucidating what multiculturalism actually hides, which is a rich history of racialized contributions that have been erased to form a sense of unity under British colonization.

Surrey was a recurring theme throughout the qualitative interviews. Participants reflected on what it was like to play sports against Surrey teams and be judged or taunted by other South Asians. They would refer to Surrey as an example of the diversity to come or reference Surrey as a main source of racism against the South Asian community because of the class stigma and crime associated with the area. Therefore, in order to understand discrimination in the Lower Mainland as it relates to South Asians, it is imperative to understand the centrality of Surrey as both a physical and imagined space.

Attempts by organizations as varied as Tim Hortons, Molson Canadian, Scotiabank, Hockey Canada, and the Canadian government to promote hockey as Canada's magical unifier have fallen short of the promise offered. Indeed, I shall argue that hockey divides the nation as much as it brings it together. The power in the mythologies of hockey and Canadian multiculturalism is not that they are outright lies but that they are partial truths: segments of truth that serve to represent the whole. As a result, this is a call to action to provide a more nuanced, honest, and historical account of Canada's multicultural rhetoric and ideals.

2

Narratives from
the Screen

Media and Cultural Citizenship

Cinematic depictions are often graphic indicators of changing cultural trends. In this regard, consider the movie *Breakaway* (Lieberman, 2011), the first major cinematic treatment of South Asian Canadians in hockey. The film tells the story of Rajveer (Raj) Singh (played by Vinay Virmani), a Brampton (Ontario) born and raised Punjabi Sikh Canadian, who wants nothing more than to reach his hockey potential. His father, however, wants him to forget about hockey and learn how to earn a living by working for his uncle's trucking company, Speedy Singh. *Breakaway* is the Canadian version of *Bend It Like Beckham*, a story about the conflicts and victories that can be found in multiculturalism and sport. As Abdel-Shehid and Kalman-Lamb (2015) synopsize, *Bend It Like Beckham* is a film about transcendence, whereby institutional oppression can be outworked and out-willed, and it reproduces the notion of "culture [clashes]" (p. 143) between traditions that have immigrated versus inherited national norms. In each film, the host nation is written as the hero and sport serves as the vehicle to achieve this national truth.

Akin to *Bend It Like Beckham*'s storyline, Raj struggles to balance his Canadian and Sikh identities. The hockey rink represents escape, potentiality, and difference. It is an escape from his stereotypically overbearing father. It represents his potential as a hockey player when he demonstrates that he is able to play with the local semi-pro team, the Hammerheads. Raj assumes that once the coach sees his skills he will invite him to play with the Hammer-heads; unfortunately, after his impromptu tryout where Raj demonstrates that he is capable of competing with the Hammerheads, the coach responds, "I'll make sure there's a ticket for you when we play in the finals [Skating away from Raj]. Don't feel bad kid; you weren't going to make the team anyway." Raj's difference is situated as fodder for humiliation and discrimination. Field (2014) critiques the film, stating, "in a post-multicultural Canada, such lines are meant to draw the audience to the side of the underdog, while collectively shouting 'no, that's not our Canada'" (para. 22).

For the remainder of the film, hockey and Canada become integral—and innocent—actors. Difference is overcome at the rink just as easily as it is made visible. Raj's coach, Dan Winters (played by Rob Lowe), gives a pep talk to the team where he explains that a win will help erase their racialized difference. This speech cements hockey's innocence, because, as many sports films have taught us previously, winning is the definitive response to racism. At one point, the Canadian *Charter of Rights and Freedoms* is trotted out to deflect any criticisms of systemic racism (something that scholars such as Denis [1997] contend is Western in conception and reproductive of the whitestream itself). Raj's love interest in the film, Melissa Winters (played by Camilla Belle), a law student and the sister of Coach Dan, describes what happened at the tryout as "a human rights case. The Canadian Charter of Human Rights clearly speaks against this kind of organized harassment." The charter is used both as an apparent buttress and national alibi against racial oppression that renders discussions about racism unnecessary because everyone is assumed protected by the law.

Narratives that exist on the screen, whether big or small, offer an important entry point into this study. *Breakaway* attempts to depict certain tensions that exist in Canadian society (white vs. brown, tradition vs. modernity, religious identity vs. national identity), yet it also reproduces the common belief that respect for difference (and a love of hockey) ultimately prevails. In this chapter, I argue that the *Hockey Night Punjabi* broadcast offers us a real-life example to further explore such tensions and points of friction as they occur in the landscape of ethnic sports media. An examination of narratives in *Hockey Night Punjabi* enables an exploration of what separates South Asian participation in hockey from that of any other racialized group.

Hockey Night Punjabi

In 2008, the Canadian Broadcasting Corporation (CBC) experimented with multicultural broadcasting during the NHL playoffs by offering hockey commentary in Mandarin, Cantonese, Italian, Inuktitut (Inuit language), and Punjabi. Only the Punjabi version was successful enough during the trial run to garner weekly broadcasts the following NHL regular season. It would play concurrently with Canada's longest-running broadcast and the CBC's most lucrative program, *Hockey Night in Canada* (*HNIC*) (Shoalts, 2014), on digital channels and via online streaming. After spending four years in a small room being filmed on a handheld camcorder in Toronto, the Punjabi broadcast briefly moved to Calgary and has been in Vancouver since 2014 (personal communication, April 18, 2016). When Rogers Communications bought the rights to *HNIC* in 2013 (Canadian Press, 2013a), OMNI television (a Rogers subsidiary) made a pitch to move the Punjabi edition to Vancouver and adopt the old Sportsnet set.

The current broadcast team consists of Harnarayan Singh, Randip Janda, Harpreet Pandher, Gurp Sian, Taqdeer Thindal, and Mantar Bhandal, with Amrit Gill as the social media host. Previous broadcast iterations also included Bhupinder Hundal, Bhola Chauhan, Parminder Singh, and Inderpreet Cumo. It is a privately funded program with Chevrolet as the title sponsor. As of late 2017, viewership was estimated at 209,000 viewers per game (personal communication, November 21, 2017). Considering that hockey is nationally broadcast in only English and Punjabi,[1] *Hockey Night Punjabi* truly is symbolic of hockey culture changing on the fly.

Hockey Night Punjabi has built the program around play-by-play commentator Harnarayan Singh. A native of Brooks, Alberta, Singh was groomed for the broadcasting industry from a young age. He and his older sisters grew up during the 1980s when the Edmonton Oilers dominated the NHL, winning five Stanley Cups between 1983 and 1990. His sisters passed their hockey fanaticism to him, and Singh turned that fandom into a love of broadcasting:

> My sisters tell me that I was running around the living room all the time re-enacting the players but also commentating at the same time . . . I wanted to be Ron MacLean and I pretended to host hockey awards shows and I had my own hockey radio show. So, they got me a little Radio Shack kids microphone stand and stuff so that I could do that. I guess no one realized it at the time but they were nurturing that whole thing and encouraging my interest in hockey and the broadcast side. (Personal communication, April 18, 2016)

Singh has publicly recounted on numerous occasions that hockey became a vital connection point with other children growing up in Brooks (Sax, 2013). Wearing hockey shirts deflected some of the attention away from his turban and the questions that accompanied being the only Punjabi family in the area. He shared positive memories from his time in Brooks, still his difference was always apparent. When I asked if he ever noticed that he looked different from all the people he admired in hockey culture, Singh answered:

> Yeah, it did resonate with me because of the fact that people pointed it out to me at a very young age. I remember going to our family doctor and he asked my

dad, "What does he want to do when he grows up?" And, my dad said, "Oh, he wants to go into TV/radio, he wants to be a broadcaster." The doctor goes, "You have to be realistic! The chances of that happening are so slim. Have you looked at what people look like on TV? They don't look like you." (Personal communication, April 18, 2016)

Singh described the doctor's reality check as "devastating." He further reflected that teachers and professors along the way tried to dissuade him from sports commentary in particular and instead encouraged him to try the news side of broadcasting (seemingly to protect him from disappointment). While Canadian media has its own diversity issues, Singh's personal history suggests there is a broader recognition that sports media sets even narrower confines. Singh continued his reflection: "I had this postcard of every announcer; every commentator at the time that was working for *Hockey Night in Canada* and it was on our fridge. So, you know, whenever I'm going to get a carton of milk for my cereal, I would look at it and yeah, it wasn't the most diverse group to say the least. So, all the heads were put together on this postcard and I would wonder, "Do I fit in there?" (Personal communication, April 18, 2016).

Singh's narrative is important because it exposes conflicting realities. On the one hand, it highlights a specific set of hurdles that exists for racialized Canadians with regard to self-doubt and the power that a homogenous media presence has on public perception. On the other, it represents an important story of hope and potential; it means that the next generation of Sikh Canadians, or South Asians more broadly, will not have to *wonder* if they fit into hockey broadcasting—they can simply focus on making it happen. This immediate effect was demonstrated during the 2016 Stanley Cup playoffs when a young man tweeted that *Hockey Night Punjabi* "may have altered [his] dream [from becoming] a sports journalist to becoming a Punjabi sports journalist" (Singh, 2016). Even social media host Amrit Gill explains that it is rare for a South Asian person to be involved in broadcasting: "There's no one in our culture that does anything like this so my extended family and my friends are always saying, 'You're doing something different. We like talking about it.' One of my aunties, she's always telling me that we always talk about what our kids are doing and it's always the same thing, nursing blah blah blah but then I bring you up and they're very interested because it's so different" (personal communication, February 25, 2016).

In 2004, the percentage of racialized Canadians working for daily papers was noted as 6 times lower than their demographic presence and that there is no real urgency from media agencies to diversify their staff (Miller, 2005). Amira Elghawaby (2014), a journalist and communications director at the National Council of Canadian Muslims, argues that part of the lack of representation may stem from an inability of racialized Canadians to envision a career in the media, coupled with the traditional devaluation of media jobs in certain families. Thus, the presence of people like Singh and Gill on national television arguably helps embolden the contributions of minoritized communities and their value as citizens.

I conducted a social media analysis during the 2013–2014 regular season and observed that, at the time, the broadcast was met with equal parts support and resistance (Szto, 2016). The most unsettling pattern that developed through Twitter comments about the show was laughter at both the concept of the show and its commentators. Half of the tweets coded as resistant to the show included overt expressions of ridicule such as, "LMFAO [laugh my f—ing ass off] HOCKEY NIGHT IN PUNJABI!!!!!!," "Hockey Night in Canada Punjabi is arguably the funniest thing in professional sports [attached photo of commentators]," and "Hahaha! Hockey Night in Canada Punjabi. #lolololol [attached photo of commentators]" (p. 214). As the show has grown in popularity and reach, the support on social media now seems to overwhelm the few racist comments that trickle in; still, the fact that the sight of men with turbans on sports media can elicit a pattern of laughter from Canadian citizens illustrates the harm in reproducing a racially and ethnically homogenous media. A few years ago, *Hockey Night Punjabi* existed outside the realm of possibility to more Canadians than we would probably like to admit, but, oddly enough, the Rogers buy-out of Sportsnet turned out to be extremely beneficial for *Hockey Night Punjabi*.

When the broadcast moved to Vancouver the new physical resources enabled it to expand its capabilities by adding pre- and postgame segments and live social media. It is also offered in high definition (a key feature for any legitimate sports production) and aired on a publicly available channel. In addition to the logistical changes, personnel additions enhanced the potential for depth of programming. Bhupinder Hundal, former on-air host and occasional producer, explained that previously the show did not fully embrace the uniqueness of its position: "There wasn't a manager working on it looking at it from a business perspective. There wasn't [sic] the tools or the resources that could really lift the show" (personal communication, April 28, 2016). For Hundal, a veteran of the broadcasting and media community, it was crucial that the broadcast move away from looking like a side project and more toward a legitimate hockey broadcast: "I think that was kind of important for the evolution of, not only just that broadcast, but the connection the community is going to have with it. This is not just a novelty. This is a real, live, robust hockey broadcast for us that's at the same level as what you would get elsewhere and that was kind of a goal" (personal communication, April 28, 2016).

Now in its 11th broadcast season, *Hockey Night Punjabi* has become the leading edge of ethnic sports media. In the National Football League (NFL), the Carolina Panthers have hosted Spanish commentary for the last seven years, with the commentators becoming "cult heroes among English-speaking Panthers fans, and rock stars to Spanish speakers" (Jones, 2015). *Hockey Night Punjabi* has garnered similar cult fandom, largely developed during the 2016 Stanley Cup Playoffs when Singh's goal call, "Bonino Bonino Bonino!" became a social media sensation, drawing the attention of non-Punjabi fans and the entire Pittsburgh Penguins hockey organization (CBS Pittsburgh, 2016; C. Johnston, 2016a; Szto & Gruneau, 2018). Teams such as the Chicago Blackhawks (2016) and Florida Panthers (C. Johnston, 2016b) have added Spanish commentary for their games, demonstrating the growing prevalence of not only racialized fans but also the (economic) value of minoritized (fan) communities.

Ethnic (Sports) Media

Ethnic media refers to media created for or by immigrants, minoritized groups (whether ethnic, racial, or linguistic), and/or Indigenous populations (Matsaganis, Katz, & Ball-Rokeach, 2011). Ethnic media serve as one metric of globalization by highlighting human movement and settlement. In 2007, Matsaganis et al. (2011) reported that Canada hosted over 250 ethnic newspapers and 40 ethnic television channels, making Canada (along with Australia) the most hospitable nation(s) for ethnic media to establish a presence and potentially flourish. Yu (2016) points out that the growth of ethnic media is also a reaction to the consistent misrepresentation and underrepresentation of racialized people in mainstream media. In fact, ethnic print media is the "only print media sector that is growing in the United States" (Pew Research Centre, 2006 as cited in Yu, 2016, p. 344).

Vancouver is an important contextual component in the ongoing success and progression of *Hockey Night Punjabi* because, as of 2008, the city boasted over 100 ethnic media outlets serving "nearly twenty-three language groups, other than English and French" (Yu & Murray, 2007, p. 100). Studies conducted in the mid-1990s and mid-2000s observed a larger total circulation of ethnic newspapers in Vancouver than the city's two largest English-language papers (Grescoe, 1994/1995; Murray, Yu, & Ahadi, 2007). Thus, the geographic location where ethnic media are produced is key to their success, along with *how* such media are produced (Shankar, 2015). To understand ethnic media is to deal with the reality that there is no single model that can be transplanted from one location to another or from one group to another.

Aside from the few other analyses of *Hockey Night Punjabi* (see Stewart, 2012; Szto, 2016; Szto & Gruneau, 2018), the only other (English-language) academic work on ethnic sports media focuses on Spanish commentary of the Los Angeles Dodgers Major League Baseball (MLB) team. When the Dodgers moved from Brooklyn to Los Angeles in the late 1950s, they became the first team to offer radio broadcasting in both English and Spanish for every game. This decision, in part, reflected a growing interest in Fernando Valenzuela, a rookie pitcher from Mexico, who helped symbolize "a period of arrival for Latinos in the United States" (Regalado, 1995, p. 281). Similar to multi-language broadcasting for *HNIC*, Spanish baseball commentary started out as a cautious project with limited funding, which meant the Spanish commentators did not travel for games with the team and instead provided studio recreations. By the mid-1960s, the Spanish broadcast team of Jaime Jarrín and René Cárdenas were able to cover all Dodgers games live.

Jarrín, the so-called "Latino Vin Scully," has been calling Dodgers games in Spanish since 1958. In 2016, Vin Scully, the Dodgers' iconic English commentator, embarked on a year-long farewell tour and *The Guardian* aptly attempted to shine part of that light on Jarrín (Carpenter, 2016): "Lost behind the year-long farewell to Scully is a remarkable story. It's a story many baseball fans don't know because when they think of the Dodgers they think only of Scully. . . . Even as they mourn Scully's October retirement, they have barely heard of the regal 80-year-old legend in Scully's shadow. Nor do they realize that for 58 years, millions of southern California Latinos have had a Vin Scully of their own. And that without him the Dodgers might not be the $2 [billion] franchise they've become" (para. 3).

Jarrín and Cárdenas were pioneers in ethnic sports media, and their legacy has opened doors for a generation of Spanish (radio) broadcasters who express their gratitude any time they meet Jarrín. This legacy is one that is central to *Hockey Night Punjabi*'s goals: Does this program open doors for future generations, and does the broadcast give young South Asian broadcasters the ability to hone their skills for opportunities in mainstream media?

Regalado (1995) stresses that Spanish broadcasting "brought a new element to baseball in the United States and expanded the game's horizons well beyond its borders" (p. 289), but perhaps more significantly, ethnic sports media helped solidify the value of Latino players and the existence of the broader Hispanic community. These examples of ethnic sports media offer one avenue for historically marginalized communities to write onto the national narrative and contribute alternative visions of what is possible for both media and citizens. Ethnic sports media can help bring citizenship into new areas of concern (Vega & Boele van Hensbroek, 2012), such as the intersections of culture and media.

Breaking Barriers

One significant difference between *Hockey Night Punjabi* and the Dodgers' Spanish commentary is that Jarrín would translate Scully's commentary;

thus, the dominant English commentary carried through to the Spanish-speaking community. In contrast, *Hockey Night Punjabi* commentators have free reign to call games as they see fit and, arguably, it is this freedom that has made mainstream broadcasting take note.

Hockey Night Punjabi commentary is loud, boisterous, comedic, musical, and informational. The broadcast team will draw equally from Bollywood and Indian food references as they casually slip in popular culture references to wrestling or the television show *The Simpsons*. This variety helps them speak to multiple generations in one family, since it is a common occurrence for South Asian families to have extended family living under the same roof. It is an effect of their broadcast that the team never saw coming. Singh explains:

> You have this dynamic where there is such a cultural divide within one household, and it's not only language but it's technology, it's the customs of the country, and the cultural norms are so different. So, there's nothing to really bring everyone together because the differences are so vast where I've had grandparents come tell me that our grandkids don't even talk to us. They don't want to sit with us, they think we are so old or we don't know how to work iPhones. I've had teary-eyed grandmothers tell me that because of the show now it is a Saturday night tradition and their grandkids are sitting with them thinking that it's so cool that my grandma is watching hockey and she knows who the [Toronto Maple] Leafs are, the Canucks. She's become a fan. (Personal communication, April 18, 2016)

Other research participants often echoed similar sentiments that their grandparents or aunts and uncles, who were newer arrivals to Canada, really enjoy the broadcast. Prav, 20, grew up playing minor hockey and explained that his grandfather used to watch hockey but he never understood the game. Now his grandfather is able to discuss the game and provide Prav with game updates (personal communication, September 1, 2016). Sonia, a 26-year-old former player, spoke of the excitement from her extended family when they discovered the broadcast: "That group of people who don't speak English that much and are working these jobs, when that *Hockey Night in Canada Punjabi* broadcast came out it was the talk of the town. It was so exciting because it's like we can follow along and not just listen to this thing and watch the tv. It's a big deal, I feel especially for, when I think of my uncles or my aunts, they can follow along in a more meaningful way" (personal communication, December 1, 2016).

Ethnic sports media represents a complicated convergence of the desire and/or necessity to assimilate into the dominant (white) culture, while also retaining cultural difference. As Justin Trudeau, then Liberal Party leader and current prime minister, once tweeted about the show, it is "multiculturalism at its finest." Whether or not *Hockey Night Punjabi* symbolizes the full potential of multicultural policy or its intentions is debatable, but it does foster cultural citizenship where it did not previously exist.

Coauthoring One's Existence: Cultural Citizenship

Cultural citizenship, as defined by Boele van Hensbroek (2012), privileges meaning-making. It does not attempt to replace fundamental rights as core to notions of citizenship, but it does want to layer the need for meaning on top of access to decision-making. For Boele van Hensbroek (2012), "the essence of the idea of cultural citizenship is then: *to be co-producer, or co-author, of the cultural context (webs of meaning) in which one participates*" (p. 78, emphasis in the original). This perspective is useful for framing issues of exclusion and representation. The initial stages of this particular framework involve freedom to participate in cultural practices as the first stage, but coauthorship is not merely content with participation: "The idea of the whole exercise is to provide reinterpretations of history, to challenge or enrich existing views, in short, to have an impact on the cultural consensus. This deeper aspect of participation is captured well in the idea of co-authorship, for if deviant historical interpretations remain in a cultural niche and the ruling images are not challenged, then there may be cultural freedom but no co-authorship. Without some impact on the construction process of the cultural consensus there would still be deficient cultural citizenship" (Boele van Hensbroek, 2012, p. 82). The conscious desire for *Hockey Night Punjabi* to coauthor the Canadian hockey narrative is central to its potential for breaking down barriers and creating a new space for South Asians in Canadian media and sports.

Drawing from the work of S. Hall (2005), culture is viewed as a production that enables citizens to "produce ourselves anew, as new kinds of subjects" (p. 556); consequently, culture both writes on itself and writes itself into being. This notion of writing onto an existing narrative that has generally only allowed limited authorship is evident in Hundal's dream for the broadcast:

> What I would like to see is that there [are] a few South Asian players who are in the NHL and are having success in the NHL. And, their parents put them into the game because they were able to understand the game better because of the broadcast. I think ultimately that's kind of what we want to see. I think if that were to happen [it] would let me know that we have achieved the legacy that we wanted to with the broadcast. The whole idea is to break down barriers, right? If we're able to break down the barrier and warm up the game of hockey to parents who typically might not be hockey moms and hockey dads, and their kids are able to achieve the highest pinnacle of success, even just making the NHL or playing regularly in the NHL would really put a stamp on what this broadcast has meant. (Personal communication, April 28, 2016)

In this sense, authorship comes in the form of attempting to have Canada's people represented in the nation's game—writing through physical inclusion. Understanding the game is a necessary first step to ensure participation, and the hope is that participation at multiple levels will add nuance and counternarratives to a mythology that has remained insulated.

The broadcasters talked about how each of them would play NHL video games as children and commentate the play in Punjabi for fun. At no point did it ever occur to them that this opportunity might exist for them as adults. They also discussed the end goal of having a Punjabi broadcaster(s) on the English broadcast. Hundal again emphasized, "I think the goal as broadcasters is how do we get good enough that we're *Hockey Night in Canada*, as opposed to just *Hockey Night Punjabi* . . . can this be a stepping stone . . ." (personal communication, April 28, 2016). Consequently, English media maintains its dominance as the reference point for legitimate media, and ethnic media is reproduced as abnormal. With that said, during this study, Singh made three appearances on Sportsnet's Wednesday night national hockey broadcast. This was the first time that a Sikh Canadian had been included in mainstream hockey broadcasting (Dormer, 2016). Additionally, Randip Janda also secured a mainstream broadcasting position on Sportsnet 650's newly formed sports talk radio program (P. Johnston, 2017). Hundal noted that while it is possible for those working in ethnic media to transition into mainstream media, the opportunity exists only for those who lack any discernible accent (personal communication, February 10, 2016). It is essential to note here, however, that accents are cultural dimensions of speech and live "largely in the realm of the imaginary" (Hill, 1998, p. 682). Drawing from the work of Frantz Fanon, Puwar (2004) argues, "When established institutions open their doors to postcolonial bodies, they have a strong preference for those who have assimilated the 'mother country's' legitimate language. Proficiency in the legitimate national language plays a decisive role in the selection of [racialized bodies] for professional spaces" (pp. 112–113). Consequently, it is not merely the competency of a person that is up for judgment; *how* this competency is conveyed is equally important—the hegemonic national language represents the "voice of reason" (Puwar, 2004, p. 111) and accents are a distinction that helps separate racialized bodies from one another.

To continue privileging English media in a multicultural nation as the marker of achievement remains problematic, but the potential for ethnic sports media to help increase diversity in mainstream media is a tangible benefit. For example, Singh, Janda, and Hundal attended the 2017 NHL All-Star Game, where they broadcast in both English and Punjabi and were able to interview players alongside mainstream media. And, on February 18, 2016, National Hockey Day in Canada, the English broadcast threw it to Singh, Janda, Pandher, and Hundal in studio who did a short feature (in English) purely about hockey. Is this an example of the mainstream simply co-opting the alternative or are the margins writing themselves into the center? Perhaps it is a bit of both, but at this point *Hockey Night Punjabi* has situated itself in a position where it is able to expand the conversation as to who can and cannot contribute to sports media and Canada's pastime.

Hundal also reflected on the importance of being able to act in the role of a coauthor with one's identity intact. The ability to appear in hockey culture as a baptized Sikh sends an important message that aspiring broadcasters should not need to feel torn between their heritage and mainstream society. This tension was illustrated in the movie *Breakaway*, specifically with the issue of wearing a turban while playing ice hockey. The few research participants who had seen *Breakaway* tended to argue that the film exacerbated the issue of the turban and the assumption that baptized Sikhs have to choose between honoring their faith and fitting into hockey culture. Likewise, my own experience recounted in the introduction was unpacked with participants as less of an issue for those who choose to wear turbans than it is for those looking from the outside in. Singh stressed, "to an actual turban wearer it's a non-issue because there's ways around it . . . there's a bazillion styles of turbans out there so it can be very much adjusted to be worn under a helmet for safety reasons in a sport like ice hockey or football" (personal communication, April 18, 2016). Additionally, a visit to the North Surrey Recreation Centre challenges this presumed conflict between turbans and hockey because, in many of the team photos, young boys can be seen wearing turbans or patkas.

Personally, for Hundal, maintaining his chosen identity is what makes the journey worth traveling: "I think you'd be more proud if you stayed true to your identity and achieved that success as opposed to trying to compromise your identity to try and achieve that success. . . . It's going to be a much more difficult road—no doubt—but you'll overcome so much and your journey is going to be more rewarding, the end result is going to be more rewarding. And, it's going to be more inspiring to another generation of youth. I think that lasting impact is something that drives me" (personal communication, April 28, 2016).

In these examples, the mere participation of certain citizens helps provide alternative narratives to commonly held assumptions. The presence of people like Singh and Hundal helps to write other Sikh Canadians into popular existence.

What is more, the fact *Hockey Night Punjabi* is essentially accountable only to itself means it can decide which narratives to amplify. In 2016, when Prime Minister Trudeau issued an official apology for the Komagata Maru incident, *Hockey Night Punjabi* was able to speak about this tragic event with its viewers in a way that would surely seem out of place on a mainstream sportscast. Likewise, the broadcast provides a space to highlight the voices and experiences of South Asian players such as Robin Bawa, the first NHL player of Indian ancestry. Bawa, a native of Duncan, British Columbia, is noted as a trailblazer for South Asian hockey players. In their interview, the second question posed to Bawa was about his experiences with racism in hockey, to which he responded:

> I think racism is always there. When I was younger you could see it more, maybe now it's a little more hidden. I remember when my grandpa came over in 1906 they couldn't go to get a haircut—whites only. Then you go into grade one, grade two, grade three, the way I started to play hockey was one of the kids goes "Your kind doesn't play." I went home to my dad and I said, "Hey dad, is that true?" He goes, "No, not at all." So, the next day we bought a pair of skates and away we went. (Hockey Night Punjabi, 2016b)

The interview, which was conducted in English and posted in full on social media, enabled a discussion about racism in hockey that is often omitted or used only to bolster narratives of meritocracy and determination. In addition, during the winter of 2016–2017, the broadcast helped promote a stem cell drive for two young Sikh boys diagnosed with leukemia. Registration events seeking possible bone marrow donors were held at various gurdwaras (temples) in the Lower Mainland and in Ontario (Hockey Night Punjabi, 2016a). For *Hockey Night Punjabi*, race cannot be ignored.

As noted in the previous chapter, the question of *which* men are able to contribute and benefit from hockey culture is fundamental to this analysis. Hundal states, "we have to break down the barrier of hockey being an all-boys club, number one. And being an all-boys white men club" (personal communication, April 28, 2016). What is reported, downplayed, replayed, and eliminated from the media "is always the result of a complex process of selection" that tends to reproduce dominant ideologies (Gruneau, 1989, p. 134), which is why it is imperative that traditionally marginalized communities be able to control their own narratives.

Last, *Hockey Night Punjabi* offers a new linguistic development for Punjabi Canadians. It is often forgotten that English is the first language of the broadcast team. Even though they are all comfortable and fluent Punjabi speakers, the speed and spontaneity of calling a live sporting event comes with certain pressures, especially when it is not one's mother tongue. In order to prepare, Janda explains they hold their meetings in Punjabi to help them "start thinking hockey in Punjabi" (personal communication, May 3, 2016). In the beginning, the team was assisted by people who used to work on OMNI's newscast, a sort of "language committee," to help with the nuances and depth of the Punjabi language (personal communication, May 3, 2016). They also use vocabulary lists to avoid excessive repetition and to quell any desire to substitute English. According to Janda, the "preparation is vital otherwise we'd be

FIG. 2.1 Bhupinder Hundal, speaking with *Hockey Night Punjabi* fans at the 2017 Vancouver Vaisakhi festival.

speaking English every second word" (personal communication, May 3, 2016). When Janda and Singh attempted to commentate in English once for fun, Janda described the experience as "weird," because at this point Punjabi has become his first broadcasting language: "It wasn't natural at all and the assumption is I speak English all the time, this should be easy, and it wasn't" (personal communication, May 3, 2016). Pandher asserts that *Hockey Night Punjabi* may speak the most Punjabi of any programming, including many of the news reports from India (personal communication, April 14, 2016). In this way, the Punjabi broadcast makes a conscious effort to make language central to the experience. Likewise, the boisterous and humorous commentary purposely draws from Punjabi culture, forming a convergence point for language and culture to coalesce into something uniquely designed for its target audience. It is not simply hockey commentary in Punjabi, and this may explain why the other experimental language broadcasts mounted by CBC did not resonate as well with their respective communities.

The development of this particular dialect and communication technique, specific to hockey broadcasting, connects back to the fact that multiple generations of Punjabi viewers watch the show. Janda explained to me that the Punjabi he learned growing up in Canada is different from the Punjabi that people learned growing up in India, and that the richness of Punjabi means there are various levels of the language (personal communication, May 3, 2016). As a result, the broadcast mixes Punjabi for the young and old, those Canadian born and those naturalized. The creation of a new dialect unique for those watching hockey is another example of constituting a group's citizenship through language, communication, and media. *Hockey Night Punjabi* facilitates citizenship beyond participation in hockey; it produces meaning where none previously existed, all while writing itself and its fans into the cultural consensus.

Limits of Ethnic Media

The positive contributions of *Hockey Night Punjabi* outlined so far need to be balanced with some of the limitations that face both ethnic media more broadly and this particular broadcast. First, as was alluded to earlier, the separate but equal format, in many ways, reifies racialized difference as abnormal in Canadian society. To offer a privately funded, minoritized language broadcast on a multicultural channel does little to challenge the conservative, whitestream nature of hockey culture. Its existence could be eliminated at any given time, and mainstream hockey culture would not need to acknowledge this fact.

Additionally, working on a niche program such as *Hockey Night Punjabi* tends to draw attention for being different rather than for its commonalities with *HNIC*. For example, when I asked Singh if he ever gets tired of being asked to talk about diversity in hockey instead of just hockey (an offense of which I was equally guilty), he agreed that he would like to talk more about the sport and less about his personal journey but that he recognizes his personal story is an integral piece of the puzzle that cannot be forgotten (personal communication, April 18, 2016). One coach I interviewed voiced similar concerns whereby he noticed that he was only ever invited to speak about diversity in hockey instead of coaching strategy (personal communication, April 3, 2016). The separate but equal format reproduces the idea that difference should be segregated from so-called mainstream culture and that certain bodies remain out of place. Puwar (2004) notes that racialized bodies have little choice in the matter; they have special interests "'foisted' upon them" (p. 67). These observations reiterate Gayatri Spivak's claim, "I am invited to speak today for the precise reason I wasn't in the past" (as cited in Landy & MacLean, 1996, p. 194). We must learn to question: Which bodies speak about which subjects? What is this body expected to speak about? What is this body not expected to speak of? On whose behalf are they asked to speak? And, if they speak "out of turn" will they be heard? (Puwar, 2006). Singh acknowledges that having someone like him on the English broadcasts is a powerful move toward social harmony in a nation that has experienced increasing backlash against equal rights, especially when the opportunities are not limited to speaking about his experience on the margins.

A second limitation is the assumption than an expiration date exists for non-English media. Most ethnic media are relatively small-scale operations and regional in nature, making sustainability and monitoring and evaluation difficult tasks (Matsaganis et al., 2011). Presumably, as generations become more hybrid, the hypothesis is that English media will be sufficient and we will see a decrease in ethnic media outlets. Harry, a long-time hockey coach and administrator echoes this perception: "I think as time goes on it might not be as successful because gradually everybody will have English as their first language ... you require an audience and right now there's an audience for this, maybe in 15 years there won't be one" (personal communication, April 3, 2016). Kevin, who referred to the broadcast as a "gimmick," offers a comparable critique on the perceived limits of the show's growth potential: "CBC and Rogers Sportsnet can say whatever they want but it's done for a purpose, to draw more viewers, to draw more revenue. That's fine, nothing wrong with that but is it going to replace anything? No. The South Asian population is limited. There's only X [amount] you are going to reach because it's here. Are you going to get more viewers in India? No. They're not" (personal communication, November 21, 2016).

It is important to note, however, that these remain assumptions because ethnic media of this particular iteration is really only a generation old. The Canadian Radio-Television and Telecommunications Commission (CRTC) did not announce an explicit ethnic media broadcasting policy until 1999 (Matsaganis et al., 2011), and legislation for increased diversity in media was instituted in 1991. These comments also seem to ignore the fact that new immigrants continue to arrive and, even without new arrivals, ethnic media helps keep languages alive, which is vital for the survival of many communities, such as Indigenous groups.[2] Conceivably, this assumption is based on the increased saturation of the English language globally; still, the expiration date hypothesis has yet to be confirmed.

Third, despite the broadcast's attempts to create a well-respected sports production, there is a definite feeling from the younger generation that it is a sideshow. For example, Dev, a 25-year-old recreational player, expressed appreciation for the Punjabi broadcast but maintained that *HNIC* offers more to its viewers: "I'm all for it, if they want to watch it in their native language that's totally cool, but there's just that history behind all the sportscasters on *Hockey Night in Canada* that you kind of have to watch it, right, to get that full experience. Bob Cole for one, he's a national treasure. Don Cherry. I mean yeah, it's just those elements of *Hockey Night in Canada* with different language broadcasts" (personal communication, August 12, 2016).[3]

That full experience seemingly points to the history that comes with *HNIC* and its recognizable figures. Racialized deference to the whitestream is evident in this statement because we could just as easily state that viewers of *HNIC* are the ones who do not receive the full experience—there are stories that they are missing, current events they may not be privy to, and calls that they would be lucky to catch on social media after the fact. Even the conservative

American news outlet *Fox News* wrote, "The most exciting goal calls of the Stanley Cup playoffs aren't in English or French" (Bathe, 2016) in reference to the Punjabi broadcast. This sense of loss or missing out extends only in one direction.

Furthermore, the fact that none of the broadcasters have playing experience creates challenges for some viewers, such as Kevin:

> I'm jaded in the sense that being a hockey dad, the analytical side of it, I'd rather listen to Jim Hughson, Craig Simpson because I'll get the more analytical side because Craig Simpson has played hockey. The other two guys, they're very good Punjabi communicators. They're very entertaining. It is fun, here and there to flip it back and forth just to hear descriptors but that's it. Are they giving me an in-depth analytical description of the game? They are giving me entertainment value but are they giving me a true hockey perspective? No. (Personal communication, November 21, 2016)

Kevin's feelings are common in sports discourse, where playing experience is conflated with the ability to provide thoughtful game analysis. This critique is commonly waged against female commentators (Franks, 2016; Glass, 2017) and broadcasters of color (Dowbiggin, 2013); it polices who is able to speak in sports media, further marginalizing groups that were often not privileged with the ability to participate. But who is and is not qualified to commentate on sports is socially constructed, because Jim Hughson has explained that he, unlike Singh who grew up with the dream of commentating and graduated with a degree in broadcasting, "went to university, didn't finish a degree, [and] went back to work in the radio business" (Fox, 2015, para. 7). It also appears that Hughson never competed in organized hockey. What makes Hughson's analysis more qualified than someone like Singh, other than the fact that he was given the opportunity to call Vancouver Canucks games and allowed to hone his skills over the past four decades? Through Dev's and Kevin's comments, we can observe the normative power of white Canadian culture at work by positioning the English broadcast as the one true hockey perspective.

Moreover, the humor that the Punjabi broadcasters inject into their commentary seems to paradoxically solidify the sideshow nature of the broadcast for hockey aficionados, even though it is presumed welcoming for those learning about the game. Gary, 38, grew up playing hockey and articulates this cognitive dissonance created by humor where a stone-faced professionalism has come to be expected: "They're pretty funny. I can't watch it because I'm laughing half the time. Not because of the quality, I just love what they're saying" (personal communication, April 15, 2016). Notice how quality and entertainment are explained as mutually exclusive. Randy, 43, offers a similar take on the broadcast:

CS: Do you ever watch the Punjabi broadcast?

RANDY: I'll watch it from time to time. It's one of those things, I won't watch a game. I'll tune in for comedy's sake, to see the quotes they come up with.

CS: You won't consistently tune in?

RANDY: No, never. (Personal communication, November 15, 2016)

Interestingly, *Hockey Night Punjabi* seems to draw laughter from its detractors and its supporters. They are laughing for different reasons, yet both forms reproduce the show's marginality.

The informational and laid-back nature of the show that is supposed to invite new viewers appears to be off-putting for seasoned hockey fans. This paradigm again normalizes the English commentary and reproduces ethnic sports media as something that someone advances beyond, both as a viewer and broadcaster. How then does *Hockey Night Punjabi* attract a sufficient number of viewers to provide a sense of longevity for the program since it is discursively produced as training wheels for new hockey fans? Logistically, it does not make sense to merge the Punjabi and English broadcasts, but there does need to be an equal sense of value placed on both outlets and crossover segments where appropriate. While "water cooler" talk may prove to be more difficult with multiple interpretations of hockey, in order for us to make claims about the power of sport to build bridges and provide common ground, citizens must feel like their experiences are recognized and valued by the wider populace.

In asking how culture affects citizenship, we can see patterns whereby the dominant culture reproduces its citizens by confirming or denying one's visibility and their value to the national narrative. The end goal, then, of cultural citizenship is a national narrative that is no longer based on a single linear history. And, as S. Hall (2005) argues, "It is therefore not a question of what our traditions make of us so much as what we make of our traditions. Paradoxically, our cultural identities, in any finished form, lie ahead of us. We are always in the process of cultural formation. Culture is not a matter of ontology, of being, but of becoming" (p. 556). Media narratives offer an entry point to explore the lived experiences that follow this chapter with a particular set of questions in mind regarding the relationship between citizenship and hockey, the inclusiveness of the sport, and what possibilities exist for coauthoring a collective retelling of hockey in Canada.

Sara Ahmed (2012) asserts that the politics of diversity use people of color as tools to provide a façade of happiness and camaraderie. She states, "If your arrival is a sign of diversity, then your arrival can be incorporated as good practice. Bodies of color provide organizations with tools, ways of turning action points into outcomes.... We are ticks in the boxes" (p. 153). Using this logic, *Hockey Night Punjabi* and the rising stardom of Singh could be read as tools to deflect accusations of institutional racism, but it seems the way to make sure that these developments do not remain "ticks in the boxes" is to not rest. We cannot assume that this is a sign of things to come. If Singh remains the only Sikh to appear on Canadian hockey media in 10 years' time, then Ahmed would be proven right. The influential presence of *Hockey Night Punjabi* stands as a symbol of potentiality because the lives, politics, and work of Canadian "others" hold the prospect of helping us understand "both the refined and crude constructions of 'white power' behind 'Canada's' national imaginary. They serve to remind us of the Canada that *could* exist" (Bannerji, 1997, p. 37). This is not where our work ends—it is where it begins. In the next chapter, we begin to undertake some of this work by understanding how the space of the hockey rink polices racialized difference and, in turn, often putting South Asian citizenship and belonging into question.

3

White Spaces,
Different Faces

Policing Membership at the
Rink and in the Nation

Field Notes: Vancouver Giants versus
Tri-City Americans, October 23, 2016
My friend and I have seats right behind
the bench. We have never sat this close at
a hockey game before. I sit down next to
an older white gentleman, maybe in his
60s, who starts to chat me up when he
sees my camera. He asked if I was with
the press. I inform him it is just for my
own use. He tells me that he and his
friend traveled from Vancouver to
Langley for the game via public transit.
He said it was his first time in this
stadium (he used to watch the Giants all
the time when they played at the Pacific
Coliseum). I commented that I had
played in this arena (Langley Events
Centre) once but that I had never
watched anything in here. He asked if I
was a figure skater. I said, "No, I play

hockey." He paused for a second then said, "Oh yeah, that university in China is trying to get a hockey team going." I humor him and we briefly discuss the Chinese women's team that happens to be doing a mini tour in Vancouver at the time.

Of all the people to have this conversation with in the stadium, this person happened to be seated next to someone there to observe how race and citizenship intersect in the space of the arena. His assumptions seemed to be influenced by the fact that I was one of the few racialized faces in the arena. I later reflected that, while not maliciously intended, these microinsults were arguably illustrative of the shallow well from which many draw conversational material when confronted with racialized and/or gendered difference at the rink. Microinsults tend to reproduce stereotypes or insensitivities about one's racialized, gendered, or sexual identity (Sue, 2010). In this instance, the man's comments invalidated the long history of women's hockey in Canada as well as my claim to citizenship and belonging. This is simply one of many moments that demonstrate how non-white Canadian women are regularly reminded of their difference and even otherness via microaggressions, defined as subtle put-downs that can be either intentional or unintentional but all re-affirm difference and racial hierarchy (Pierce, Carew, Pierce-Gonzalez & Willis, 1977; Sue, 2010).

Sport is often cited as a powerful tool for integration and bridge building. Whether it is Prime Minister Justin Trudeau, explaining that the Stanley Cup "has a weight of symbolism and strength of binding our country together that very few material symbols do" (Canadian Press, 2017b, para. 7), former Prime Minister Stephen Harper telling *Sports Illustrated* that hockey acts as a "common denominator" for Canadians (Farber, 2010), the Institute for Canadian Citizenship (2014) arguing that sports helps new Canadians feel included, or former United Nations Secretary General Kofi Annan pronouncing sport as a universal language (United Nations, 2004), the fundamental message, from a functionalist perspective, is that sport is capable of overcoming any kind of difference.

In my view, the "integrative power of sport" is one of those partial truths that, again, stands in for the whole. It is not so much that sport is always a vehicle for the expression and transmission of sexist/racist/homonegative/ableist ideology. Rather, sport is better viewed as a contested terrain where power and difference are constantly under negotiation. Sport can still be seen as an ideological tool, but with the realization that there may be multiple hands attempting to use that same tool for very different projects. The sporting field is a space where meaning is made but not necessarily with equal input. This chapter focuses on the space of the hockey rink and how it can police difference in seemingly innocuous ways, making racialized membership, in both hockey culture and the nation, an uneasy, unsettled, and conditional experience.

Who Belongs in a Space? Who Is Trespassing?

The sports stadium, sports bar, and field/arena have been implicated in establishing and maintaining a particular boundary of belonging. The *politics of belonging* extend beyond individual feelings to involve "not only constructions of boundaries but also the inclusion or exclusion of particular people, social categories and groupings within these boundaries by those who have the power to do this" (Yuval-Davis, 2011, p. 18). In other words, what makes belonging possible for some and ostensibly impossible for others? Furthermore, Puwar (2006) emphasizes, "an altered inhabitation of space does not automatically translate into straightforward belonging. Residency and arrival can be a tenuous and precarious place, even if one takes up the most consecrated of spaces" (pp. 81–82). In Canada, the rink has traditionally represented one of those sacred spaces.

For many Canadians, it is still inconceivable that South Asians can play or have an interest in hockey. Puwar (2004) suggests new bodies that seem conceptually "out of place" (p. 8) are often forced to "endure a burden of doubt, a burden of representation, infantilization and super-surveillance" (p. 11). To understand the experience of these so-called "space invaders" (Puwar, 2004) is to expose the faults in traditional approaches to multiculturalism and diversity because every *body* that is different from the somatic norm becomes a trespasser. To Puwar's argument, some of my participants shared experiences of having people assume they knew nothing about the game, or that when they referenced hockey they must have been talking about field hockey. For instance, Gary, 39, who grew up in northern British Columbia, told of an incident that took place after he had already been playing ice hockey for a number of years: "Actually, best story is I was going to play hockey, a floor hockey league with my elementary school and, I had been playing hockey for a little while, and when I went to go sign up the coach of the team stopped, put his pen down, and goes, 'So do you actually even understand the basics of hockey?' I said, 'What do you mean? I've been playing hockey for years now.' 'Okay, are you sure?' I was like 'Yeah!'" (personal communication, April 15, 2016).

This double-take on bodies out of place is an example of the burden of doubt that Puwar (2004) references. Similarly, Kiran, a 22-year-old elite player, grew up in predominantly white neighborhoods of the Lower Mainland and often had to explain her hockey participation: "Well, usually when I tell people I play hockey they're like 'Oh yeah? Field hockey?' I'm like, 'No, I actually play ice hockey.' They're like, 'Ice hockey?' I'm like, 'Yeah, you know the sport that everyone in Canada loves—I play that one'" (personal communication, April 28, 2016).

Therefore, despite the notion that hockey is available to everyone, certain bodies are met with resistance from the very beginning—they are forced into verifying their existence, resulting in a state of conditional acceptance. The assumptions that South Asian Canadians do not understand the game or would prefer playing field hockey may be interpreted as a play on cultural stereotypes, but on a deeper level it challenges the citizenship of certain Canadians based on their physical appearance (microinvalidation), a challenge that is not equally presented to all Canadian bodies. Comparable to my opening field note, when it comes to hockey, racialized Canadians are often required to (repeatedly) create a space for themselves, whereas most white Canadian men, and increasingly white women (or those able to pass as white), have a symbolic space reserved for them.

Kiran shared an incident where her current team went to a Tim Hortons coffee shop in another province and the employee who took her order automatically assumed Kiran was not Canadian-born because of her racialized appearance. This employee had asked all of Kiran's white teammates where they were from, referring to the city, and asking why they were in town. When it was Kiran's turn the woman asked her where she was from and when Kiran answered "Vancouver" with some other information, the woman responded, "Oh, congratulations! Perfect English!" The whole team laughed aloud, as did Kiran who replied with a confused, "Thank you?" (personal communication, April 28, 2016). Even though this specific experience was told as a humorous memory it exemplifies how visible markers of difference are produced, maintained, and/or resisted in everyday interactions that, on the surface, may not intend malice but are effective at reproducing the sense that some bodies are out of place in certain situations. In Sue's (2010) taxonomy of microaggressions, these acts of microinvalidation make racialized citizens feel like an alien in their home country. They discursively create an environment where racialized citizens are never fully allowed to feel comfortable in their legal citizenship.

Being out of place often leads to the policing of one's own behavior, something that has been commonly documented and discussed amongst African Americans (Gandbhir & Foster, 2015; F. R. Lee, 1997), and more recently amongst Muslim groups (Shireen Ahmed, 2017), regarding interactions with law enforcement. Self-policing results from being concurrently invisible and hypervisible: invisible in the sense that certain bodies do not count as much as others and hypervisible because racialized bodies operate under "super-surveillance" when they are framed as trespassing (Puwar, 2006). There is an expectation that in order to avoid further discrimination one has to behave in accordance with conventional or mainstream white norms because any transgressions can be used to generalize the entire community or to limit future opportunities. Gary provided an example illustrating how some racialized individuals internalize difference, resulting in policing the group's collective behavior. During a recreational hockey game Gary had an altercation with a South Asian player on the opposing team. He details their interaction in the postgame handshake lineup:

> He actually comes up to me and goes "Hey, my teammates later on told me that it was actually my fault," and I said "Yeah." I said, "You know we have to be really careful when we're playing out here because people only see the color of our skin. This is unfortunate but that's what they see and we gotta, you gotta, always be aware when you're playing hockey that other people are watching everything you do, especially when you're a minority. You are already separated from everyone else and when you do something wrong it's amplified." He's like, "Yeah, you're right." . . . . People already notice us because we're different and anything we do is going to get amplified by two. I go, "Is it fair? Nope. Is it reality? Yes." (Personal communication, April 15, 2016)

Puwar (2004) asserts, the "movements, postures and gestures [of racialized bodies] are closely watched for any untoward behavior. Racialized optics remain suspicious of these bodies out of place" (p. 51). For these reasons, Gary felt compelled to police his opponent's "untoward" behavior because (a) not only could it create racist assumptions about this player, but more importantly, (b) his behavior could inadvertently cast doubt and suspicion on all other South Asian players by association through appearance. Gary's intervention was equally about self-preservation as it was about protecting South Asian respectability. This is another example of inhabiting an unsettled experience by being marked as a permanent trespasser.

The marking of certain acts as inappropriate in accordance to the body that performs the act is perhaps best exemplified by the scrutiny that surrounds professional tennis player Serena Williams (e.g., Douglas, 2005; Schultz, 2005). When Serena Williams verbally attacked a linesperson at the 2009 U.S. Open, her outburst reproduced the angry Black woman discourse, an image that the United States Tennis Association (USTA) felt was "bad for the image of the sport." Her "tirade" resulted in a $82,500 fine, a two-year probation, and the USTA has since "put a ban on the use of this footage" (Baird & Major, 2013). Conversely, similar outbursts by white male players such as Jimmy Connors, John McEnroe, and Andy Roddick are generally discursively produced as shows of determination, commitment, and entertainment worthy of being replayed time and again.

Moreover, individual racialized bodies tend to be used as proof of a larger cultural problem. Gary protested: "I'm tired of hearing guys saying, 'Oh we played a team of East Indian guys or brown guys or whatever and they're just a bunch of jerks.'... They probably were jerks but I know other teams filled with Caucasians or other ethnicities and they're just as big jerks. So why is it that it's that team of brown or East Indian guys that are the bunch of jerks. It's no, that team was just a bunch of jerks" (personal communication, April 15, 2016).

Gary reflected on the weight of having to represent his entire racial group in a positive light by explaining that he is prepared to educate his daughters about the expectations that come with their racialized difference. For Gary, being a racialized Canadian means being an ambassador for Indian culture, because he understands that the actions of one will stand in for the actions of all, a correlation that white privilege manages to deflect. He describes this imposed ambassadorship as "a bit of a burden" but not one that he would trade for anything (personal communication, April 15, 2016).

As an elite-level player, the burden of representation for Billy, 20, is even greater. After some injuries and not performing to expectations, he would occasionally visit hockey forums and notice people comment, "You're a disgrace to our culture" (personal communication, July 20, 2016). Upon reading those kinds of comments the weight of representing a culture and community of people became tangible for him: "I remember reading that and I think that's when I really realized, as much as I'm just playing for myself and my family, you're playing for a lot of other people as well. You represent a lot of other people, so it comes with a lot of pressure and you learn how to mature quicker because you got to understand there are other people who are looking up to you and watching you" (personal communication, July 20, 2016).

Thus, regardless of whether one is playing recreational or elite-level hockey, to invade this space means accepting a litany of responsibilities for the opportunity. Billy reiterates this collective responsibility to represent an entire racialized community, which is a responsibility that elides the vast majority of white male athletes.

Brian, 25, who originally identified as a hockey player more than being East Indian because he never grew up around other East Indian families, retold a story of exclusion that concretized his difference on the team:

> It was provincials in Bantam and we were playing in [small town in British Columbia] and we played a game in the morning and we lost. I was really upset about it. I think I actually had a chance to either win the game or tie the game and I missed the net. I remember breaking my stick over the post and then feeling terrible because it was a $300 stick my mom just bought [laughs]....
> I came back and my mom right away had a meal for me ... and she told me you need to have a nap and be ready for the game. While I did that apparently the coach went and knocked on everyone's door and [the team] went to the [local

brewery], which was a little trip. I woke up and the first thing I do is get my sticks ready. So, I start taping my sticks and I go to the room because everyone plays Xbox or Play Station—nobody is around. And I remember a huge argument my mom had with my coach in the parking lot of the hotel [about] why everyone was going [without me]. And, this was the third time this happened that year. (Personal communication, September 11, 2016)

I asked Brian if an experience like that made him feel like an outsider on the team:

Yeah, I think it does. And that was one of the times where I felt maybe I should play basketball because I was very athletic, I could jump very high and everyone at that time was doing the whole stereotype: "Oh, you can jump high because you got pigment in your skin type of thing." And you start to identify with minority things. . . . I still listen to country music and stuff like that but there was a big time in my life when everybody was doing that and then me and my brother and my two cousins that grew up in that town went into gangsta rap music because it was all very aggressive and it was about being a minority. So, you start to get pumped up about being an outsider. You honestly start to feel that way after a while, but I think once you learn how to own it, it's a lot more powerful to you. You start going to tournaments in Vancouver and you look around and my parents go, "You're the only East Indian kid playing here, you should be proud of that," instead of being like I got no chance because of it. You should be proud that you are even here and you're at this level and there's so much more potential for you to keep going on. (Personal communication, September 11, 2016)

Brian's turn to gangsta rap is noteworthy because it speaks to marginalized experiences and is an important cultural outlet for citizenship where racialized difference is celebrated instead of downplayed. Hip-hop culture, which encompasses graffiti, rap music, DJ-ing, and break dancing, is a valuable outlet for negotiating racialized identity (Forman, 2000; Jeffries 2011; Kubrin, 2005). Rap music represents a voice for Blackness, marginality, poverty, and social struggle (Jeffries, 2011). More specifically, gangsta rap "is considered a product of the gang culture and street wars of South Central Los Angeles, Compton, and Long Beach, and the retromack culture (pimp attitude and style) of East Oakland" (Kubrin, 2005, pp. 360–361). This was a distinct departure from earlier forms of rap that were more inclined to give voice to the Black experience; gangsta rap is a declaration for the "black underclass in the ghetto" (Kubrin, 2005, p. 361). But what does an East Indian boy from northern British Columbia have in common with Black youth living in the "ghettos" of California? Brian needed to find a different space where his racialized identity could be empowered by and through his difference, which is something that rap music (as a form of politicized art) makes far more accessible than sport.

According to Sharma (2010), the connection between second-generation immigrants in North America and the impact of Black culture has been under-analyzed. Despite Prashad's (2000) argument that brown bodies are used as a tool to oppress Black bodies, "Blacks continue to represent the most visible example of a minority identity for South Asians of all generations" (Sharma, 2010, p. 16). Admittedly, this embrace of Blackness can also be understood as the commodification and co-optation of alternative culture, but Sharma asserts that through hip-hop music, Desi (a term often used for South Asians in America) artists use music to reconcile their difference: "They engage in *making race*: changing the nature and meaning of existing racial categories by producing their own versions" (p. 89). This connects to Brian's reflection about suddenly accepting his difference and finding power in his existence along the margins. Music, like sport, is an integral practice for cultural citizenship because it eluci-dates the struggles around who is counted as a citizen and in which ways (Avelar & Dunn, 2011). In Brian's case, music offered a form of resistance neither easily found nor generally accepted in hockey. Because Brian's membership in hockey was, at times, an uneasy one, music allowed him to settle some of the feelings caused by being marked as a trespasser.

Bodies out of place are often recognized as trespassers not only on the ice but also in the stands. A number of players discussed incidents that made them feel protective of their parents' right to inclusive public space. For instance, Gary described how he could hear rude comments made from the stands about his skating skills while he was on the ice: "Then my parents would go watch hockey and then they'd feel uncomfortable too right. They're already having a tough time fitting into Canadian culture and now they're hearing things said about their son and they're like we don't even know what to say" (personal communication, April 15, 2016).

Sonia, 26, described similar protective instincts with her mother:

> I remember that part, that she was connecting with mainly Asian folks who, I don't know what their experiences were, but I remember almost feeling protective over the way some people spoke to my mom over certain things. . . . Then when I heard some white kid make a comment about my parents it would hurt so bad. I remember crying a few times. "What the f—- is your problem?" . . . At that age when you're starting to become aware of those dynamics but you're not quite sure how to articulate those thoughts you kind of internalize them. (Personal communication, December 1, 2017)

To this day, Sonia associates condescending comments toward her parents with hockey. Growing up, this internalized difference made Sonia want to disassociate herself from her Punjabi identity by not speaking Punjabi at the rink or volun-tarily pointing out her racialized difference. One year, when another Punjabi girl joined Sonia's team, she remembered this player saying something to the effect of "my kind," in reference to Punjabi people: "I remember being like, 'I don't want to engage in this conversation.' I remember that moment. That's weird but it totally happened. I would never speak Punjabi with her. Now, if I ever see a Pun-jabi person, we're like 'talk talk talk' because I don't care but before, no way, I would never have brought it up" (personal communication, December 1, 2016).

The desire to minimize her difference is indicative of feeling like someone perpetually trespassing on private property where the space is never wholly yours. There may not be an overt declaration that racialized players need to shrink themselves to fit into hockey culture, but there is certainly a patterned interpretation by racialized players that this is the path to survival. These nar-ratives demonstrate that anti-racism requires more than a lack of racist dis-course. In order for hockey to reconcile its whiteness and earn the diversity it so desires, those in power must actively create space for difference to be respected, not tolerated, at the rink. Another way that difference can be policed is by never having the ability to name one's self.

Self-Identification

Before moving any further, it is important to revisit the term South Asian. When I asked each of the participants how they racially or ethnically identi-fied, the majority immediately answered Canadian. Twenty-two out of 26 interviewees were born in Canada, and those who were born elsewhere now hold Canadian citizenship. Unfortunately, racialized Canadians learn at a young age that answering Canadian usually signals the start of a much longer conversation instead of the end of it. The constant need to qualify one's exis-tence is part of how an uneasy and conditional membership is created by the nation. As a result, when probed further on the common question posed to all racialized Canadians, "Where are you *really* from?," most participants offered a term relating to their South Asian heritage. Gary describes this liminal space where Canadians of color are forced to redefine themselves for the benefit of other Canadians: "When people ask me where I'm from, I'm from [Northern BC] and I'm Canadian. But I don't even say Indo-Canadian anymore. I just say I'm Canadian. My culture, well my background is Indian—where I'm from, where my parents are from, what I'm teaching my kids too [is] that we are Indian as well. We gotta embrace that but I look at myself as Canadian more than any-thing else. It's tough though because not everyone looks at you as Canadian" (personal communication, April 15, 2016).

Kevin, 46, expresses similar identification patterns: "It's funny. I always say, nowadays, I always say originally, I'm from Vancouver and now I live in [suburb].

And they go, 'No, no. Back!' Okay, if people pry then you tell them where in the Punjab you're from and the city you were from, and where your family is from. Or people shift and they'll go 'Where are your parents from?' But I identify myself as Canadian, which I am" (personal communication, November 21, 2016).

The implications of racialized citizens never being allowed to define themselves has been discussed at length elsewhere (e.g., Canessa, 2007; Ghee, 1990; Ghosh, 2013); however, it is important to recognize that participating in hockey is not enough to verify the citizenship of certain Canadians. Hockey may be common, but it does not denominate us equally.

The chosen self-identifications of my research participants ranged from Indo Canadian, Indian, East Indian, Punjabi, and/or brown. Parents like Randy, 43, in fact confirm Canadian-ness for their children: "I teach my kids, you know you're East Indian. You have to be proud of where you're from and where your grandparents came from but you're Canadian" (personal communication, November 15, 2016). For those with a variety of ethnic heritages, it can be difficult to explain in passing conversation, so some people, such as Amit, 24, truncate their identity for the sake of time and effort:

AMIT: When somebody asks me what nationality I am, I say mainly Fijian.
CS: Mainly?
AMIT: Haha, yeah. We are a mix of stuff but I am mainly Fijian though.
(Personal communication, May 16, 2016)

Amit was the only person who strayed from the dominant (and mostly imposed) terms of Indian, East Indian, and so on.

For others, it was clearly an uncomfortable task when asked to label themselves:

Well, I guess the best answer if someone asks you what you are is I'm a human being, right? I just, it just keeps going, you can go nationality, your race, your origin. So, I mean, here in Canada, we're Indo Canadian but I don't like that term personally.

CS: How come?
I feel like . . . well, here's the thing, if somebody comes from Europe and they're from Scandinavia we're not calling them Scandinavian Canadian—they're just Canadian right? So, if somebody is Canadian, they're Canadian. You can say that, yeah, he's a Canadian of such and such descent, I think that makes sense . . . if you're going to say it for one ethnic group then you should be saying it for all. Like he's such and such Canadian. But here, because I feel we're visibly a minority, you know we're kind of labelled into this group. Sometimes you hear South Asian. I don't know if that's the proper one either, but I guess it is.

CS: Does it have any meaning for you? Like would you ever say I'm a South Asian guy?

No. I think the best way to put it for me is I am a Punjabi Canadian and you don't hear that one because literally that is my culture, that is my language, that is the origin where I'm from. (Hockey Night Punjabi representative, 2016)

I had a similar exchange with Greg, a 47-year-old hockey parent who moved to Canada from the United Kingdom in his early 20s: "I don't care one bit. Call me a Hindu, call me whatever. I don't care one bit. I just see myself as a human being—that's #1. If anyone sees me as anything different than that, then I don't really care. If somebody comes up to me and says yeah, you're South Asian or whatever, listen I'm a human being we don't need to get into those details" (personal communication, November 21, 2016).

The problem with labeling individuals into any category, whether related to race, ethnicity, gender, or sexuality, is that it reifies boxed identities and reproduces a singular experience. Yet, for Barthes (1972), it is precisely in the details, the processes, and the repetition of everyday experiences where myths and our common human-ness starts to unravel: "Doubtless the child is always born, but in the general volume of the human problem, what does the 'essence' of that action mean to us compared to the child's modes of being, which indeed are perfectly historical? Whether the child is born with ease or difficulty, whether or not he causes his mother suffering at birth, whether the child lives or dies, and, if he lives, whether he accedes to some sort of future—this, and not the eternal lyric of birth, should be the subject of our Exhibitions" (p. 198).

Therefore, even though the color-blind version of self-identification may seem to equalize citizens, it is far from equitable. In an attempt to offer some semblance of South Asian identities for the purpose of social justice requires concentrated attention on specific citizens that have historically not been seen as equal to others. To refer to oneself as human *first* performs an inadvertent erasure of the context necessary to advocate for equality (Barthes, 1972).

Sonia demonstrated "situational ethnicity" (Stayman & Deshpande, 1989), whereby racialized people often draw on multiple presentations of their self-identity depending on the context. This is also known as "code switching" (Oswald, 1999), where minoritized people, in particular, learn to quickly navigate through the multiplicity of their existences for the sake of appropriateness, belonging, and/or safety. It can be read as an act of agency for racialized people to emphasize or downplay certain aspects of their identity (Georgiou, 2006). De Fina (2007) explains, "participants in social activities 'do' identity work and align with or distance themselves from social categories of belonging depending on the local context of interaction and its insertion in the wider social world" (p. 372). Drawing from sociolinguistics, ethnic identities are negotiated and "indexed in subtle ways rather than openly declared, and that they often contradict expectations and stereotypes about received ethnic boundaries" (p. 374). Citizens are able to connect with certain values and ideologies through communicative acts, such as their choice in language (Brown, 2002). Sonia articulated this internal negotiation when asked if she uses the term *brown*:

> SONIA: Depends. I feel like we use it internally, when I talk to other Indian kids, "brown kids," whatever we say it to each other but if I heard a white person call me a brown person, I don't know. I would be like "What do you mean?" That can mean so many things, like the color of your skin? I don't really get it, but I think, also in the Lower Mainland, it has a very specific connotation and usually refers to Punjabi people. You think like Surrey, Abbotsford, that sort of thing.
>
> CS: Would that be a negative connotation?
>
> SONIA: Sometimes. Yeah, I think so. (Personal communication, December 1, 2016)

In this way, the conscious choice not to self-identify as brown serves as a way to downplay some of the negative associations tied to the label. This demonstrates some of the work that racialized Canadians are forced to do when living in a multicultural white settler nation where racialized membership is always contingent.

Brown

One way that South Asian Canadians have dealt with the unease of being racialized Canadians is to create a new identification—one not defined by the Government of Canada. Brown comes with a litany of geographically delineated interpretations. Studies in brownness have tended to center Latinx experiences in the United States (e.g., Aldama, 2005; Milian, 2013; Muñoz, 2007; Rana, 2015). Muñoz (2007) likens brownness to blackness, whereby both groups are positioned as social problems: "Feeling like a problem, in commonality, is what I am attempting to get to when I cite and exercise the notion of feeling Brown . . . Feeling Brown is feeling together in difference. Feeling Brown is an 'apartness together' through sharing the status of being a problem" (pp. 443–444). However, as was briefly discussed in chapter 1, brown people around the world, inclusive of those from Southeast Asia, South Asia, Hispanic nations, the Middle East, and Indigenous communities, are not universally marked as problems. Al-Solaylee (2016) writes that brown people "are not as privileged as whites but not as criminalized as blacks" (p. 7), which is a debatable statement considering Latinx immigrants have been labeled rapists and drug dealers by U.S. President Trump in an attempt to rally support for stricter immigration controls through the Southern border. Nonetheless Al-Solaylee describes racialized brown skin as "possibly the biggest prison of them all" (p. 8). What is shared between studies of brownness is "a political awakening from the outside in" (Al-Solaylee, 2016, p. 9). He contends that for too long brown people have been identified externally, particularly by their music and foods—falafel, curry, tacos—and it is now time to both self-identify and self-authorize one's existence.

Even though no one originally introduced or identified themselves as brown, in every interview the term brown was used, usually once a certain level of comfort was established. When participants were asked to explain the meaning and use of the term, it raised a feeling of self-consciousness for some: "Well, when I use it, I use it in a jokingly manner, probably with my friends. 'That's such a brown thing to do,' kind of like stereotyping ourselves but just within our circle. That's really it, like I, sometimes to point out a brown person for lack of better words. This is a really embarrassing question" (Hockey Night Punjabi representative, personal communication, 2016).

Another participant followed up with me once I stopped recording our interview, worried about his answer to my question of brown. I interpreted this concern as stemming from the local (negative) connotations that Sonia raised earlier and how brown in the Lower Mainland of British Columbia may have more unwritten rules attached to it than geographically determined or state-imposed labels. Conversely, Gurp, 25, who grew up playing minor hockey, asked me before our interview began what I meant by South Asian because it did not resonate with his own identity: "Like I said, I don't use South Asian. Brown is the best term I can come up with because that's what is most commonly used and to me that's everyone from Indians to Pakistanis to Sri Lanka, Bangladesh, Middle East, basically that entire South part of Asia" (personal communication, May 10, 2016).

This was the broadest interpretation of the term provided, with most other participants correlating brown with their own ethnic group. In other words, if one identified as Punjabi then brown referred to other Punjabi people, if one identified as Indian then brown referred to other Indian people, and if one identified beyond the nation-state borders of India, the term brown expanded to include the group with which they identified.

For some, brown is a positive identification and it can be used freely within the broader South Asian community or among teammates: "My hockey team, now they call me the brown girl on the team and I'm fine with that. I know their intention isn't to insult me. It's just a play on words. That's fine. That doesn't bother me" (Suki, personal communication, June 15, 2016).

Similarly, Sunny, 20, used the term brown with his teammates to help make *them* feel more comfortable, which opened the door for jocular humor (personal communication, July 21, 2016). This self-identification signaled to his non–South Asian teammates that he was comfortable with his difference and, in turn, gave them permission to also acknowledge his difference.

For others, being reduced to a color conjured discomfort and emphasized difference that was beyond their control:

> You know we shouldn't be classifying ourselves as a color. I mean . . . you know I'm proud of who I am, my nationality, my culture, my background but I don't know about being proud of your color. Because I just, honestly, I think of myself as an equal. (Hockey Night Punjabi representative, personal communication, 2016)

> Like as much as we say white, Black, or brown, yeah, I guess technically I'm brown. That's correct [laughs]. I get it's an easier way of people identifying who's who . . . yeah, good for you . . . The shade of color [I am] is not even really brown. It's not even really the color brown, which is a very deep and dark color. (Kiran, personal communication, April 28, 2016)

To understand shades of brown is an important aspect in theorizing brownness. Those with darker shades of brown skin tend to be further racialized within brown communities. The spectrum of brown skin mirrors the white–black hierarchy, with darker brown skin connoting lower-class labor (Al-Solaylee, 2016). For many brown communities, to marry a white person is seen as the highest aspiration because they are literally altering the color code and setting their children up for enhanced social mobility. Al-Solaylee (2016) writes of a similar perspective to Kiran with regard to shades of brown where, as an Egyptian, he was once referred to as a "Paki": "It had never occurred to me that I would be lumped with South Asians on the racial-slur spectrum, because I had thought of myself as lighter-skinned than most of them. They were dark brown; I was light brown. Couldn't these racists tell the difference?" (p. 6).

Consequently, it can be jarring to find out that one's light skin can still be marked *dark enough* to warrant the gamut of racial slurs. These narratives highlight that racialized bodies cannot escape racism based on a technicality, because to be brown is to exist in a hierarchy of brownness (Al-Solaylee, 2016) ensconced within a hierarchy of white to Black (both of which privilege light skin and oppress darker skin colors).

As with any word, *who* uses it is always an important factor. Kiran explained how her teammates refer to her, which was neither approved nor denounced by her: "No one refers to me as Indian—it would definitely be brown. I don't ever hear anyone ever say 'Oh, we have an Indian girl on our team.' Instead it's 'Oh, we have a brown girl on our team'" (personal communication, April 28, 2016).

When others have not been given permission to identify someone as brown, it is hard to know the impact that this simple term can have on an individual. For example, Kiran remembers joining a new team and walking into the locker room as a rookie and having the first statement be, "Perfect, we're so excited that we finally get to play with the brown girl" (personal communication, April 28, 2016). It is common for hockey teams to refer to teammates by surnames only or a team-designated nickname, but for Kiran throughout the year some of her teammates continued to refer to her as "the brown girl" without ever asking if this name was acceptable to her. This external identification can be read comparably to Frantz Fanon's experience of being pointed out by a little girl on the street as, "Look, a Negro!" (as cited in Puwar, 2004, p. 109). In that moment, the look "imprisoned" Fanon and he became an object; the look placed a weight on his shoulders and "'challenged [his] claims on the world: on where he could be and what he could be'" (as cited in Puwar, 2004, p. 41). Kiran's story resonates with a comparable embodied experience whereby the words from one body imprint on the Other. This represents an opportunity for coaches to check in with their racialized players because players may not feel comfortable challenging other teammates about their language; therefore, coaches play an important role in either forming anti-racist spaces or reproducing racist ones.

Kiran further explained that because she grew up in predominantly white areas of the Lower Mainland, aside from interacting with her family, she does not feel a particularly strong connection to other brown people:

> By saying brown, you are kind of throwing in all the stereotypes of that and I don't think that is really fair. That is saying that this person is like this person and this person is like this person. That's not really fair for me at this point. I have more similarities with people who aren't brown. So how is that fair for me? You are throwing me in a category that I don't even belong in. So, what does that do for my sense of belonging? Where do I belong? . . . I really don't have very many brown or Indian friends who do both sports and grow up where I live. So, for me, I really hate that term because that puts me in a spot where I'm alone. (Personal communication, April 28, 2016)

I will further unpack this sense of being alone in the next section, but here it is reproduced by her teammates through language, in addition to a lack of physical representation in hockey. Brown represents a paradoxical existence for many—to be simultaneously seen and invisible (Al-Solaylee, 2016). It is the racial category that is able to expand and contract most easily depending on the ideological or political context at play, relegating the people who occupy the space of brownness to live in constant instability. Most importantly, we must recognize that brown is a heterogeneous term in itself and continues to be negotiated on a daily basis.

FIG. 3.1 Waiting their turn to play ball hockey at the 2017 Hometown Hockey event in Surrey.

Being the Only One

Unlike conditions identified in the research conducted by Daniel Burdsey (2007) and Thangaraj (2015) on South Asian experiences in British soccer and American basketball respectively, the current make-up of hockey necessitates isolation for many South Asian Canadians. Noticeably different from Burdsey's (2007) and Thangaraj's (2015) studies was the fact that most of my research participants experienced much of hockey culture as the only one:

> When I used to go to my brother's practices when I was younger, I did feel like my family in the crowd was very different from everybody else. So, it did feel like, oh . . . maybe the color of my skin did isolate me from everybody else. (Hockey Night Punjabi representative, personal communication, 2016)

I was the only Indian person around and I was very aware of that at a very young age. (Sonia, personal communication, December 1, 2016)

All through my years of playing I was the only one. When I would go away for tournaments in Saskatchewan, Calgary, Winnipeg, anywhere, I was the only one colored. Everyone else was just white . . . or Asian. (Suki, personal communication, June 15, 2016)

These narratives echo what Val James, the first African American to play in the NHL, experienced during his hockey career, and most notably in Canada. He wrote in his autobiography, *Black Ice: The Val James Story* (V. James & Gallagher, 2015):

Of course, when I was subjected to racial abuse on road trips, I could count on the support of my teammates. They always said the right things but, try as they may, they couldn't really sympathize with what I was going through. An old Midland teammate recently brought up an incident when opposing fans threw bananas at me. What the hell could my fellow teenagers on the Flyers ever say to make that better? They would be offended on my behalf but, not being black themselves, they just could not relate to the pain and humiliation and anger that I was experiencing. In that sense, I was very much alone. (p. 49)

It is important that we not confuse these narratives with loneliness, because no one used the term lonely to describe their experiences—even when I explicitly used the term. As a number of them explained, to be part of a team means rarely being lonely. To be lonely by definition is to lack friends or company; yet, an isolation that exists within a team dynamic, surrounded by people, is, as James describes, something completely different. It describes a lack of *shared* experiences, despite sharing *similar* experiences. As Suki further clarified, especially when she was younger, "I felt kind of left out and kind of uncomfortable, and then I was kind of self-conscious" (personal communication, June 15, 2016). In addition, Brian recounted a story where he and the opposing team's captain were both South Asian and that, despite the competition at hand, he felt like his "best friend on the ice was the other Indian guy on the other team" (personal communication, September 11, 2016). There is an emotional component in recognizing one's alone-ness. It is vital to understand that the journey for many racialized hockey players, to-date, has been one undertaken as an isolated entity. This isolation helps contribute to the overall sense of unease and being a trespasser.

Bourdieu and Wacquant (2002) believe that to be *of* a space feels like being a "fish in water" (p. 127) because one is a product of his or her environment; "they merely need to be what they are in order to be what they have to be"

(Bourdieu, 1990, p. 11). Conversely, that same space can make racialized people "feel the weight of the water" (Puwar, 2004, p. 131). The politics of belonging and the policing of space are integral for understanding how citizens and national subjects are constituted and/or rejected. For white, cis-male, able-bodied citizens, their bodies are irrelevant—a non-issue—but for racialized citizens their body precedes their being. Racialized appearance is the first impression, and it means that these bodies are required to constantly reclaim space and membership for themselves. Perhaps the best way to synopsize South Asian experiences as space invaders in hockey is through this off-the-record statement from a South Asian coach: "It's f—-ing hard."

Near the end of my field research I experienced a similar interaction as the one that leads this chapter. Here is an excerpt from my January 15th, 2017, field notes from the Hometown Hockey Event in downtown Vancouver:

> While I'm sitting and half-watching the circus act waiting for the *Hockey Night Punjabi* crew to arrive, a middle-aged white gentleman sits down next to me and asks if I am a professional photographer. I answer "No." He then asks me if I am a big hockey fan. I reply, "Yes, are you?" even though I'm really not in the mood for chatting. He says, "Of course, I grew up with hockey. But I guess you did not grow up with it." I give him a wry smile and say, "Actually, I'm from here." He replies, "Oh, well then I guess you did."

Once again, it would seem as though my body (and camera) were out of place. It should be noted that this man spoke with, what I discerned in the moment as, a heavy Slavic accent. Thus, I found it even more significant that he was questioning my hockey fandom and belonging given that, through my ears, I sound pretty Canadian, am at the same hockey event as him, and am wearing my Vancouver Canucks toque. Clearly the "Canadian costume" that I have been curating for the past 30-plus years is not enough to distract from the Asian-ness of my body—I was regarded as a trespasser. The work that is done in and around hockey culture and at the rink to confirm, deny, and/or question Canadian membership is made possible by the very notion that there can be bodies out of place. We must ask: if hockey is for everyone and Canada is a country that values diversity, then how can anyone be out of place?

4

Racist Taunts or
Just Chirping?

> I am not obliged to keep hitting that
> wall. . . . But not to speak anger because
> it is pointless is not the answer. After all,
> even if we use softer language, we are
> already a sore point. We might as well do
> things with these points. To speak about
> racism is to labor over sore points.
> —Sara Ahmed, 2012, p. 171

It is not uncommon to hear of racist tirades at European soccer matches. For example, in February 2017, Serbian soccer fans spent the entire game making monkey noises every time Black Brazilian midfielder Everton Luiz touched the ball; as a result, Luiz left the field in tears (Kerr-Dineen, 2017). Hockey fans have also been known to throw bananas on the ice at Black players (NHL, 2011), and once fans dumped alcohol on Indigenous children at a game in South Dakota (Griffith, 2015). However, these incidents are consistently treated as abnormal events in hockey culture and blamed on a few unruly fans, instead of being understood as a broader social issue. The soccer community, in contrast, has created a number of anti-racism campaigns/organizations such as Say No to Racism, FARE (Football Against Racism in Europe), and Kick It Out, and regularly fines teams if their fans use racial/ethnic slurs.[1] Conversely, hockey leagues have never openly admitted to having a problem with racism. It may be fair to critique soccer's various anti-racism initiatives as window-dressing, but at least there is something to critique, something to improve upon, or somewhere to direct one's energy. Hockey, on the other hand, provides no such space or direction; there is no place to resist that which is (supposedly) not a problem. At the end of 2015, the NHL partnered with the Ross Initiative in Sports for Equality (RISE) "to raise awareness and combat racism" (para. 1) and created a public service announcement against discrimination that was shown at the annual outdoor Winter Classic that year (NHL, 2015). Still, this partnership remains a suspiciously quiet arrangement. In October 2018, the NHL, under the leadership of Kim Davis, executive vice president of Social Impact, Growth, and Legislative Affairs, published a policy brief titled, "Shifting Demographics and Hockey's Future" (NHL, 2018). This document acknowledges that minoritized groups represent growing markets and increasingly powerful forces that must be considered in the strategic planning of hockey at all levels. But it only hints at racism as an ongoing issue for the game. Similarly, it is important to note that even though race is *part* of the focus during *Hockey is for Everyone* month and the overall campaign, the word racism is never explicitly used.

Daigle (2016) contends that in Canada there is a tendency to "Canadiansplain" racist incidents away. "-Splaining" is described as a manner of explaining or commenting in a "condescending, overconfident, and often inaccurate or oversimplified manner, from the perspective of the group one identifies with" [derived from the original term "mansplain"] (Daigle, 2016, para. 1). Raj provided an example of what Canadiansplaining looks like in practice: "Maybe in the Deep South there is still a lot [of racism] but in Canada it seems, you hope that people don't express it as they did back in the day" (personal communication, June 21, 2016). Ergo, to Canadiansplain involves a concession that racism (and in specific anti-Black racism) exists in Canada but never to the extent that it does in the United States (Daigle, 2016). This belief often stems from the fact that slavery was abolished in Canada nearly 30 years before it was abolished in the United States (Everett-Green, 2014). As a result, Canada became a home to many escaping enslavement (to whom Fosty and Fosty, 2008, attribute a significant portion of the development of Canadian hockey). Nonetheless, too often this question of historical difference is muddied with an exaggerated sense of moral superiority. While the racial histories of Canada and America are both different and similar, to Canadiansplain implies that multicultural policies will ultimately prevail. Therefore, any concerns about racism are often dismissed as frivolous, unfounded, and/or offensive. This patterned behavior has also been referred to as the "angel complex" (Colour Code Episode 4, 2016).

This inclination to point out more egregious wrongdoers in order to deflect attention away from racism within Canada's borders would be slightly less problematic if the statistics did not prove otherwise. According to *The Globe and Mail*, there were more recorded hate crimes in Canada (per capita) against Indigenous peoples in 2014 (3.7 per 100,000 people) than in the United States against Black Americans (1.85 per 100,000) (Grant, 2016, para. 32). And yet, as Takeuchi (2014) argues, hate crimes against Black Canadians accounted for 42% of all racially/ethnically motivated crimes in 2014 (para. 8). Hate crimes against Muslims doubled between 2012 and 2014 nationwide (Paperny, 2016), and the Toronto Police Hate Crime Unit reported an increase in Muslim-directed hate crimes following the resettlement of 25,000 Syrian refugees (Toronto Police Service, 2015). Amidst these reports, it is common to find someone such as Amira Elghawaby, spokesperson for the National Council for Canadian Muslims, express the need for more anti-racism education and then quickly follow up this call with a hedged statement such as, "Canadians are overwhelmingly warm, generous, compassionate people who respect diversity" (Paperny, 2016, para. 23).

Even though the United States, and increasingly the United Kingdom, have long been icons of disdain for racialized difference, several writers have claimed that both of these regions have conducted more research on the experiences of racialized people in white-dominated settings than Canada (see Lewis, 2001; Ramsey, 1991; Varma-Joshi, Baker, & Tanaka, 2004), arguably because race is seen as a viable discussion topic. The comparative lack of race-related research in Canada gives the illusion that racism is a non-issue, resulting in a general lack of urgency to discuss racism in any productive manner. To illustrate, when *The Globe and Mail* created a podcast about race in Canada called "Colour Code," the hosts prefaced the podcast by explaining that the word "Code" in the title alluded to the Canadian "code of conduct" whereby "we don't talk about race, and that should change" (Colour Code Episode 4, 2016). Moreover, the popular representations of cities such as Toronto and Vancouver as utopias of diversity give the impression that all of Canada is diverse, when the reality is that the majority of Canada (while not necessarily still homogenous) is far from being the multicultural mosaic we promote (Varma-Joshi et al., 2004). To illustrate, the *Vancouver Sun* reported, "only one in 40 immigrants live in small town or rural Canada, compared to one in five who are born in the country" and almost 75% of new immigrants move to Toronto, Montreal, and/or Vancouver (Todd, 2017, para. 4). Even though the racial divide may not be as stark as it once was, it is important to recognize that all spaces (urban, suburban, rural) come with unique challenges to racial inclusion, equality, and justice. Therefore, by limiting research on race in Canada to the more diverse metropolitan cities, we do not present an accurate depiction of discrimination. Despite the fact that the research conducted for this study took place in Vancouver, the space of hockey remains a white-dominated one and becomes useful in expanding our understanding of racial acceptance, or lack thereof, in contemporary Canada. As chapter 3 highlighted, many of my research participants had to endure racism by themselves, which parallels (although not exactly) the little research that has been conducted in less diverse regions of Canada. When research on racism is conducted in predominantly white spaces there is a noted resistance to acknowledge the presence of it (Varma-Joshi et al., 2004). The intersections of discourse, racialization, and citizenship undergird the remainder of this chapter.

Just Chirping?

On-ice racial taunting was a common theme among my research participants. Unsurprisingly, the longer one was involved in hockey, the more instances one usually experienced; however, participants were typically reluctant to name more than one incident:

> I got called butter chicken once. (Billy, personal communication, July 20, 2016)

> I've heard this one, "Get back on your rug" or something like that. (Sunny, personal communication, July 21, 2016)

> I remember it because it was the funniest one I've ever heard. One guy, we were playing in [American city], and he had bleach blonde hair and he said, "Why don't you go back and play soccer with your elephants." I was like, that has nothing to do with me, that's maybe Africa, but that's not where I'm from. (Shane, personal communication, September 1, 2016)

These slurs range from the derogatory to the humorously inane, but the pattern of interest, for me, is not so much the slur itself, it was how participants tended to downplay these instances as merely trash talk, known in hockey nomenclature as chirping. For example, Prav, 20, explained to me that chirping is merely gamesmanship occasionally verbalized as racism: "With the chirping, it's just that they want to get in your head and if you're more focused on your game, and when they see you actually perform and do good in the sport then they might think to themselves, even if they don't say it to you, they might think I shouldn't have said that to this person because their skills are showing that they can actually play the sport" (personal communication, September 1, 2016).

In explaining how racist taunting is *just* used to get a player off of their game, Prav rationalizes skill as a potential defense against racism. However, the fact that the elite-level players in this study often had more to say about racist experiences on the ice seems to counter Prav's assumption (or hope).

In a tongue-in-cheek hockey article titled, "The Art of Chirping," the author describes chirping as "so deeply rooted in the essence of competition that it becomes its own game ... like any skill, it takes years and years of practice to achieve perfection" (McKinven, 2015, para. 1). Notwithstanding the fact that these incidents commonly end up in physical altercations, the general consensus is that to be the target of chirping is a compliment because you have been deemed worthy of such attention, and, on the whole, these interactions are "relatively harmless" (McKinven, 2015, para. 11). This assertion also counters Prav's assumption that chirping, or at least the racist version of it, is reserved only for lower-skilled players. Chirping supposedly fosters camaraderie with one's teammates and serves as a way to galvanize "Us" versus "Them," but when does chirping cross the line into hate speech? A quick search of "Chirping 101" guides on the Internet reveals a variety of tips including attacking someone's looks, skills, age, and equipment, but none appear to champion racist slurs as part of the overall strategy. Thus, if there is an unwritten rule that chirping stops short of racism, why did the players in this study willingly give the benefit of the doubt when it came to racist comments on the ice? Or as Dixon (2007) points out, why is trash talking accepted when the same comments made off the playing field would certainly be deemed unacceptable?

Suki, 21, an elite-level player, detailed a racist and homophobic incident that ultimately led to a fight on the ice. In my view, her narrative downplays any intended malice while also attempting to reconcile the incident in her own mind:

> We were just about to play our final championship game for [a major tournament] and one of my teammates, who is white, she loved Indian music and ... my dad made her a CD disc with a bunch of music and she loved it. For that game, she really wanted to play it during the warmup, no one cared, they said go for it. So, she played it and the other team who was all white, thought it was my tape and they targeted me during the whole game ... "Nice music faggot Indian," they would make all these different comments to me. I would be skating by, they would say something to me. You know it didn't bother me, I was like they are just trying to get in my head, we're the better team and it didn't get to me. It actually fired me up more because I started scoring goals and then that pissed them off, whereas the comments got worse throughout the game ... one of them actually fought me. She tripped me over the blue line and I fell, she jumped on top of me, started punching me while I'm on the ground. ... It didn't really bother me because they were trying to get into my head and the fact that I was scoring. I just kept my head up high. It didn't bother me, I mean it did bother me but you know I fought through it. I think that was probably my worst experience with racism. (Personal communication, June 15, 2016)

Suki repeatedly assured me that the verbal taunting and the fight did not bother her until ultimately, she had to admit to herself (and to me) that it did bother her, but she made a conscious decision to persevere. Suki's story also contradicts Prav's earlier assertion that once someone's skill is established the taunting should subside because one has earned their place. It is unfortunately true that (physical) intimidation is regarded as a fair hockey tactic, especially against skilled players; however, racial taunting is an additional barrier experienced by racialized players.

Racial taunts or slurs are expressly prohibited in the official rules of the NHL (NHL, 2014), major junior leagues such as the Western Hockey League (WHL, 2015), and the recreational Canada-wide Adult Safe Hockey League (ASHL, 2016). The NHL, for instance, states in section 4 under Types of Penalties, "racial taunts or slurs" (p. 35) can result in a game misconduct penalty. Players explained that at the higher levels of hockey it became much harder to get away with racist comments on the ice, which may also facilitate the illusion that racism is not a problem for the league, especially compared to the days when Val James played during the 1970s and the entire stadium would shout racial epithets at him (V. James & Gallagher, 2015).

Research conducted outside the realm of sports on racist name-calling observes that victims "overwhelmingly felt that name-calling was a particularly insidious form of violence, specifically because of its harmless reputation" (Varma-Joshi et al., 2004, p. 178). In this way, there is something unique to the context of hockey (and sports more broadly) where racial taunting is less deplorable. I suppose, if fist fighting results in only five minutes in the penalty box, perhaps the dismissal of racial taunting represents an accurate (yet problematic) response. In Varma-Joshi et al.'s (2004) study of racist name-calling in New Brunswick schools, white teachers were observed to discount racist slurs and taunting as a form of violence. Comments made by teachers such as "it's just names," and the misguided "sticks and stones may break my bones, but words will never hurt me" adage were used to minimize the significance and consistency of racism in schools. The York Region District School Board in Ontario is under similar scrutiny, with a recognized pattern of staff dismissing complaints about racism (Javed & Rushowy, 2017). Pointing out the fact that racialized communities are responsible for population growth in the area, the school boards must be accordingly proactive in addressing the needs of these communities. Deracializing racist comments insinuates that both parties are equally guilty of making trouble (Essed, 1991). Varma-Joshi et al. (2004) contend, "when victims refuse to turn the other cheek, their reaction is framed as the actual problem, rather than the supposed childish name-calling" (p. 189), and thus there is an overall reluctance to speak up about these incidents because they can result in a second victimization.

When I first asked Amit if she had ever experienced any discrimination in hockey, she answered confidently that she had not. Toward the end of our interview I wanted to confirm her answer and, even though she repeated her initial answer, the probe ended up revealing an important aspect of Amit's hockey experience:

CS: You said going through the hockey system you never experienced any discrimination, nothing negative directed at you?

AMIT: No, never.

CS: That's very good.

AMIT: Yeah, yeah. Trying to think, I feel like there was a situation but I just can't recall it right now. Okay well just playing other teams, and you know how you get girls, girls are very verbal whereas boys are very like, they'll just body check you or something. I definitely, on the ice, have been called names. So yeah, but that's like the only type of racial slurs or bullying I've ever received was usually from an opponent. Well it's only been from an opponent, never from a coach or anything just from the players when you're on ice. Usually it's like a cheap shot and they'll say something, or they'll just try to get you riled up and they'll start saying stuff. Just being darker and stuff a lot of people think I am half black or I am of that descent, so I've totally been called the N-word before on ice.

CS: Really?

AMIT: Like a lot actually, so has my sister. My sister is darker than I am and she gets called that a lot. My hair is very curly too, like [an] afro, so when my hair is down, when I play hockey I tend to leave it wild, so a lot of people would definitely assume I am African American and they would be calling the N-word on the ice . . . that definitely was the only racial anything that I received was on the ice and it was used, it was another player like of an opposing team and they just try to get to you, the verbal names. (Personal communication, May 16, 2016)

Again, there is this notion that racism spawning from the opposing team is somehow acceptable because they are the enemy and, therefore, expected to hold contempt for you. Crucially, if racism is conceptualized by some participants as relational and a label placed only upon those assumed to be part of one's in-group, we must consider how this definition greatly alters the perceived presence of racism in hockey.

One would also think that being called the N-word throughout one's hockey career would be a significant memory, but clearly it took some probing to summon these memories for Amit. This forgetfulness could stem from the fact that these instances were quite hurtful and Amit chose to bury them, or they were so common that, unfortunately, no one instance stood out. When I asked Amit how these racial misidentifications made her feel she explained, "I take offence to it not because I'm being misidentified but I take offence to it because [even if I were black] why does that make it okay for you to call anyone that?" She ultimately stated that these comments were not only meant to "get under [her] skin but there's usually some sort of internalization of that culture . . . that causes you to say it." The guise of chirping slowly unravels.

Even though Amit played junior hockey in the Lower Mainland and Brian played in northern British Columbia, he experienced similar racial misidentification before 9/11: "A lot of the racial slurs I got before were African-American racial slurs because people just didn't understand the difference and that's a lot easier for me to go to my mom and dad and be like, 'Oh why did you cross-check that guy in the face?' Well, he said this to me, and my dad goes 'That doesn't even make sense. You understand why he's saying it right, because he's mad'" (personal communication, September 11, 2016).

In these instances of misidentification, the ignorance of the offender seemingly blunts their words because he "doesn't know what he's talking about." Brian noted that after 9/11, the misidentifications pivoted from being Black to being Muslim: "When 9/11 happened that's when it really took off because those phrases like terrorist and stuff were never anything linked to us at that time." The ease with which Brian was able to transition from Black to Muslim is evidence of how quickly brownness can be manipulated to fit the political environment. Moreover, Brian mentioned an instance where he got into a fight at school and he claimed that the other boy "called him a terrorist," which was a lie, but teachers came to his defense. This was an interesting act of agency for a young Brian, who recognized that his racialization, at times, could be used to his benefit. This was, however, an anomaly among my research participants.

Trash talking in sports, at one point, was considered a moral panic because this lack of sportsmanship was interpreted as "the decline of civilization" (Bruning, 1994 as cited in Eveslage & Delaney, 1998, p. 239). In Eveslage and Delaney's (1998) study of trash talk amongst a high school basketball team in Philadelphia, they observed that "insult talk" frequently stressed and confirmed team hierarchies, included personal insults "often as calls to defend masculinity and honor," and objectified "objects defined as 'feminine'" (p. 241). Moreover, the authors argue, within teams, there are clear boundaries of trash talking with sensitive issues being off limits as a demonstration of empathy for one another. Opponents, though, are not as deserving of empathy. Accordingly, "in all-male highly competitive settings with high insecurity levels, insult talk dominates" (Eveslage & Delaney, 1998, p. 248; see also Bissinger, 1990; Raphael, 1988) but, as Amit's and Suki's statements above demonstrate, insult talk has also found a place in women's sports. Dixon (2007) contends that players take pride not only in their ability to dish out trash talk but also their ability to tune it out. Suki's narrative above confirms this perspective, when she stated that as the racial comments intensified, the more "they fired [her] up" and ultimately served as badges of honor along with the goals she scored.

Still, even if players interpret (or rationalize) on-ice racial slurs as games-manship, sociologically speaking, trash talk/chirping is a discursive practice of power where dominance is asserted, resisted, and/or negotiated. Previous research has noticed that some people are marked as more deserving of trash talk than others. Eveslage and Delaney (1998) observed from their research, "the boys no doubt were choosing what they perceived as 'easy targets' gar-nered from larger cultural messages and were attempting to buttress their masculinity" (p. 248). Additionally, it is hard to brush off trash talking as lacking malice when the act itself is premised on disrupting an opponent's mental state; in other words, the need to "block something/someone out" implies the existence of an unwanted presence (Dixon, 2007, p. 99). As a result, even if subjects of racism acquiesce to racist acts, this does not make racism appropriate.

Was It Really Racist?

Racial prejudice is both hard to prove and relatively easy to deny. Some par-ticipants felt that racism was a strong word with a narrow definition. For example, when I asked one of the *Hockey Night Punjabi* commentators whether they had experienced any racism as part of the broadcast they responded, "No. I don't, racism is a strong word" (personal communication, 2016). This narrow interpretation of racism would become a theme among the majority of inter-view participants, that the label of racism should be reserved for only the most egregious and unequivocal acts of hate. But one has to wonder, if we cannot label racial slurs and physical violence as racist acts, what is left to call racism? Hockey parent Kulbir similarly hedged his answer when talking about a lack of playing time for his daughter, "I'm not saying it is racism, but [there's] still something there" (personal communication, June 15, 2016). Conversely, others were simply never sure what they had experienced: "Like again, everything in my career, nothing has been like no that's bad, that's racist. Everything is kind of underlying, you can assume, you can make assumptions and stuff like that but there's nothing really like—that's bad. So, it's hard. It's hard to see and decide and what's good and what's not. . . . There's always that hesitation. Was that a moment of an underlying prejudice?" (Kiran, personal communication, April 28, 2016).

Just as sexism teaches women that "they are not reliable witnesses to their own lives" (Solnit, 2014, p. 8), so too does racism teach self-doubt to racialized citizens. Part of the work performed by institutionalized racism is to make those on the receiving end unsure of its existence.

Goldberg (2015) describes this inability to pinpoint racism as part of racial dismissal in a postracial world. Postraciality does not mean that race no longer matters or that we are beyond caring about racial difference; indeed, it is the exact opposite: that race matters more than it ever has but in new articulations (Goldberg, 2015). He states, "race (as we have known it) may be over. But racism lives on unmarked, even unrecognized, potentially for ever" (Goldberg, 2015, p. 6). According to Goldberg, the dismissal of race or racism makes it exceptionally difficult to expose because postraciality renders the structures responsible for oppression and privilege opaque. Hence, when Canada reiterates the fact that we actually thrive off of the difference that exists within our borders, it makes it exceptionally hard to be confident in claims against racism because there is no foundation for belief. To speak of racism is to inhabit the space of *being the problem* (Sara Ahmed, 2012; Du Bois, 1996).

Sara Ahmed (2016) claims that in anti-racist work "you are not allowed to be sure" (para. 69). In her ethnographic research on diversity work she reflected on how the word *racism* rarely emerged and that she had not explicitly used the word. Similarly, I did not use the word *racism* in my interview questions. My intention was to avoid leading my participants down any specific path and instead, referred to it as "discrimination," a "lack of diversity," or the sense of being "unwelcome." The problem, however, with not saying the word *racism* is that we become complicit in its erasure. To suggest that diversity work is needed inherently means that racism is present (Sara Ahmed, 2012).

Furthermore, even when participant experiences were filed away as racist there was a general reluctance to talk about them. Sonia reflects on not wanting to exacerbate her racialized difference: "I think I probably didn't share it or explicitly explain how it made me feel because I didn't want to bring attention to the fact that I was brown. Because . . . you would see on the boy's team, there would be select Indian guys and stuff like that but for the most part, when I was growing up, it was mainly white girls. If that difference is pointed out to me I would feel shitty about it" (personal communication, December 1, 2016).

Sonia continued to reflect that her parents were also unwilling to talk about racism:

> But it also is what my family associates with being Canadian. Because I think a lot of the time, especially in my family, stories about exclusion or stories about experiences of racism in the early days are never really talked about because it's kind of a deep dark twisted memory and it doesn't feel very good. I notice that [my parents] would never want to talk about it because they never wanted to expose us to [it]. "No, we went through that so you guys can do shit like this, play hockey." That was a key thing that, that's a key piece of hockey culture. We made it! We can play now. My dad always said, "I always wanted to play hockey but we had no money; I couldn't get skates, I didn't want to show up wearing someone else's skates that were too big for me." . . . Especially for him, me

playing hockey was "We made it!" But those stories of why it's meaningful are sometimes just pushed aside or kind of covered up because you don't have to deal with it anymore. (Personal communication, December 1, 2016)

Sonia's story is significant in two ways. First, she observes that her reluctance to speak out about discrimination is rooted in the fact that to do so would further amplify her difference. Therefore, in an institution such as hockey where difference is not only discouraged but also generally maligned, pointing out one's racial difference by calling out racism amplifies a possible reason for exclusion. Second, she recognizes that her participation in hockey was key for her father's sense of citizenship; having his child participate in hockey meant that he had finally secured his own Canadian-ness. It meant that he was financially able to participate in the national culture and that he had successfully integrated his family. Sonia surmised that her parents' reluctance to talk about negative experiences from hockey somehow diminished the dream of being Canadian. In other words, to give weight to racism—to give it voice and life—denies the Canadian mythology of multiculturalism and challenges one's citizenship. Kari, Sonia's mother, echoed this reluctance in a separate interview: "I've felt it sometimes but I don't want to think about it. . . . If you keep thinking and keep bringing it up then sometimes it gets bigger than it is. Just go with the flow" (personal communication, January 16, 2017). Happiness and national repair are possible only if immigrants let themselves be included and they can do this by "playing the game" (Sara Ahmed, 2012, p. 166) or as Kari says, "Go with the flow." The "game" here is understood as both the national sport but equally as the "national field" (Sara Ahmed, 2012, p. 166). If those wearing the label of immigrant remain attached to the injury of racism, they facilitate their exclusion; "to show our gratitude, we must put racism behind us" (Sara Ahmed, 2012, p. 168). Consequently, the unwillingness of hockey culture to admit that hockey is not for everyone (or at least is not *always* for everyone) denies its participants a space to be honest about their experiences. There is no room for negative feelings under the *Hockey is for Everyone* banner.

Brian shared a comparable story about his father's silence surrounding racism at the rink. He told me that he would see his father physically fighting in the stands with other parents (personal communication, September 11, 2016). At the time, Brian's father tried to shield him from what other parents would yell at him while he was playing, but as Brian matured and asked his father about those incidents, he eventually shared the details as a lesson to be learned. Brian did not share the details of what was said with me. Parents were identified by every player as critical in learning about how to deal with racism. Parental advice ranged from ignoring offensive comments or players to confronting the offender. But the overarching instructions were the same: Do not pay too much attention to it, but if you have to, leave it on the ice. In this way, racialized children are taught to avoid naming racism, which also alters our perception of the presence of racism in hockey culture. They are taught to be docile citizens (Foucault, 1977). They are taught to make excuses for racist acts and speech.

In addition to narratives about avoiding any talk of racism, Brian shared a story about consciously trying to divert his personal narrative away from one that centered on racism to a more positive discussion that would hopefully encourage more South Asian participation. A local media outlet interviewed him and another South Asian player, and Brian disliked that the interviews were being framed around race/racism:

> I almost felt bad after because I talked to [player] too and I know they almost, the questions they asked prompted him to make it seem like it was very racist for him. And we kind of went in the same boat, the kid played in [junior league] for five years and now he's going to [an elite league], those things might have existed but it didn't stop him from being successful so why focus on the negative? Talk about your positives about being Indian. . . . I came in and basically said I don't like the race card . . . you need to get over the fact that your kid is probably not making the team because he's just not good enough. Whether that's the reason or not, that's what the kid needs to believe. . . .
>
> They were, again, they were like well this situation happened—what do you think about it? And I just kept siding with the other side, whether I believed in it or not I didn't want them to market it like that and especially put it on TV. . . . They're going to air it like that and I didn't want these parents to sit there and have someone feed them all these things that they already thought or they already know and that's their first introduction to hockey. They knew it, that's why you didn't make that team. Watch this! (Personal communication, September 11, 2016)

Brian's desire to control the narrative about South Asian experiences in hockey is revealing for a number of reasons. First, he reproduces liberal rhetoric about succeeding in the face of adversity, which presents adversity as inconsequential and fails to acknowledge that this adversity is not distributed equally. Second, he talks about the race card as a maneuver used to gain sympathy. Race card rhetoric, akin to playing the victim, stems from affirmative action programming whereby quotas for minoritized citizens were instituted for university admissions, hiring, and other opportunities under the assumption that these individuals lacked the credentials to be included and were gifted opportunities over more deserving applicants. To speak of the race card conjures assumptions about differential treatment, because to bring attention to one's race in a negative manner seems like an unnecessary attempt to dredge up the past—a past that is, supposedly, no longer relevant. However, it also ignores the fact that everyone has a race card to play and whites have been found to increasingly use their race card as a countermove against attempts to foster equality (Hammon, 2013). Third, Brian contends that even if racism is at play, South Asian children must believe that they are being judged solely on their merits. While this is a patterned coping mechanism, it again denies a space for players to talk about their personal experiences with racism. Fourth, he admits that he may have been dishonest in this interview in order to maintain the innocence of hockey. Brian referred to hockey as a "culture and a religion" in his interview (personal communication, September 11, 2016). He also spoke of karma, explaining that players have to trust that things will eventually work out. Brian's trust in the church of (Canadian) hockey speaks to the mythological power of both the sport and multicultural discourse; to criticize discrimination is unpatriotic *and* sacrilegious. The discursive (re)production of hockey as a religion in Canada is telling because it speaks to its power, meaning, and the purpose that the sport provides individuals, while also explaining the reluctance to speak truth to power. Hockey "becomes the subject of feeling, as the one who must be protected, as the one who is easily bruised or hurt. When racism becomes an institutional injury, it is imagined as an injury to whiteness" (Sara Ahmed, 2012, p. 147). Thus, we need to ask what implications manifest when individuals feel the need to protect the sanctity of the game, when that protection is not reciprocated. Last, Brian did not want South Asian children to be dissuaded from participating in hockey with the proof of racism serving as the deciding factor. Brian's actions may have been well intentioned but avoiding racism does not make it go away; and, arguably, it is better to prepare racialized children with an honest account of what can happen and impress that others share their experiences, instead of letting them be shocked when the racial taunts begin.

At first, I assumed that the reluctance to share experiences must have stemmed from these memories being too traumatic to discuss; hence, the generalizations, pivoted discussions, and the desire to avoid re-traumatization. However, we must also acknowledge that silence represents an act of agency. Tapias (2016) elucidates: "Silence provides a subtle cultural mechanism through which relations of power and intimacy are contested, subverted and/ or negotiated. When narrativity is self-censored and strategically silenced, what are the reasons for doing so? ... As a meaningful speech act, silence reveals as much as it conceals" (p. 174).

In Tapias's (2016) research with Bolivian migrants, she contends that silence becomes a preventive health measure, whereby the refusal to not disclose trauma, stress, and/or discrimination serves to "protect the self from the ill wishes of others" or to "prevent distress and possible illness in those one loves" (p. 175). We can certainly see evidence of this agency through the acknowledgment that parents often hid racist incidents at the rink from their children, and the reluctance to divulge any specific incidents may function as a form of self-care.

Unfortunately, what can be expressed as an individual act of agency also serves to suppress the collection of narratives limiting the potential for broad-scale change. For example, Kiran described her hockey career as a constant battle that others never really understood: "It's a topic that you don't really want to bring up. . . . It's something that I've always thought about but never really truly expressed my feelings about because no one's asked me" (personal communication, April 28, 2016). Sara Ahmed (2016) muses, "What is phantom for some for others is real. What is hardest for some does not appear to others" (paras. 18–19). This is the difficulty in attempting to advance discourses of racism as institutional oppression because the proverbial wall that one bangs their head against is not an actual wall. For the majority of Kiran's teammates, the wall that she has battled her entire career remains an invisible hindrance felt only by Kiran; and it should be acknowledged that the locker room is a difficult space to begin describing this "wall," especially as the only one who recognizes its existence. For these reasons, anti-racism training should be a mandatory component of coaching certification programs, in addition to providing anti-racism workshops for players and parents. Similar to the *You Can Play* project LGBTQ+ advocacy workshops that address heteronormativity/homonegativity in locker rooms (MacDonald, 2016), anti-racism workshops should be led by independent organizations and instituted at a consistent level for all players (e.g., every U-12 team undergoes anti-racism training at the beginning of the season). The Truth and Reconciliation Commission of Canada's Calls to Action include anti-racism training for sports as a national responsibility and commitment. This call to action is more specifically meant to decolonize the sports system, but it provides a significant entry point for discussions about racism more broadly.

The way participants downplay racism or avoid talking about it contributes to Robin James's (2015) interpretation of a multiracial white supremacist patriarchy (MRWaSP, pronounced Mr. Wasp). She refers to it as multiracial because this neoliberal form of oppression invites racialized people (and women) into their own capture by rewarding those who "share in the destruction of other men and women of color who are vulnerable, disenfranchised, and rapidly being eviscerated through the policies of a multi-racial white supremacy" (Sheth as cited in R. James, 2015, p. 12). This does not mean that racialized people necessarily take pleasure in contributing to racial oppression but that the rewards for adopting and adhering to existing power structures are more readily accessible to those who "play the game." There will be *less* racism for racialized folks who take on a Westernized name, follow the Christian faith and its traditions, and downplay their racialized difference, among other things. It is basically the path of least resistance to a form of contingent acceptance. This is an understandable response in the face of discrimination and marginalization, but we need to be very clear that this path reproduces racialized oppression and colonial relations.

An Archive of Evidence

My original hope was to use the stories shared in this study as a way to move sport policy representatives to action by providing evidence of consistent racism in contemporary Canadian society; conversely, as this project came to life, I started to reflect on the evidence that I had gathered and wondered if it was enough to lodge a case of discrimination against the institution of hockey. And is it enough to advocate for more inclusive national narratives?

Sara Ahmed (2016) postulates on her personal blog that evidence is what you accumulate when you are not given places to go: "Add it to the archive is an expression that allows us to think that an experience however difficult might have use value as evidence (we have somewhere to put it; we have a place for it to go). But of course when I say 'add it to the archive' I say so with a degree of skepticism; if that archive is already stuffed, more evidence might be what we do not need" (para. 34).

This study is a perfect example of having an abundance of evidence with no place to take it. Overwhelming evidence of oppression and discrimination is unfortunately useless when the system is built on devaluing the evidence available along with its witnesses. Ergo, while archives of struggle may be cathartic and create necessary support networks (e.g., collective storytelling projects such as the Everyday Sexism Project and the iHollaback initiative that expose general sexism and street harassment, respectively), what value does this body of evidence have when it comes to dismantling systems of oppression? And, what *counts* as evidence? As I moved through the interviewing process for this project, I wondered: For whom are we really gathering evidence? Could the supposed need to collect evidence be an activity that supports oppression through distraction?

Evidence-based medicine (EBM) has been identified as the inspiration behind the need for evidence-based policy making (Little, 2003; Oliver, Lorenc, & Innvær, 2014). The initial drive for more evidence stemmed from a desire to reduce ineffective and/or harmful clinical interventions, and so a movement toward systematic review, randomized trials, and meta-analyses developed. As a result, the discourse of evidence connotes objectivity and quantitative data become synonymous with scientific proof (Little, 2003). Even though there is little theorization on the concept of evidence itself, some in the health and medical fields have pointed out fundamental flaws with this new applied research field, such as a lack of clarity regarding "what constitutes and defines 'evidence' and 'policy'" and "how evidence is supposed to improve decision-making"

(Oliver et al., 2014, p. 35). In addition, there is a mismatch between what policy makers define as evidence and what academics define as evidence. Perhaps most pertinent to the discussion of racism is the fact that evidence is supposed to produce instability but, as Little (2003) protests, "this may not be a problem if it can be accepted and accommodated but it is wrong to create the impression that today's truth will be the same as tomorrow's" (p. 180). Western society has positioned evidence as something we are supposed to react to, so what then happens when we present evidence that counters the desired outcome? What do we do with *unwanted* evidence? If evidence is always supposed to be under review (Little, 2003) and, as such, a society that privileges evidence must also be one that accepts conflict over certainty.

How useful is evidence of systemic oppression or patterned discrimination if the system does not allow you to do anything with it? The politics of evidence itself must be questioned because traditionally oppressed groups have been providing evidence of marginalization for decades only to be met with scoffs of derision and advice to "lean in" (i.e., Sandberg, 2013). It is too easy for evidence to be deemed the wrong *kind* of evidence or insufficient, and unfortunately "evidence of walls does not bring the walls down" (Sara Ahmed, 2016, para. 41). Subsequently, if racism works by disregarding evidence of racism, as Ahmed proposes, what good are testimonies of racism?

The answer may reside in cultural citizenship, in the need to know that you belong even if you are not counted. "Doubts about evidence become doubts about persons who are providing evidence" (Sara Ahmed, 2016, para. 5), which is precisely why dismissing evidence of racism concurrently dismisses the citizens, and citizenship, of those who present it; to make evidence of struggle disappear is to make those who struggle disappear. The ability to feel like one's experiences are of equal value to the opportunities provided and that one's words are heard with equal attention to anyone else are central to *feeling* like a citizen. Proponents of cultural citizenship argue that affective components of citizenship have been downplayed because, as a legacy of white, male domination, citizenship sees rationality and feeling as opposing traits (Cho, 2011). But, *feelings* of exclusion are required to truly understand the power of racism and its limitations on access to full citizenship.

It becomes even more important that we learn to speak of racism when we perceive it to be present and that we use the word itself—racism—because to avoid this word means that we are complicit in the disappearance of our fellow citizens and the injustice that makes it possible. This is not to say that labeling racism is sufficient in overcoming it, but this label makes resistance possible; it means there is something tangible *to* resist. If evidence cannot be used to prove injustice, then we will use it to prove existence: "Our archive is an archive of rebellion. It testifies to a struggle" (Sara Ahmed, 2016, para. 31). Evidence, then, should be conceptualized not as a way to dismantle the walls but as essential in "rallying the troops," to develop solidarity for the movement that lies ahead. It is through collective resistance that we are able to make discredited, dismissed, and disappeared evidence matter.

If speaking "about racism is to labor over sore points" (Sara Ahmed, 2012, p. 171), then this chapter makes it clear that many in hockey culture prefer to avoid this type of labor. The implication of this, unfortunately, is that nothing really changes. It is difficult to hear racialized citizens express the need to brush off these sore points as inconsequential—this is a learned behavior. Young athletes *learn* that accepting chirping on the field of play is simply part of the game. They *learn* that pointing out racism simply highlights your presence as the problem. They *learn* to accept racism as an inevitable part of sports. It is time our athletes learn that anger aimed at injustice and discrimination is not only warranted but is a necessary part of being an active and equal citizen. It is a right that too few racialized Canadians choose to exercise—the right to express anger and the right to speak honestly about one's experiences. To demonstrate anger, especially in public spaces, is a (racial) privilege. In the next chapter, I will discuss how gender further complicates racism and continue to unpack how racialized participants learn to accept and downplay racism as part of the game.

5

South Asian Masculinities and Femininities

Hockey, like most Western sports, is a gendered activity. When research participants were asked to name their hockey heroes, the NHL game was almost exclusively reproduced as the epitome of the game. Pavel Bure, Sidney Crosby, Steve Yzerman, Jonathan Toews, Joe Sakic, Markus Naslund, Alex Ovechkin, and Bobby Orr were some of the idols referenced during interviews. Only once was a racialized player named as a role model (Paul Kariya) and only one participant talked about women from the Canadian Olympic team as her role models. While masculinities (e.g., Allain, 2010, 2015; MacDonald, 2016) and femininities (e.g., Theberge, 1997, 2000, 2003) have been previously explored with respect to Canada's game, rarely has gender been explored in combination with racialized experiences. As a result, this chapter seeks to complicate how whiteness informs and enables particular gendered performances, while constricting other racialized performances that take place at the rink. I then move into more focused discussions about the intersection of gender and South Asian racialization.

The Irony of Hockey Performativity

Gender is a performative social construct. Adopting Judith Butler's (1988) stance, it is something that is produced and reproduced throughout our lives until it is solidified into some semblance of an authentic self. Being a hockey player adds an additional subcultural layer of performance to already complex intersectional lives. Hockey invokes a very particular performance that is often equated with white culture, but, in my view, that is a grossly simplified explanation. Rather, hockey comes with a specific aesthetic and embodiment that privileges an amalgam of classed, gendered, raced, and sexuality performances.

As Dev points out, "You walk down the street and you can tell who hockey players are cuz of the way they are; they're very arrogant sometimes but they're very confident" (personal communication, August 12, 2016). Sunny further expands on the performativity of hockey culture: "I know there's guys that will live the hockey culture on and off the ice, the way they act, the way they talk, stuff like that, and for me, I don't think I talk and live the way that a lot of them do" (personal communication, July 21, 2016).

"Living hockey culture on and off the ice" can stereotypically be identified by performances invoked through clothing (i.e., baggy shorts, T-shirt, baseball cap, flip flops/sandals) (MacDonald, 2015), hairstyle (i.e., a mullet or hairstyle that is long enough for the hair to flow out from underneath a baseball cap), language (i.e., sexist and homonegative language), excessive alcohol consumption, and hypermasculine sexuality (MacDonald, 2016). To illustrate, Brock McGillis, the first openly gay male hockey player to have played professionally (in Europe), had to do a lot of work in order hide his sexuality from his teammates: "McGillis did everything he could to fit in. He put on a hypermasculine guise, chewed tobacco, used a more rugged voice and walked around with a cocky swagger. He slept with as many women as he could . . . he even used homophobic language himself" (Mendelsohn, 2019, para. 3).

It's not hard to see why the NHL has never had an out male player, either present or former, when so much is required from the boys and men who choose to enter and remain in what can be a very toxic sporting environment. But this narrow gender performance is further compounded by class and race.

To the unfamiliar eye, much of this performativity appears to evoke a working-class aesthetic despite the fact that today the vast majority of white Canadian male hockey players come from privileged class positions. The leisure brands they adorn (i.e., Gongshow, Bauer, Beauty Status, Sauce) are priced for upper-middle and upper-class consumers, with a Gongshow hooded sweatshirt costing up to US$60. Gongshow describes its hockey lifestyle brand: "To take the essence of hockey, the freedom of the ice, and the memories with our teammates and put that all into an apparel brand that lives and breathes the hockey lifestyle and its culture on and off the ice. We are 'BUILT IN THE LOCKER ROOM'" (Gongshow, 2019).

On Gongshow's website, the story behind the brand speaks to the supposedly humble, unpretentious roots of hockey by describing how the brand came to life over "a few cold ones" at a "local Ottawa pub called Father and Sons." It symbolizes "what hockey players [are] all about." Shoppers are supposed to interpret this as down-to-earth, blue-collar folks illustrated by images of pick-up hockey on outdoor rinks and someone lacing up their skates in an old barn, all predominantly buttressed by white apparel wearers. Aside from the prices of the merchandise itself, there is a giveaway that the hockey lifestyle is a class exclusive, and ironic, one. In one image, a person sits on top of a net with their legs dangling over the mouth of the goal. Out-of-focus shinny takes place in the background but the skates that are the focus of the image happen to be a pair of Bauer 1S skates that were originally priced at some retail outlets for US$949.99 (Hockey Monkey, 2019).[1] Thus, as much as hockey likes to promote a working-class ethos, it is difficult to get away from the corporatization and exclusivity that is now central to the game.

Women and girls also contribute to this narrow conceptualization of hockey performativity. This may be because only recently have girls had reliable access to hockey with other girls, meaning many of the women from previous generations share the experience of being the only girl on a boys' team. This alone-ness leaves little room to challenge the dominant culture of what it means to be a hockey player. But importantly, for racialized girls and women, adopting this performativity can be a method to gain acceptance and/or self-preservation into an exclusive culture, albeit on a contingent basis. Sonia explains hockey as a status symbol if performed correctly: "This was in the '90s and there's kind of a connotation of being cool and playing hockey, so I thought that was pretty cool" (personal communication, December 1, 2016). She continues to describe the pressure associated with looking like you fit into rink culture:

> SONIA: I feel like there are so many barriers, whether it's language . . . but also equipment, price of equipment, pressure to have a certain type of look. That was always a thing I remember.
>
> CS: What's the look?
>
> SONIA: The look of having, in my day, it was when I got those Bauer Vapor skates. I remember because Brendan Morrison had them and I was like, "Mom, I have to have those skates." There were [sic] the model below it had the black patches on the back and I was like I need the blue patches. I remember it was a big ordeal, a big situation because I was like, I want that look. I want to be cool on the ice. I had no care in clothes otherwise but . . .
>
> CS: You got to look the part.
>
> SONIA: Yes! Totally. Someone who is coming, or something that has recently immigrated—no way! How do you even get involved in that if it's not inviting?

Today's version of the Bauer Vapor skates that Sonia references can cost anywhere from $200 to $800 for junior skates and $200–$1,000 for the senior skates. Therefore, the look that is desired by many players is a class distinction that challenges the blue-collar myth of hockey. It is also important to note that women-specific gear, while it exists, is difficult to find and is certainly excluded from the look of a hockey player. More importantly, the look serves as a social lubricant that, in theory, helps to minimize other differences such as race and gender, yet in reality this is a precarious way to gain entry into the group. Still, when girls and women—and racialized players—reproduce these whitestream interpretations of normative hockey performance, they reproduce a culture that ensures that other racialized participants will have to go through the same assimilation process (Ratna, 2014).

Hockey hair (also known as a player's "flow") is such a significant part of hockey performativity and culture that the state of Minnesota (colloquially known as The State of Hockey) celebrates an annual All-Hockey Hair Team (Kalaf, 2018), with the mullet representing the iconic hockey hairstyle (E. Kaplan, 2019; comment: a generous donation from Great Clips enabled it to continue in 2019). Thus, even though other cultural arbiters of hypermasculinity, such as the military, connote short hair as a sign of respectable masculinity, and commonly mark the act of any sort of hair care as feminine, hockey culture commonly privileges long hair as a masculine performance. In many ways, these "ironic masculine performances" (Ventresca, 2016, p. 154) are central to hockey culture because they contribute to the myth of hockey as a blue-collar everyman's game at a time when economic exclusion has never been more the reality.

Ventresca (2016) unpacks irony and masculine performativity in his analysis of Movember, a cause-related marketing campaign that encourages men to grow moustaches during the month of November as a way to draw attention to men's health issues. He explains that ironic masculinity enables (white) men to alter interpretations of manhood "without fear that these transformations will unsettle the gender binary or diminish faith in the 'naturalness' of male dominance" (p. 193). The NHL has become a conspicuous supporter of Movember because it aligns with one of hockey's most hallowed rituals: growing a playoff beard. The size of one's beard is a visible indicator of not only one's masculinity but also his hockey ability, because the longer one's team remains in post-season competition, presumably the larger one's beard grows (Ventresca, 2016). In *ESPN*'s 2017 Body Issue (D. Fleming, 2017), an issue dedicated to showcasing the nude bodies of high-performance athletes, Brent Burns and Joe Thornton of the San Jose Sharks, who are well-known for their full beards, were featured with beard extensions to further play up this aspect of hockey performativity and masculinity.

Facial hair, however, is not equally privileged. There are delineations between acceptable and unacceptable facial hair, with racialized men often positioned as the object of ridicule (e.g. the stereotype of East Asian men who are unable to grow a moustache and are therefore maligned as less masculine) or reduced to foreign caricatures (e.g. brown-skinned men who wear turbans and sport long beards) (Ventresca, 2016). Beards on brown-skinned men are popularly depicted as markers of difference, associated with terrorism, and/or used to stoke fears of Islamophobia. Yet, an unkempt beard on a white hockey player, Ventresca (2016) contends, exists "under the banner of irony" and allows young white men to "safely appropriate and manipulate the meanings associated with a variety of beard and moustache styles" (p. 161). He also points out that Movember has gained more traction in hockey culture than in either the NBA or NFL (arguably because both leagues are heavily populated by racialized men); and even then, the players who participate in Movember were overwhelmingly white athletes. As a result, "The NHL's whiteness . . . [is] aggressive and manly, but never dangerous or posing a threat to society" (p. 234). Racialized players, especially brown or Black players, have to navigate fitting into hockey culture but are also arguably limited by the ways in which they can conform.

Returning to the mullet as emblematic of hockey culture, the hairstyle's linguistic origins denote foolishness but the exact origin of the mullet is hard to pinpoint. In Alan Henderson's book, *Mullet Madness!: The Haircut That's Business Up Front and a Party in the Back*, he chronicles the mullet as far back as the ancient civilizations of Mesopotamia, Syria, and Asia minor. Over time, it has become a symbol of cultural identity that has been appropriated and rejected in a multitude of ways. In Canada and the United States, the mullet has predominantly symbolized white, blue-collar masculinity (e.g., David Spade's comedic film *Joe Dirt*, about a "white trash" protagonist). Alternatively, lesbians adopted the style during the 1980s as a subcultural group trait, it has been connected to Bollywood cinema as a way to depict a collision between class barriers (Gopal & Moorti, 2008,), at one time the mullet was so popular among European soccer players that it was known as the "footballers cut" (Bromberger, 2008, p. 379), and in 2010 it was one of the "un-Islamic" Western hairstyles that Iran banned for men (Dweck, 2010). Hair plays an important role in negotiating gendered and racialized performativities because it is symbolic of sexuality and culture. In 1951, Charles Berg contended "that hair is a visible and metaphorical substitute for unseen genitals," and in this particular interpretation "long hair signified unconstrained sexuality, short or tied-up hair meant controlled sexuality, and a close shave indicated abstinence" (p. 380). Thus, long hair, in all forms, aligns with hockey's hypermasculine performativity by privileging sexual conquest as part of the sporting culture (MacDonald, 2016).

What is important to consider with the mullet as part of both hockey and Canadian culture, however, is how racialized men have historically been Othered by their long hair. Baptized Sikh men maintain their unshorn hair underneath their turbans, which has caused tensions in various arenas such as the hockey rink (CBC Sports, 2008), legion halls, and working for Crown organizations such as the RCMP (CBC, 2017). Furthermore, residential schools cut the hair of Indigenous boys as an act of assimilation and violence to separate Indigenous children from their culture and identity (De Leeuw, 2007).

Two recent sporting examples illustrate the intersection of hair and racialization. At the end of 2018, a Black high school wrestler was made to cut off his dreadlocks in order to compete (Andone, 2018). The referee in charge of his match claimed that his hair did not comply with wrestling rules and he would have to forfeit the match if he did not cut his hair. Previously, the athlete had been allowed to compete with a head covering over his dreadlocks but in this instance the referee stood firm with his decision. While many valorized the player's decision to cut his hair because he was framed as the "epitome of a team player," others claimed this was the "epitome of racism" (L. Pierce, 2018), because it made very clear that the rules of the sport were designed for white performativity and sensibilities. Additionally, in January 2019, during a lacrosse game in Philadelphia the stadium announcer repeatedly made the comment "clip that ponytail," aimed at Lyle Thompson, an Indigenous player from the Onondaga Nation in New York state. Feeding off of the announcer's comments, the fans began chanting that they were going to "scalp" Thompson (Rolen, 2019). Hair represents culture and identity (Oyedemi, 2016); the cutting of hair has historically represented one form of violence used to oppress racialized people and erase their cultural difference. These examples illustrate *whose* masculinity counts and how racism can undercut masculine performances (to be unpacked further in a following section). The ironic performances that take place within hockey culture are allowed because whiteness has the power to control how such symbols are produced and consumed. Racialized citizens have not been afforded the same privilege of writing onto the culture of hockey in the same ways. Who wears a beard and who wears long hair as part of their hockey performativity illuminates the policed boundaries of hockey culture, and thus cultural citizenship. With Harnarayan Singh and other members of the *Hockey Night Punjabi* broadcast challenging what a sports commentator looks like, it is possible we may see a relaxing of these cultural boundaries. Still, we wait.

Racialized men, like queer men, tend to be reluctant in bringing too much attention to their difference because difference continues to be met with violence, marginalization, and stigma at the rink. In Nathan Kalman-Lamb's (2018) research on Canadian hockey culture, a former Ontario Major Junior player who identified as Jewish reiterated the idea that being anything but white and Christian comes with a litany of additional issues: "But it's like, oh, the Black kid does one thing wrong, he's out of here. And, you don't want to be Jewish, you don't want to be Black, you don't want to be, you *definitely* don't want to be Asian" (emphasis in the original, para. 19).

This player identifies the narrowness upon which hockey culture exists. It is not necessarily easy to pinpoint what hockey culture *is*, but it is very easy to detect what it is not, or who it excludes. Asian-ness is still largely acceptable grounds for ridicule in Canada and the United States, and it is dialectically necessary to uphold the hegemonic notions of Black and white masculinities (King, 2006). To say that Asian athletes are openly accepted as equals in most sports would be a stretch. The mere presence of Asian athletes in traditionally Canadian and American sports forces us to ask, "what are the terms of coexistence" for those citizens marked as out of place? (Puwar, 2004, p. 1).

South Asian Masculinities

White men, in Canada and the United States, are traditionally privileged with normative masculinity, a balance between brains and physicality, whereas Black men are overwhelmingly portrayed as a body without a brain (Prashad, 2000), and thus hypermasculine (Leonard, 2007). Again, occupying the "racial middle," South Asian men are relationally constructed as a brain without a body, "devoid of a body (phallus), [South Asians] are arguably unable to perform normative masculinity and fail to penetrate American-ness. South Asian bodies then stand as queer bodies in relation to white masculinity" (Thangaraj, 2013, p. 248). The paradox of the South Asian body represents a recurring theme throughout this study. Because the male South Asian body is (re)produced as queer, the persistent stereotype remains that this demographic is academically inclined but athletically inept (with cricket and field hockey remaining as convenient racist stereotypes).

S. Fleming (1995) lists some of these generalizations about South Asian bodies:

Asian children have low ball skills, low coordination and are weak.
Asian and West Indian children dislike the cold.
Where stamina is required, Asian girls are often at a disadvantage as they are usually small and quite frail.
Asians are too frail for contact sports. (p. 38)

While biological, cultural, and psychological explanations for athletic prowess have become accepted folklore, questions of access, opportunity, and discrimination continue to struggle in mainstream discussions. For many, these stereotypes become self-fulfilling prophecies where Asians internalize these ideas and "[swallow] the myth themselves" (S. Fleming, 1995, p. 40.). In fact, while attempting to explain my research project to one of my (biracial) cousins, he paused and responded with a comment about how he supposed South Asians do not have the "right" bodies for hockey. It is illustrative of how, to this day, many racialized people themselves have swallowed the myth of biological determinism and can contribute to the perpetuation of race as biological instead of social. Further building on the idea of race and biology, Greg, a hockey parent, explained to me that, "Caucasians get into their adult bodies quicker than East Asians and South Asians. Because they get into their bodies quicker . . . they actually perform better at an early age, whereas with East Asians and South Asians, they develop later. It's hereditary" (personal communication, November 21, 2016). Despite eugenics being widely debunked as pseudo-science, Greg's explanation is disappointingly common discourse in sports where the legacy of eugenics and biological determinism continue to frame race as either a competitive advantage (e.g., Kenyan long-distance runners) or a hindrance (e.g., lack of Black swimmers).

In Canada and the United States, prejudiced assumptions about Asian physicality and athleticism have only recently been challenged, which is curious given that during British colonization, Punjabi Sikhs were known as a martial race and vital to the success of the Indian army (Basran & Bolaria, 2003). Additionally, kabaddi (known by various names) is a popular Indian-created team sport that involves tackling the opposing players and no protective equipment is worn. This is a rough sport played by both Indian men and women in international competitions but is unable to challenge Western conceptions of masculinities and femininities because it exists far away from Western sports media consumption. Gary proposed that part of the South Asian interest in hockey is the comparable physicality that can be found in kabaddi: "One of the big games in India is Kabaddi and it's very physical [laughter]. So, Indo-Canadians like that" (personal communication, April 15, 2016). He also mentioned that South Asian men were stereotyped for their rough play: "I've had a Caucasian guy once say, 'You brown guys are all alike, just think you're tough guys'" (personal communication, April 15, 2016). It seems an odd comment to make considering hockey culture is built on intimidation, toughness, and physical violence; hockey-playing men have been socially constructed and privileged as "tough guys." The interpretation, then, is that toughness is valued and accepted in some bodies and in others it is seen as a disqualifying attribute. Thangaraj (2015) reveals in his research on South Asian basketball players that queer bodies are able to invert emasculating constructions by demonstrating athletic prowess where little is generally expected of them; but, this opportunity to contradict normative assumptions about race seems far more limited in mainstream hockey.

All Asians represent a paradox in the white imagination. During the early 1900s, Chinese and Japanese immigrants were used to stoke fears of "yellow peril," an Asian invasion that was premised upon high population numbers, cultural differences, and legitimate military strength. The opposite side of this coin, however, is the model minority myth (to be discussed further in chapter 7) where Asians are thought to be academically inclined and self-sufficient. By constructing all Asians as self-sufficient, we need not worry about anti-Asian sentiments because they can take care of themselves (unlike racialized groups who are a "drain" on the system); yet, when Asians "over" achieve they quickly reproduce the fear of "yellow peril" by putting white entitlement into question. In essence, the racial middle is a demographic who are used as tools to achieve or suppress racial justice in relation to other groups depending on the political time and context (Kawai, 2005).

For South Asian men, the paradox is that they are academically inclined, and by extension, athletically inept. Still, this physical weakness is juxtaposed against media representations of South Asian men as "violently patriarchal," with young men often growing up in "testosterone-fuelled [environments]" (Bakshi as cited in Walton-Roberts & Pratt, 2005, p. 174). Canadian media and the government (Citizenship and Immigration Canada, 2012) have contributed to these Orientalist notions by connecting South Asians and Muslims with "honor killings." Between 2002 and 2010, the *Globe and Mail* reported 12 honor killings—murders committed by male family members against women who supposedly bring shame to the family. These killings are framed as barbaric and old-world traditions that are unacceptable to Canadian sensibilities. The Orientalist nature of these stories assist in the erasure of domestic violence more generally in Canada because between 2002 and 2007, 212 Canadian women died at the hands of their domestic partner (Caplan, 2010). Gerald Caplan highlights the racialized hypocrisy by stating: "Women killed by partners are known as domestic homicides, and, unless especially gruesome, are barely worth a mention in the media. Maybe there's just too many of them to be newsworthy. . . . Yet both kinds of murders have a common root. Both are honour killings, reflecting a twisted, pathological male sense of honour" (para. 3 & 8). Too much testosterone, then, only becomes cited as a problem when exercised by racialized bodies, otherwise it is simply part of life in Canada.

These Orientalist notions find their way into the locker room. Dev talked about how individual South Asian men are often asked to explain the conduct of *all* South Asian men:

CS: So, what would one of those borderline racist questions be?
DEV: Well, just things about culture, like "I heard this thing on the news about brown people. I think it was in India there were a couple of girls who got raped on the bus and the guys got off literally scot free." It was just one of those questions like, "What's the situation with women's rights and stuff like that in India?" (Personal communication, August 12, 2016)

The racial equivalent would be to ask a white player, "What's up with white women's rights in Canada?" as a follow-up to a rape or domestic violence news item. Violence associated with certain bodies becomes named violence, whereas violence stemming from white bodies is all-too-often generic (and normalized) violence. This is another example of why race needs to be a talking point in hockey culture, because these discussions are already taking place but very few have the appropriate tools to make the most of these opportunities.

Surrey, British Columbia, as discussed in chapter 1, is produced as a criminalized and racialized space. Since the mid-1990s, South Asian immigration has spurred ideas about "Sikh youth violence" and "criminal gang activity," (Tyakoff, n.d., p. 3) despite the fact that research has demonstrated that crime is not race-related, and further reproducing the idea that brown bodies are both insufficiently and excessively masculine. This constructed reputation also came up during a couple of interviews. Gurp raised the issue of South Asian gangs as a possible reason for a lack of South Asian talent at the higher levels of the game:

> I just thought of this but the reason why there may not be as many South
> Asians, I mean, I don't know what the Surrey teams look like and how many
> Indians are there but, gangs. It's very possible they're not joining because they're
> involved with gangs and what not. All being about hard and not playing sports
> and whatever else. I have no idea; I don't know how many South Asian youth
> are actually involved in gangs, but I do know South Asian gangs are on the rise,
> so who knows. (Personal communication, May 10, 2016)

Black and brown citizens are overrepresented in gang activity, and the media often reproduce the idea that racialized people are more prone to criminal activity, despite the fact that all ethnic groups are susceptible to gang activity (e.g., Freng & Esbensen, 2007; Wortley & Tanner, 2006).

Continuing with the idea that South Asians filter themselves out of the game, Sunny pondered a stereotype that he had heard but not one with which he agreed: "I've heard in the past that we have like a reputation where it's, like you get to a certain level and you just want to party or something like that . . . how we have a reputation where we get to a point and we don't care anymore and we just kind of ruin it for ourselves" (personal communication, July 21, 2016). This seems like a convenient excuse to be placed on South Asian hockey players who consistently have a more difficult path to the elite levels of the game. Gary also voiced concerns about a lack of discipline amongst South Asian youth:

> I'm kind of worried about our generations because they're into partying . . .
> they're into partying and drinking and all that kinda stuff and I've seen some
> kids, and not just in hockey but basketball, soccer, who are really, really good

and they just throw it away for their drinks and they're partying and the girls or the boys. Yeah, I just think that's a huge part of it right now, especially in the Lower Mainland. . . . I don't think the kids are as disciplined enough to understand how important it is to go to your practices, have a good diet, have a good lifestyle, be good role models. (Personal communication, April 15, 2016)

Accordingly, we can see that South Asians are starting to reject the idea that they physically cannot play hockey; yet, they have replaced biological determinism for cultural determinism in stating that there is something wrong with South Asian culture that limits their own potential. This aligns with new racism rhetoric where social inequality is positioned as a cultural deficiency, rather than something hereditary. Structural racism is rarely pinpointed as a possibility for exclusion from the highest levels of the game.

Verbal Trauma and the Body

There was a small, but noticeable pattern in my interviews whereby women participants were more willing to share specific experiences of racism in detail with me. The men, on the other hand, often replaced the opportunity to talk about their experiences with a declaration that, even though racism was present, it could be subdued (even if only in their own minds) by physically enhancing one's muscularity and/or other assertions of physical dominance. This gendered difference may stem from ingrained gender roles whereby women are socialized to embrace their feelings in ways that men and boys are generally discouraged from doing; but it may also point to a form of empowerment that is available to men through the body that is not as easily accessible or as valuable for women.

Racism and masculinity are closely intertwined. The intersection between race and gender for South Asian men is based on the historical connotation that Asian men are effeminate and weak because white masculinity is mythologically constructed as he who triumphs over the Other. The celebration of Rome's victories over the barbarians, or—in our own time—the triumphs of cowboy over Indian, hero over villain, civilization over anarchy, West over East (Hoch, 2004) are all examples of racialized men being excluded from their own self-determination. Goff, Di Leone, and Kahn (2012) contend that because masculinity is premised on "control over one's outcomes" (p. 1111), challenges to one's racialized identity are equally challenges to one's manliness. For example, if financially providing for one's family is fundamental to masculinity then job discrimination is an example where racialized men can be emasculated. Raj described an incident from when his grandfather immigrated to Canada saying, "There was racism in jobs back then. You know my grandpa came over . . . went to work in [small British Columbia town], and my grandpa and uncle went, and they came back and they didn't get paid" (personal communication, June 21, 2018). The ability to deny a South Asian man his pay because of his skin color is also a way to deny him his masculinity. Accordingly, Asian men in the early 1900s in Canada and the United States were forced into typically "'feminine' work such as laundry, housekeeping, and cooking, which translated into restaurant work" (Takaki cited in Shek, 2006, p. 381); hence, the persistent stereotypes of low-credentialed workers as racialized citizens.

Presumably because white men have denied access to full masculinity (and cultural citizenship) for South Asian men, the men in this study generalized and downplayed their marginalization by referring to racism as "it" or "that" when talking about their experiences (chapter 4) and then quickly proclaimed their physical dominance/competence as an act of agency. Dev cited his physical size as a deterrent for racism: "I'm a big guy so they don't really tend to say anything too bad. But I'm sure if I was [sic] smaller they would probably. I don't know" (personal communication, August 12, 2016). Raj also recounted how as his body changed, so too did his response to racism. He described himself as a "scrawny little kid" growing up, which meant that opponents "could say anything" to him (personal communication, July 21, 2016). As a young player and a goal scorer he was unable to fight other players because that would have been a waste of his skill, but as he matured and his uncle taught him how to fight, he realized he did not have to stay silent any longer:

I had enough. Then no one said nothing because they knew I was going to fight them or beat them up. So, it's different. That was my way of releasing my anger or my vengeance towards that because it really bothered me when I was a kid. It did. But what was I going to do about it. You can't really do something about it, you had to take it. But boy when I played against some of those kids [at a higher level] that I played in [lower levels] I got paybacks. Paybacks from hell—it felt good. (Personal communication, July 21, 2016)

Fighting became catharsis for Raj, who described his physical transformation as connected with his racialized liberation: "When I started working out and got tougher and stronger then I was at peace with myself." The notion of being at peace with oneself is noteworthy and how it was his ability to respond to racism that afforded him that state of mind. It should make us question how many racialized Canadians live in a state of unrest because we have been taught to accept, or turn a blind eye to, racism in one way or another.

Chan (2001) posits that because white men overwhelmingly represent normative masculinity, Asian men are essentially "given a false choice: either we emulate white American notions of masculinity or accept the fact that we are not men" (as cited in Shek, 2006, p. 156). This inability to self-determine one's existence undercuts the fundamental privilege of masculinity in a patriarchal society, leaving some South Asian men at a loss for options: "But on the ice, it was basically anything goes . . . you hear some things. It was, ya, you hear some things. It's not great, but what are you gonna do right? You can't stop anyone from doing anything and you're not gonna go and maul the kid cuz he said anything. I'm not going to screw my team up for a personal vendetta" (Gurp, personal communication, May 10, 2016).

Hockey invites racialized bodies into their own capture because docility is required by the culture; yet, this docility also enables racism to persist. Players are limited in their options in dealing with racism if they want to continue a hockey career; it would seem that the promotion of anti-racism (as a player) and advancing one's hockey career are mutually exclusive in today's hockey system. This is where zero-tolerance policies are crucial, and coaches and officials need to be able to step in and either escalate incidents through procedural mechanisms or be empowered to stop play as a practice of anti-racism. To play through the acknowledgment of racism is to accept its presence.

Hockey parents Kulbir and Greg talked less about their physical size but certainly referenced their ability to physically impose themselves in an assertive/aggressive manner. Kulbir stated, "I don't take any crap from anybody. I always go after—you have a problem? Then nobody says anything." He told me that because of his personality "parents are always nice to me"; however, when I tried to clarify if parents actually made him feel welcome, he replied, "Well, not really. Especially when you go to Toronto to play, Winnipeg, Calgary, they always look around. . . . But I don't think I have any problem because I am very nice with them too" (personal communication, June 15, 2016). Here again, it is important to note the difference between being welcomed and merely having the ability to deter overt racism. Greg expressed a similar method of avoiding confrontations about race at the rink by being frank with other parents:

CS: Have you ever been made to feel unwelcome in the hockey community?
GREG: Yeah but I'm not the kind of guy that will take it. I'll honestly and come out and tell ya, "Do you have a problem?" Right from the get-go: "Do you have an issue?" Right from the get-go guards go down, wording is changed and it's different. (Personal communication, November 21, 2016)

In these narratives, it is evident that marginalization exists but there is a refusal to give racism attention or any real acknowledgment so long as a show of physical strength/imposition is usually enough to deter any potential incidents. Notably, physical dominance/muscularity does not eliminate racism; instead there is a sense that it can, at the very least, provide relief (or a semblance of safety) for individuals. This is problematic in the way that teaching women self-defense to avoid sexual assault is problematic—it does not address the under-lying cause. In the case of sexual assault, the underlying cause is male entitle-ment to the female body, and in the case of racism it is that certain bodies are socially devalued. This method of physically deterring or silencing racism also contributes to the skewed presence of racism in hockey because it is allowed to exist as a collective problem but never identified as an individual problem.

These accounts of physicality support existing research connecting racism with performances of masculinity. Cheng, McDermott, Wong, and La (2016) were the first to examine the relationship between racial discrimination and the drive for muscularity among Asian American men (defined in their study as inclusive of Chinese, Vietnamese, Indian, Korean, Bangladeshi, Cambo-dian, Filipino, Hmong, Japanese, Malaysian, and Pakistani). Asian men have been observed to have a "higher drive for muscularity and lower body satisfac-tion than [do] Whites and Blacks" (p. 216; see also Barnett, Keel, & Cono-scenti, 2001; Grammas & Schwartz, 2009; Kelly, Cotter, Tanofsky-Kraff, & Mazzeo, 2015; Keum, Wong, DeBlaere, & Brewster, 2015), suggesting that this desire for muscularity is connected to racial positioning. Cheng et al. (2016) concluded that "Asian American men who experienced greater perpetual for-eigner racism reported higher levels of attitude toward achieving muscularity" (p. 221). Perpetual foreigner racism refers to the assumption that any Asian person must be foreign born and therefore remains forever foreign in the white imagination.

The ability and opportunity to enhance one's muscularity becomes a way to cope with racism because participating in Canada's game is, by itself, not enough to erase racial difference. Gurp recalled an incident where violence was chosen as the answer because his teammate had reached a breaking point: "I don't even remember if we won or lost but this guy on my team he just, dur-ing the handshake line he wound up and decked the kid. Knocked him out right to the ground . . . but he had just had enough. . . . He was an emotional guy, but he wasn't, I had never seen him that explosive" (personal communica-tion, May 10, 2016).

Similarly, Varma-Joshi et al. (2004) have observed that for some victims of racism the only defense available was "proactive violent behavior" or the threat of physical violence (p. 196). Thus, in a world where social, economic, and cul-tural capital is contingent and only partially in one's control, physical capital offers the most accessible route to (the illusion of) equality. Particularly when operating in a liberal ideological framework that stresses individual responsi-bility, fortitude, and innovation, developing one's physical stature becomes one of the few individual solutions available to address systemic injustice.

Raj's previous narrative is illuminating because he states that enhancing his body put his mind at peace. This peace was unavailable to him as a younger player and apparently only through the body could racism be acknowledged and resisted. More research needs to be conducted to determine whether or not physical empowerment works in the same way for women, although a comment made by Kiran suggests it might: "Over the ice, there's been moments where I have almost caught a few people almost going to say something, but they stop themselves. There have been moments where I'm like, 'Oh, you're gonna say something.' But I don't know, I get pretty intense on the ice so maybe they got scared of me [laughs]" (personal communication, April 28, 2016).

It may be relevant, for example, that recent research on perceived racism among Asian American women observed a direct link with disordered eating as the common coping mechanism (Cheng, 2014). Future research needs to question what role the body and physicality may play in downplaying, avoiding, and/or coping with racism for women athletes.

South Asian Femininities

In 1989, Nancy Theberge stressed that all women are constructed within the myth of female frailty; however, not all women are marked as equally fragile. Sojourner Truth, one of the first known intersectional feminists, highlighted this racialized difference in 1851 when she stated: "That man over there says that women need to be helped into carriages, and lifted over ditches, and to have the best place everywhere. Nobody ever helps me into carriages, or over mud-puddles, or gives me any best place! And ain't I a woman?" (Fordham University, 1997).

Understanding how race complicates, or "fragments" (Douglas, 2002, p. 5) the experiences of women is central to achieving anti-racist work, or any other justice-oriented work. Theberge (1997) contends that the very existence and popularity of women's hockey should challenge the myth of female frailty, still this resistance is often countered by the complaint that it isn't real hockey, meaning men's hockey (Theberge, 1997, p. 84). In the scramble to legitimize women's hockey (e.g., MacDonald, Szto, & Edwards, 2017), white women's experiences have been serviced to represent *all* women's experiences in the game, or as Goudge (2003) states, "Gender is on the agenda but racism isn't" (p. 51). Following Ratna's (2011, 2018) calls for more attention to be paid to women of color and their complicated sporting experiences, I attempt to shine a light on a sliver of South Asian women's experiences in Canadian hockey culture.

Broadly speaking, the assumption that Asian women embody tradition through normative gender roles often results in a representation of physically weak and passive women (especially in comparison to white women). Walton-Roberts and Pratt (2005) note that transnational movement into "Western society" can in fact embolden patriarchal power, rather than dilute it, because immigration exists through a patriarchal lens. Referring to Canadian immigration policies specifically, Thobani contends that "immigration policy reinforces and produces patriarchy because it casts immigrant women in a literal state of dependency on male household heads (as cited in Walton-Roberts & Pratt, 2005, p. 175). In Thangaraj's (2015) work on South Asian basketball leagues, he observed that South Asian "women are not seen as having the bodily or cultural toolkit to navigate the competitive realm of the basketball court" (p. 191). In fact, some of the women in his study viewed participation in basketball as a marker of being a bad Indian because it went against traditional gender norms. Conversely, the South Asian women in this study offer necessary counternarratives about passive and fragile women.

Nanayakkara (2012) historicizes the relationship between sport and South Asian women explaining, "Sport has been accepted as an integral part of the Indian culture for both men and women since ancient times" (p. 1889). The relationship dates back to 3250–600 B.C. with evidence of participation in dancing and swimming. Military training during the Vedic period also emphasized female strength and self-defense. River games, archery, and ball games were some of the many activities that South Asian women participated in until European colonization altered the social, economic, and political status of South Asian women. Once Western education was instituted in the colonies, sport participation was mostly limited to Western sports that had international competitions. "Unfortunately, urban non-missionary school girls and rural girls who were unfamiliar with western sports were not capable of taking part in any international competition and were underrepresented in global sport competitions" (p. 1892); hence, it is imperative to situate South Asian female sports participation in a broader discussion about the long-term implications of British colonization on South Asian women and girls. The way sports are framed and *which* sports are promoted have a lot to do with (re) producing racialized notions about who can and does participate in sport. The South Asian voices included in this study are proof that Indian culture is not a monolithic barrier to sport participation for South Asian women. We must acknowledge that research on South Asian female sporting experiences remains one of the least explored areas for social enquiry (Nanayakkara, 2012), and that family values are very dependent upon those who make up the family.

The stereotype that South Asian parents are strict and protective was evident through quotes such as, "my parents were very strict on my growing up so they'd always be like 'Don't go out too much. . . . Stay inside,' and with that, if I was going to stay inside I was obviously going to watch hockey" (personal communication, Hockey Night Punjabi), or as Raj elucidated, "They were so strict on me it was crazy. . . . I couldn't even get on the phone to talk to someone, [had to] sneak around and do that" (personal communication, June 21, 2016). Sonia reflected on how her gendered and racialized identities were externally imposed upon her. Teammates would ask her questions about Punjabi culture, positioning Sonia as a cultural educator, in turn asking her to contribute more labor than is generally asked of white hockey players (to be further unpacked in chapter 6): "What did they ask me? Something about 'Are you allowed to do . . . this?' Do you have super strict parents or whatever? I remember, 'Do you have to get an arranged marriage?' Shit like that" (personal communication, December 1, 2016).

Kari reflected on her family restrictions growing up in India: "I was more a triathlete: run, long jump, and that kind of thing . . . in college and school too. But over [in India] girls are very reserved in those days, not anymore. My father didn't . . . sometimes I was playing something, I won something I didn't want to tell him that I play. Eventually he found out. He's okay but I was so afraid" (personal communication, January 16, 2017).

It would seem, however, that the restricted or less privileged upbringing of many South Asian immigrant parents is what can facilitate sport participation for their Canadian-born children. Kari explained that because she never had the opportunity to openly excel at sports as a child, she wanted to ensure that her daughters would have those opportunities: "My dream was that [my daughter] could go up to a high level. I'm happy" (personal communication, January 16, 2017). Kiran shared a similar story about her parents:

> My mom, growing up, she was born in India and she didn't play, see my parents never got the opportunity to play sports so when they did have the luxury of putting us in sports and I've been blessed that they have put me in sports. . . . My mom always loved sports. She'll watch the Canucks . . . she'll watch baseball if it's on. . . . My mom said, "Ah, I would have been so good at hockey if I got to play" [laughter]. But she didn't actually play any sports but she herself is pretty athletic. . . . He was actually born and raised in Fiji so it was a smaller place and his mom really kinda said, "You know that you have to look after the house. You have to help out. You gotta work. So, he was kinda restricted too."
> (Personal communication, April 28, 2016)

Kiran's family's class position enabled her parents to enroll all three children in various sporting activities. Therefore, where we often see culture as the barrier to increased sport participation, we must be careful not to confuse cultural barriers with class barriers, or even issues of access.

All of the women interviewed for this study attributed their hockey participation to their parents and their willingness to challenge traditional gender norms in one way or another. Parental labor is central to the sporting system and athlete success (Gruneau, 2016). It is one of those factors that is easily overlooked but speaks to gender norms, class position, type of employment, and family structure. Kari had no idea how time-consuming being a hockey parent would be when she started: "No idea. No idea. Now when I sit back I think—it was a lot of time! But that time when you're going through [it] I didn't have the time to think about how much time it was. Go! Go! Go! Practice once or twice, then game. Games [are] always far [away] and you have to be 1.5 hours early, then 1-hour game. It's like your day is gone. You are lucky on the way if you get some groceries or things" (personal communication, January 16, 2017).

Being a hockey parent adds additional labor to traditional gendered expectations because Kari still had to take care of groceries and other errands. She continued by explaining that hockey is in fact more demanding on families than other sports such as soccer: "But my eldest she was already involved in soccer and I think that was enough. The problem was my husband was so busy he could never take a weekend off and I cannot manage all three kids at three different rinks plus work. Soccer was easier. The parents voluntarily [took my daughter] or I can drop them off, they can pick them up. The games were a little bit closer than hockey, the fields" (personal communication, January 16, 2017).

The distance and availability of rinks further compounds the difficulties for hockey families. Amit spoke of similar gendered expectations in her family, referring to her mother as "the typical hockey mom." She described the role as, "The minivan, like three kids. She would drive us, like my sister was playing ringette as well so she would drive the three of us to three separate games and then just try to pick everyone up, take us home, cook dinner and then if one of us had practice later for something else she'd drive us there. So, we like lived in the minivan."

Even though I interviewed more South Asian men than women, only the women spoke about hockey parenting as gendered labor. None of the men talked about also having to balance groceries or other household activities as part of their responsibilities. This, again, could be a gendered conversational response but it could also illustrate the fact that not all parental labor in support of hockey is equal in participation.

Moreover, as vital as it is to amplify the voices of South Asian women who challenge dominant notions of South Asian female oppression, it is equally important to recognize that South Asian men play a large role in enabling and/or hindering their children's sport participation. As an example, Suki's father was instrumental in both her and her sister's hockey careers: "He was like, you know equality for all my kids. If my sons want to play hockey, sure. If my daughter wanted to play hockey, sure. It wasn't really a problem, but I do tend to see that and that's what my dad tried to do with the community was bring light to what I did and what my sister was doing—let all of them play hockey, not just the boys" (personal communication, June 15, 2016).

Hopefully these narratives can help nuance dominant constructions of South Asian men as overly masculine, traditional, and overbearing with South Asian women being universally weak, passive, and uninterested in physical contact sports.

The Noisiness of Women's Hockey

In its roles as national symbol and everyday pastime, hockey produces a
very ordinary but pernicious sense of male entitlement: to space, to status,
to national belonging.
—M. L. Adams, 2006, p. 71

When I was an undergraduate student at the University of British Columbia,
I was at a stick 'n puck session (open ice for practicing) and a man asked me if I
played on a team. I replied, "I just play for a women's recreational team in Burnaby." His response has been seared into my memory to this day: "Well yeah, all
women's hockey is recreational." I have no recollection of what he said after
that. He was trying to pay me a compliment, but this compliment simultaneously devalued all of women's hockey in Canada. He made this comment to
me after the Canadian women's Olympic hockey team had won back-to-back
gold medals at the Salt Lake City and Turin Games; and, little did he know, at
the time, that they would go on to make it four consecutive Olympic gold medals. The truly upsetting part of his statement was that it was more accurate than
it should have been. Despite the dominance of the Canadian women's Olympic
hockey team between 2002 and 2014, women's hockey remains recreational in
the sense that the ability for women to make a living wage from playing professional hockey is almost nonexistent. In September 2017, the *Globe and Mail*
published a photo essay on the women and girls who play hockey in Canada
asserting, "The story of women's hockey is a complicated tale of great progress
and inarguable disparity" (para. 1) and that women's hockey has "only scratched
the surface of how far there is to go" (Paterson, 2017, para. 8). Women's hockey
in Canada has been locked in a perpetual state of becoming.

Women's ice hockey has a long history in Canada. In the late 1800s to early
1900s, girls and women began participating in unorganized/semi-organized
hockey, and soon women's university teams were popping up at McGill, Queen's
University, and the University of Toronto (M. A. Hall, 2002, p. 32). Alberta
held its first women's provincial championship in 1906 (M. A. Hall, 2002,
p. 37). Scholars such as C. Adams (2008) and Theberge (2000) have noted
that despite "little public support or interest in women's hockey (p. 2)," girls
and women have always participated in Canada's game and often in excep-
tional ways.

It was not until the 1990s, when the International Ice Hockey Federation
(IIHF) held its first World Championship (1990), and women's hockey was
added to the Olympic program (first contested at the 1998 Nagano Olympics),
that financial resources and player development gained any real traction. Still,
as mentioned above, even Olympic validation has done little to displace the

"NHL-style customs and values [that] remain those ones that really 'count' in the sub-culture of Canadian hockey" (Gruneau & Whitson, 1993, p. 162). During this growth period, racialized women have been further marginalized and underrepresented in Canada's game; yet, rarely have they challenged the system itself. In fact, activism beyond women's equality leaves a deafening silence in the women's game.

The women I interviewed neither critiqued the gendered nature of the game nor its binary sex segregation. Only Amit positioned women hockey players as her idols, naming Canadian Olympic stalwarts Caroline Ouellette and Hayley Wickenheiser. Kiran was the only woman player who was in a position to think about her future, or lack thereof, in hockey:

> KIRAN: I know there's a few more leagues sprouting up. I know there's the NWHL and the Canadian hockey league right now but, you know, after next year it's kind of the time of my life where I probably want to focus more on developing a future and a career, and looking for some career options instead of hockey options. . . . I know those leagues; they exist but they're not exactly where I want to be and not exactly what I want. They don't pay as much and you're kind of put into a job that you maybe don't want.
>
> CS: Let's say you could play and make an actual living wage from hockey. Would that be option #1 for you?
>
> KIRAN: Yes. That would be option #1. At the end of the day, I have put in so much work and so much time and so many sacrifices that it's an obvious, obviously I still love it. And I do feel like this has been my best few years of hockey. I feel like, it tears me apart that I have spent all these years to get to better and get really good at hockey, to have to leave the game. It's almost my peak. So, it's unfortunate that way but it's reality and I'm okay with it.

Kiran touches on some of the more significant inequities that exist for women hockey players: the lack of a living wage, the need to work in order to support one's hockey career, and university/college hockey as a common end point for elite women players. When Canadians see the amount of money thrown at NHL players it is commonly assumed that women's hockey receives relatively the same benefits, especially considering how much media attention the women's Olympic team garners every four years. Sadly, the way women professional players have been treated in Canada is one of the many inconvenient truths that challenge the notion that hockey is Canada's game.

While preparing this book, the Canadian Women's Hockey League (CWHL) announced its abrupt closure on March 31, 2019 (Spencer, 2019). Neither the players nor teams' general managers were prepared for a league closure. It folded after 12 years of operation and had only begun offering stipends (between C $2,000 and $10,000) to its players during the 2017–2018 season. The National Women's Hockey League (NWHL) was created in 2015 as an American rival league to the CWHL and immediately offered salaries between US$10,000 and $26,000 per season. However, by November 2016, the NWHL announced that it would have to cut player salaries by 38% due to financial issues (Rutherford, 2019). Regardless of which league players choose, even the best salaries only offer poverty-level wages.

Professional women hockey players happen to be some of the most educated women athletes because ice hockey is only offered at a limited number of NCAA (National Collegiate Athletic Association) schools (predominantly on the East Coast of the United States), and some of the most competitive teams tend to be Ivy League schools. (Ironically, Canadian university teams are commonly seen as second-tier options compared to NCAA competition, but this is slowly starting to shift.) As a result, Olympic rosters are inundated with Harvard, Cornell, Princeton, Boston University, Boston College, Yale, and Brown graduates. Yet, when these women sign up to play in a professional league, unless they are a member of a national team program, the vast majority of professional players require full-time jobs to support their hockey careers (Pardy & Szto, 2019a, 2019b). Financial planners, real estate agents, teachers, engineers, lawyers, and graduate students are representative of the women who play elite-level hockey. In fact, both the NWHL and former CWHL are/were made possible *because* of the labor contributed by the non-national team players who work nine-to-five jobs, give up their evenings for practices, and their weekends to travel for games (Szto, 2018). Moreover, the scant media coverage provided for women's hockey further contributes to its Otherness and marginalization (MacDonald, Szto, & Edwards, 2017).

Girls' and women's hockey have managed to equalize opportunities for participation with great strides since the late 1990s, but the inequality of conditions continues to be staggering. Women's professional hockey remains a labor of love. It also offers an important case study in understanding gendered citizenship and how "rights, participation, entitlements and voice" contribute to belonging and social value within a supposedly democratic society (Danielsen, Jegerstedt, Muriaas & Ytre-Arne, 2016, p. 2). Danielsen et al. (2016) pose a simple question that perfectly encompasses the struggles that women's hockey faces in Canada: "Is it possible to act out citizenship if you do not have access to representation?" (p. 4).

Arguably, because women's hockey has been playing catch-up for so long, issues of racial justice seem like a distant concern, including for racialized players. Sexism in the game is generally agreed upon as a collective issue whereas racism is framed as a "bug but not a feature" of the institution in question (R. James, 2015, p. 85). For this reason, white feminism is rife in women's hockey (de la Cretaz, 2018; Hayden, 2019; Shah, 2019a). Women's hockey fans and media point out that there are very different expectations placed on women's hockey because the fan base tends to be made of marginalized groups from queer and racialized communities. As Zoë Hayden, editor of the *Victory Press* (an intersectional women's sports site) has lamented, the lack of justice-oriented activism from women's professional hockey is perhaps "the greatest disappointment...because they have this great opportunity to be different from men's hockey" (de la Cretaz, 2018, para. 8). The longevity and sustainability of hockey is directly affected by its overwhelming whiteness in both the men's and women's games. A look at the Canadian girl's U18 national team continues to broadcast the whiteness of Canadian hockey (Hockey Canada, 2018). Sarah Nurse, one of the two racialized women on the 2018 Canadian Olympic hockey team, explained that growing up playing hockey in Southern Ontario other players would suggest that she might be better suited to playing basketball. Nurse's response to these taunts is that "hate is just noise" (La Rose, 2019, para. 15). This individual response unfortunately enables racism to persist as an inevitable part of the game. It is also a noise only heard by certain players.

Kiran told me a story about a rookie-hazing experience from when she was approximately 12 or 13 years old, when the seniors on her team dressed up the rookies in assigned costumes: "They dressed everyone up, my friend was [cartoon character]...and then they got to me, '[Kiran], we're going to make you white today!' So, they painted my face white and they're like 'You're not brown today. You're white today!'" (personal communication, April 28, 2016).

The fact that race can be interpreted as a costume to be worn speaks to the history of blackface minstrelsy in Canada (Gilbert, 2003), America (Lott, 2013), and Britain (Pickering, 2008). Immaturity may be implicated in this particular incident, but to think of skin color as something that can be adorned and/or left behind is true only for those who are able to move about without ever realizing that they too wear a "costume." Racialized ridicule was central to the practice of minstrelsy. This experience demonstrates the necessity of deploying anti-racist education and policies in hockey programs that address the whiteness of hockey. Youth hockey players are negotiating and reproducing racialization without the appropriate tools to do so or resources to seek support when needed. Presumably, this was not a malicious act but at a subconscious level, Kiran's teammates recognized her difference as an outlier in hockey culture and through the act of white-facing her, reconfirmed the normative expectation of hockey as a white space.

Sonia also recounted incidents where her difference clearly outweighed any collective feminist struggle facing girl's hockey:

I remember the only fight I got into on the ice was because of a girl calling me a Paki and I just lost my shit. That was one of my breaking points of probably being in grade 10—it was pretty intense. When you're trying to run from [your difference] and not acknowledge it and then an opponent is like "You're a

Paki!" or "You brown this." . . . That is a thing that came up, people would say
that on the ice, "You brown this," "You brown that," "brown bitch," you'd hear
that stuff. (Personal communication, December 1, 2016)

These examples trumpet the need for an intersectional feminist approach to
advancing hockey for women and girls, because we need to ask *which* girls and
women are being uplifted, and *which* are subjected to further marginalization.
The advancement of women's hockey is not experienced equally for all women.
If white women are the "feminist killjoys" of hockey, then racialized and queer
women become the institutional killjoys through their intersectional complaints (Sara Ahmed, 2017). Sadly, the racist taunts and microaggressions that
women shared in this study, as stated by Nurse, become background noise in a
sport where girls and women are too busy fighting to establish themselves as
real hockey players with a viable future. In other words, we have taught young
women that responding to the cacophony of noise they face when entering the
culture of hockey comes with a hierarchy of responses. Responding to the noise
of sexism is acceptable, but the noise of racism is either too overwhelming or
not significant enough—we can only deal with one noise at a time.

To borrow from Robin James (2015), racialized women "can cause toxicity"
by pointing out injustices, "but they cannot experience it" (p. 105). Consequently, racialized women are invited to downplay their racialized differences
to avoid creating a toxic environment that would be noisy for everyone involved.
This particular kind of color-blind equality is illustrative of third-wave feminism or postfeminist perspectives that focus more on individual empowerment
and success, as opposed to challenging the inequitable system itself (McClearen,
2018). This in turn creates competition between men and women and amongst
white women and racialized women. These seemingly never-ending calls for
more can bring about "equity fatigue" (Sara Ahmed, 2017, p. 98), both for those
in positions of power and for those clamoring for change because so much
needs to be done. None of the problems facing women's hockey can be solved
by individual empowerment alone, and institutional racism benefits from the
sound-proofing that racialized players provide. That is to say that racialized
participants help insulate racism within the hockey community through their
individualized responses. One way to resist institutional racism is to amplify
those background noises for all to hear. R. James (2015) refers to this as "talking
back," a way to turn the noise back on itself and to expose the perpetrators of
oppression and discrimination. She encourages activists to turn background
noise into the sounds of a political resistance. To speak about racialized experiences with all the pain, joy, and ambivalence they come with can help destabi-
lize a system built on gendered and racialized docility.

Understandably, in leagues where the players are barely paid and often run
on volunteer labor, adding racial justice onto the plate of women's hockey may

seem like an unreasonable ask, or a low priority. Still, the growth of women's hockey requires participation from racialized women and the narratives featured throughout this book highlight the fact that racialized women are actively being deterred from advancing their hockey careers, and if they choose to persist it is in spite of the racism they encounter—not because racism doesn't exist in the women's game.

Building on the last chapter, I argue that we have groomed racialized hockey participants to brush racism off as an inevitable part of the experience. We reward players who downplay racism as background noise because they supposedly *overcome* racism without ever pointing a finger directly at it. As coaches, officials, parents, fans, and administrators, we do a disservice to players by rewarding their docility. Racialized citizens contribute to institutionalized discrimination by individually avoiding racism instead of challenging it. In the next chapter, I continue to problematize docile reactions to racism with a discussion about forms of capital and a theoretical critique of resilience as, perhaps, the most valuable form of capital under neoliberal governance.

6

Hockey Hurdles and Resilient Subjects

Unpacking Forms of Capital

How much does the economic cost of hockey limit opportunities for South Asian players? In what ways might patterns of recruitment in youth hockey be influenced by cultural preferences and choices? There are some intriguing hints at answers to these questions in the literatures that focus on factors that limit or encourage participation, such as gender (e.g., Coakley & White, 1992; Cooky, 2009), class (e.g., Gruneau, 1983; Hasbrook, 1986), and race (e.g., Carrington, 2010; Smith, 2007). It is notable, however, that research on such factors is far more limited when looking at access to hockey. The hockey scholarship that examines these factors is either dated or heavily swayed toward gender discrimination (e.g., C. Adams, 2014; M. L. Adams, 2006; DiCarlo, 2016; Eaton, 2012; Pelak, 2002; Slade, 2002; Stevens & Adams, 2013; M. Williams, 1995). More recently, *The First Shift*, an initiative sponsored by Bauer Hockey and Canadian Tire, surveyed 875 Canadians in Ontario and Nova Scotia targeting parents of children aged between 4 and 16 and reported that 90% of Canadian children do not participate in hockey (*The First Shift*, n.d.), again challenging the idea that hockey is Canada's game. The results identified four *perceived* barriers to participation: Hockey is expensive, time intensive, dangerous, and overly competitive.

Understanding the structural factors that limit participation are important; still, what deters people from joining and what restricts equality once inside the game are intertwined but unique discussions. If we conflate equality of opportunity with equality of conditions, we mask the structures that help maintain the status quo of a social institution. Pierre Bourdieu's work on the forms of capital is useful for adding nuance to issues of access; he believed that there were "hidden entry requirements" (Bourdieu, 1984, p. 217) such as family lineage, early socialization, and one's dress and conduct that generally helped reproduce existing hurdles.

Navigating Forms of Capital

The participants in this study identified four hurdles that make it difficult for South Asians to get into hockey and stay involved long term: cost, language barriers, lack of hockey knowledge (e.g., time commitment, equipment needs, where to register), and gatekeepers (e.g., coaches and scouts). These hurdles loosely coincide with Bourdieu's classification of forms of capital: economic, cultural, and social. Bourdieu (1986) describes capital as something that is accumulated and has the ability to reproduce or expand itself. He contends, "It is in fact impossible to account for the structure and functioning of the social world unless one reintroduces capital in all its forms" (Bourdieu, 1986, p. 83). Economic capital is simply money or access to it. Cultural capital lives in three forms: the embodied state, such as genetics or comportment; the objectified state, which exists as physical cultural goods, such as works of art; and the institutionalized state, referencing certain socially valuable qualifications. Social capital is the sum of one's group memberships that enable access to specific members and/or credentials. For Bourdieu, class struggle exists at the very heart of culture because it symbolizes the fight over representation, self-definition, and boundaries of membership. The following sections unpack the challenges of access to hockey for South Asians as outlined by the hockey players, parents, and coaches I interviewed, with respect to economic, cultural, and social capital.

Cost, Time, and Interconnections with Other Forms of Capital

Cost represents a challenge at multiple levels. Ice rentals, equipment, skate sharpening, additional lessons, conditioning, and tournament travel are some of the regular costs that occur throughout a season. Additionally, unlike most sports, the registration fees for hockey are not a set amount. Parents have to pay registration and tryout fees at the start of the season, but other fees (such as extra ice times or tournament registrations) have to be paid at the end of the season.[1] For example, Greg, a hockey parent, explained for Rep hockey teams (short for Representative—the most competitive level in minor hockey), it was not uncommon to pay $800 registration and then another $800 or $900 at the end of the season (personal communication, November 21, 2016). In the

Lower Mainland of British Columbia, the Richmond Minor Hockey Association's (n.d.) webpage warns parents that the demands of Rep hockey often bring more "expense, travel and time commitment," for which many parents are unprepared. As such, all hockey families need to have a large amount of disposable income to cover unforeseen costs. Every interview participant in my study felt that cost presented the most noteworthy hurdle to participation, a consideration that must be weighed against other opportunity costs. For example, former elite player Raj described a personal debate between investing in hockey versus investing in a private school education:

> RAJ: You can pay $15,000 or $20,000 to go into a [hockey] academy or am I going to send my kid to [private school] and go there for $20,000 a year? . . . If my kid goes to [private school] for four years/five years, he is guaranteed to go to a good school somewhere and he's going to [get] his doctor's degree or he's going to be making a couple hundred thousand dollars a year. Now if I go spend $20,000 on hockey . . .
>
> CS: It's still a crapshoot.
>
> RAJ: Yeah! (Personal communication, June 21, 2016)

Raj raises an important point, because too often hockey is promoted as an opportunity that opens additional doors to things such as athletic scholarships, but less often do we question the educational or work opportunities lost along the way in the pursuit of an elite career. Programs such as *The First Shift* attempt to address the inaccessible costs attached to hockey, which may partly explain a noticeable influx of racialized hockey participants at the grassroots level. However, beyond entry levels, hockey makes drastic class exclusions.

Hockey parent Kulbir referenced paying $10,000 to $11,000 per season for his daughter's under-18 hockey participation (personal communication, June 15, 2016). Hockey player Gary referred to hockey as a "rich man's sport" and suggested looking into subsidized programs through the schools as one way to possibly lower costs: "Hockey needs to take a page out of the American system in terms of basketball, football, you've got to make it part of your high school curriculum. . . . Minnesota has better programs than some of the ones in Canada" (personal communication, April 15, 2016).

Considering that hockey is Canada's national winter pastime, the fact that it is largely unavailable through the Canadian school system undermines the notion that it is a valued national pastime. But as Gruneau (2016) notes, "there has never been much political will to even begin to consider how the challenges of class inequality affecting access to sports might be met" (p. 242). Accordingly, we are left with a sporting system that has amplified class discrimination while failing to address how issues of class can be compounded by existing race- and gender-based discrimination.

In addition to access to capital, the culture of the game also requires a certain kind of middle-class/upper-class lifestyle and sensibility. Sonia, 26, explained how her experience as a racialized hockey player was influenced by a confluence of economic and cultural factors:

> I also didn't understand why I didn't go snowboarding on Sundays. . . . [Teammates] would be like, "What do you mean you don't go snowboarding on Sundays?" I was like "Uh, I don't know, I have to go to my family shop? I have to go to temple? What do you want me to say?" I think that whole weekend culture thing that is based around a very specific job identity or working identity, I didn't have that even though my parents did everything they could to make sure I was good." (Personal communication, December 1, 2016)

In other words, even though a self-enterprising model minority has worked themselves into an economic position to participate in hockey, there are other challenges associated with class, race, and gender. For example, *when* parents work, and what their expectations are for their gendered children, including such things as the perceived cultural appropriateness of participating in hockey for girls or boys, and if children are expected to contribute labor to the family business, all impact one's opportunities to participate. Sonia noted how her experiences were strongly shaped by the family's changing economic conditions, explaining that as her family became more economically stable her hockey career directly benefited because she "could go to those extra tournaments" and participate in additional training opportunities (personal communication, December 1, 2016). Sonia's experience helps add nuance to the assumption that registration and equipment fees are the main hurdles to participation. As her family's class position ascended, so too did her hockey potential. Here, we are able to draw a visible line between opportunity and class—one where merit does not enter the conversation.

Time, which is in many ways a commodity unto itself, is another factor that affects participation in hockey. Similar to the cost of playing, time is closely intertwined with class position: the privilege of free time. The extra opportunities that Sonia spoke of are not as optional as they may seem. Randy, a 43-year-old hockey parent, explained:

> My kid plays Atom hockey, he's in the average mix of Atom. . . . Monday he's powerskating, Tuesday he has practice, Thursday he has a home game, Friday he powerskates, Saturday he has development, Sunday he has practice. So, it's a lot. One of the powerskating sessions is optional but everybody does it . . . if you want your kid to excel, there's not a kid in the association that doesn't do some form of powerskating.[2] (Personal communication, November 15, 2016)

The fact that Randy's child is on the ice six times a week and competes at an average level provides some insight into how those requirements might intensify as players advance through the system. Another hockey parent, Sara, also referenced needing to "have your weekends open ... because you don't know what's going to happen" (personal communication, October 20, 2016), as vital to surviving hockey parenthood. Having free weekends again reflects a certain type of work schedule and/or parental structure that can facilitate participation.

Parents are expected to volunteer their time to help with team operations. This not only means having the time and energy outside of work to volunteer, but the types of volunteer jobs assumed are themselves influenced by class position. For example, Gruneau (2016) points out how the increasing professionalization of community sports clubs and associations has created demand for accounting, administrative, managerial, and business expertise that can lie outside the skill sets of many working-class Canadians, even when they are able to find the time to volunteer. A number of my respondents also referenced the need for jobs such as safety manager, off-ice conditioning coaches, cooking, and chaperoning. One parent, Kari, explained she was uncomfortable doing administrative tasks for the team but volunteered to wash the team jerseys, a task that required arriving at the rink approximately 90 minutes early and waiting to collect everyone's jerseys after games (personal communication, January 16, 2017). Life as a hockey parent can easily become an all-encompassing lifestyle. Time has been observed to be a major factor for rates of attrition in hockey irrespective of race (*The First Shift*, n.d.; Knapp, 1999); still, with racialized families, time demands compound the influences of other factors such as occupation, economic condition, and cultural capital.

Language and Other Aspects of Cultural Capital

Language as a barrier to physical activity is the most obvious example of a lack in cultural capital. This particular barrier has been detailed at length by many other scholars (e.g., Conn, Chan, Banks, Ruppar, & Scharff, 2014; Doherty & Taylor, 2007; Frisby, 2011; Netto, Bhopal, Lederle, Khatoon, & Jackson, 2010). I will not rehash the arguments except to say that the inability to communicate in English greatly hinders the ability of parents to integrate into the hockey community and makes the registration process more difficult (if advertisements exist only in English media). But there are other, subtler cultural barriers to hockey, not the least of which is the culturally specific nature of hockey knowledge.

Part of what makes hockey culture distinct is that Canada's game manages to retain an air of exclusion and intimidation. Some of this can be attributed to the notorious (although not inaccurate) stereotype of overly invested hockey parents. Hockey parent Sara indicated that this stereotype frightened her when she first enrolled her son in hockey: "I was, to be honest, quite scared at first because a lot of my friends, a lot of my colleagues have their kids in hockey and I heard a lot of horror stories.... I went in there thinking I have to be mindful of what's going on there and still make this fun for him" (personal communication, October 20, 2016).

But the physical space of the rink itself can be intimidating too: cold, drafty, loud, and far outside the cultural experience of many racialized immigrants. Harry, a coach and parent, noted: "I hear where folks say 'I didn't know I had to spend this much money each month on my kid. I didn't know there was a five o'clock in the morning practices.... I didn't know it was so cold in the rink'" (personal communication, April 3, 2016).

Barthes (2007) asked: "What is a national sport? It is a sport that rises out of the substance of a nation, out of its soil and climate" (pp. 46–47). The Canadian climate is represented as an unforgiving one, and so too is the sport of hockey. The layout of many rinks, especially those separate from community centers, lack any kind of front desk or welcome area (or they are often unattended); therefore, new visitors are forced to wander through this space without much direction. Even as a seasoned participant, venturing into new arenas to find your rink and locker room can be slightly uncomfortable experiences. It is important to acknowledge that "just going to the rink and being comfortable" (*Hockey Night Punjabi* representative, personal communication, 2016) is a very real barrier for new hockey families. The space of the rink prefaces a culture of intimidation, where one must learn to claim space but where little is simply given. This is where we can extend M. L. Adams's (2006) critique of male entitlement to space in hockey culture by contextualizing the fact that not all men feel entitled to the space of the rink. As Ronald Sundstrom (2003) argues, "when we sort people by categories, we do so spatially. Our system of race carries with it a spatial extension" (p. 93); hence certain Canadians are more likely to feel uncomfortable in hockey spaces, partly because new spaces tend to induce anxiety in everyone, but also because there is no cultural tie to that particular space.

I asked another parent, Randy, what the learning curve was like for him as a hockey parent, and he impressed the need to learn on the fly: "It was so hard! Like I was scared. I didn't think I could properly tie his skates. I actually remember on his skate I wrote with a Sharpie "L" and "R" [signifying left and right] ... now you know the logo is on the outside, you learn stuff like that but ... it is really tough. For the first month or so I always made sure my wife went so he was in the right gear, but now it's like second nature" (personal communication, November 15, 2016).

Now he is comfortable in the space of the rink, but he recognizes that other new parents have to go through the same learning process. He talked about a Chinese mother who had no idea that her son's skates needed to be sharpened regularly, something that could easily be explained at an introductory meeting. Growing up with hockey equipment around the house or having siblings who participated is a form of objectified capital in that equipment is "transmissible in its materiality" (Bourdieu, 1986) but is most valuable when it is integrated with embodied capital through a family member who has the knowledge of how everything works in concert.

Sara was born in Canada and grew up a hockey fan, but she was still reluctant to ask other hockey parents for help because it seemed like everyone just seemed to know what to do without being taught: "I think a lot of people . . . they've got maybe older kids who are in it. They know so much about it when you go in it, you're just like, "Oh, am I going to look stupid asking them now? . . . Are they just going to look at me thinking 'You're putting your kid in hockey and you don't know what he needs?'" (personal communication, October 20, 2016).

This distinction between those who just know and those who must learn is an aspect of any sporting subculture, yet here it can also be read as the dominant hockey culture imposing its very existence on newcomers. Bourdieu (1984) explains that what appears *natural* is based on the power to define "excellence which, being nothing other than their own way of existing, is bound to appear simultaneously as distinctive and different" (p. 255). The fact that Sara is Canadian born (and grew up a hockey fan) does not appear to have given her any advantage when actually entering hockey culture, which again speaks to a lack of embodied capital in certain Canadian families.

Brian, 25, a former elite player and current coach, recognized that the rink exacerbated his family's racialized difference, as "that's where it became apparent that we were a minority because at school you never see it. . . . We didn't have accents or anything like that, no one ever treated us any differently. It's when it came to parent meetings where my parents didn't understand, they needed someone to tie our skates, they needed someone to tell us what stick to use" (Brian, personal communication, September 11, 2016).

He continued: "Going to my brother's first practice with his elbow pads on the outside of his jersey. Photos like that, you chalk up to having foreign parents." Such experiences demonstrate the need for a more conscious and coordinated effort to offer informational meetings that go beyond administrative details to truly welcome and educate new hockey parents about how to wear equipment, the time commitment, and other cultural norms. This also requires an acknowledgment from the sport that it is not naturally welcoming.

In addition to knowing how hockey works, hockey parents are expected to be uniquely invested in their child's career. Unlike dropping a child off at tennis lessons or soccer practice, hockey parents are expected to spectate practices in addition to games. For example, Sonia points out: "I remember hearing people and parents have a certain type of culture, like a 'hockey culture' and my family zero per cent fit into that. I remember kids comment that, 'Why do your parents drop you off and pick you up? Why don't they stay the whole time?' Shit like that. That, I remember was really hard. And being aware of it a young age obviously I didn't think about it until I'm an adult and I reflect on that time, but that was a big thing" (personal communication, December 1, 2016).

Hockey parents Harry and Kevin expressed similar sentiments about the inability to "just drop them off and leave" (Harry, personal communication, April 3, 2016). Kevin recounted a story about a family friend who played hockey and, because his father worked at a mill, was unable to integrate with the other hockey parents (personal communication, November 21, 2016). His father was always on the way either to or from work. Thus, it is not necessarily a language or cultural barrier keeping some parents from the rink; rather it is a class position that dictates the (in)flexibility of work conditions. This expectation also relates to that particular class privilege that Sonia spoke about that enables a parent to dedicate numerous hours each week to being present at the rink. Still, even if parents such as Sonia's move up in class position and are able to increase their child's access and opportunities to excel, gatekeepers continue to play an integral role in determining what the future of hockey looks like. Unfortunately, these gatekeepers often manage to escape criticism as players in an influential web of social capital.

The Gatekeepers

Coaches and scouts wield a lot of power in hockey. Coaches dictate playing time, line assignments, and which players get the opportunities to shine. Coaches are also the direct line to scouts, suggesting which players should be considered to advance through the system. The vast majority of coaches and scouts are former players, meaning that the role of gatekeeping is noticeably more racially homogeneous than the player pool. There are currently five racialized coaches out of 315 positions in the NHL, and of the 524 NHL scouts working at the end of the 2016–2017 season, only three could be identified as racialized.[3] Each NHL club will staff anywhere from 13 to 32 scouts, all working at various levels to identify talent. In the field notes I took during a Vancouver Giants WHL game, I commented on this lack of representation among scouts: "Bunch of NHL scouts sitting around us—five or so. I see Edmonton Oilers' sheets but not sure if they are all from Edmonton. They all look alike: older, white-haired, white men. [My friend] also recognizes the similarity: 'What's up with them all looking alike?'" (Field notes, January 30, 2016).

In addition, of the 700 or so NHL players, I counted 23 racialized and Indigenous players at the time of this study (approximately 3% of the league).[4] Similar racial homogeneity can be found at the feeder levels as well. The WHL and BCHL (Junior A) each list two South Asian coaches among their 39 teams and four racialized scouts in the WHL but none noted on BCHL team websites.[5]

Former elite player Raj very bluntly explained that the lack of diversity in hockey can be attributed to gatekeepers, such as general managers, presidents, and owners, having an "old school" mentality that results in a regurgitation of "all the old coaches" and a lack of interest in "[trying] to bring up anybody new or any minorities" (personal communication, June 21, 2016). As Raj points out, there must be a concerted effort to include those who have been previously marginalized; otherwise the system reproduces itself. Raj was one of the few research participants who spoke about this structural discrimination. The NHL is notorious for recycling existing coaches. During the 2017–2018 season, 34% of coaches received second and third opportunities with an NHL team, a percentage that is higher than any other major professional men's league (Gretz, 2018). Sometimes teams even re-hire previously fired coaches instead of finding someone new to bring into the system. As Gretz (2018) puts it, "The NHL always seems loathe to explore [new] options in the name of playing it safe or going with experience. Even if that previous experience was not always great" (para. 28–29). This cultural propensity to regurgitate existing members reproduces a system that discourages diversity and equality.

For players trying to reach their full potential, these gatekeepers play a crucial role in determining what the future of hockey will look like. Both Raj and women's elite player Suki recounted instances where they expected to be named the Most Valuable Player (MVP) at a tournament but were passed over. Here is Raj's experience: "I was supposed to be MVP and something happened in [city] and I didn't get it because I was Indian. I was easily the hands-down best player in the tournament. . . . It's just a part of life. I think it made me stronger, made my skin a little thicker. But it's sad, as a parent it is hard to see your kid going through that. I'm sure it was tough for my parents to see, to tolerate that" (personal communication June 21, 2016).

It is noteworthy that Raj brushes off the impact of the incident for himself but recognizes that it must have been difficult for his parents. This further amplifies the need for scholars to reach out to parents of athletes to better understand how discrimination and racism affects them, separate from their children. Especially since parents are supposed to protect their children from the injustices of the world, how do parents make sense of their agency in a system where they have little control?

Coach Brian shared a similar story of being passed over for team selections: "I had parents from other teams, when they did the selection process, would come up to me and say, 'Oh you're going down to play [tournament]' and I would say, 'No I didn't get selected.' And they would look at me and be like, 'What do you mean you didn't get selected? You're leading the league in points!' . . . You've got parents coming up to me when I'm 11 or 12 years old and essentially telling me that's bullshit" (personal communication, September 11, 2016).

As noted in chapter 4, the presence of racism in any selection process is never directly evident. Unless a coach or scout states outright that a player was not chosen because of their race, there is little that a player or parent can do. The subjectivity of scouting and identifying talent contributes to maintaining a racially homogeneous sport. With respect to capital, denying certain players credentials that could help them advance their hockey careers represents the policing of social capital. Bourdieu (1986) explains that credentials entitle group members to a credit and potential access to new networks. Those privileged with membership are responsible for reproducing the limits of the group: "Because the definition of the criteria of entry is at stake in each new entry, he can modify the group by modifying the limits of legitimate exchange through some form of misalliance" (Bourdieu, 1986, p. 89).

In 2016, I attended The Hockey Conference, a biannual conference that brings together practitioners and academics from the hockey world. Luc Gauthier, a scout for the Pittsburgh Penguins, was one of the keynote speakers. He described the talent rubric that scouts use, which boils down to the following areas (in order of importance): hockey sense (i.e., decision making with and without the puck, anticipation, positioning, etc.), skating, skill, compete level, and character. Gauthier admitted that scouting is not an exact science and that hockey sense is the easiest area where a player can be knocked out of contention. The fact that technical skills such as skating and stickhandling are often seen to be secondary to one's hockey sense leaves the door open for scouts to dismiss players that they may not like, for a variety of reasons.

Furthermore, Gauthier stated that 60% of the evaluation takes place off the ice, with scouts talking to coaches, parents, billet families, and teachers to learn about a player's character and to determine whether or not a player fits into the team's culture. As such, the subjective nature of talent identification tends to privilege those with a lineage in the game. Coach Brian refers to these players as "purebreds":

That's why Max Domi, [Matthew] Tkachuk, all these guys that have NHL dads get drafted to the NHL because they have a guy that has been through it and understands it and the kid is just very well coached at home and away. . . . You're going to take him knowing that this kid knows how to handle himself before a game, after a game, if we cut him we're not going to have to deal with anything because the dad has been cut, the dad understands a lot of that stuff. (Personal communication, September 11, 2016)

The bloodline argument is commonly used to explain the prevalence of athletic families in every sport but as Norman (2014) highlights, what these explanations elide is the role that cultural and social capital play in providing enhanced "access to resources and connections to help [athletes] reach the top levels of the sport" (para. 4; see also Agergaard & Sørensen, 2009). Scouting represents the intersection of embodied and social capital, with players carrying the embodied capital needed to reaffirm group membership and scouts providing and denying access to limited social capital.

According to Bourdieu (1984), "embodied cultural capital of the previous generations functions as a sort of advance (both a head-start and a credit)" (p. 70). Where we talk about purebreds and bloodlines in hockey, Bourdieu refers to "eternal life" (p. 72) as one of the most invaluable social privileges. By "eternal life" he means the way that accrued forms of capital become "eternal" when passed on to future generations. It is a symbolic form of capital because this advantage is not easily recognized as capital; instead, it is perceived "as legitimate competence" (Bourdieu, 1986, p. 86). Similar to Bourdieu's (1986) analysis of the education system as a conveyor of privilege, we can interpret hockey scouting as a social structure that sanctions "the hereditary transmission of cultural capital" (p. 85). Maxi Domi and Matthew Tkachuk, both sons of former NHL players, possess sought-after names that carry inherent social capital. These specific credentials are privileges disguised as inherited skill (or act in combination with the necessary skill). Bourdieu (1986) claims these credentials have the ability to morph "circumstantial relationships into lasting connections" (p. 90). As a result, ability and talent are the products of investing in time and cultural capital for the purpose of access to social capital.

In Kiran's experience, as an elite-level player, one coach became a barrier to her success merely because he assumed that she did not want to further her hockey career. Kiran's mother became fed up with the lack of opportunities provided for her daughter to excel and eventually confronted the coach. Kiran later learned that the coach assumed her hockey career was ending. She then informed him that she was committed to play with another team the following year (personal communication, April 28, 2016). The coach had predetermined Kiran's hockey future without consulting her. This could be chalked up as poor coaching but could also reflect the assumption that South Asians have no place in hockey; that their presence, while allowed, is somehow fleeting or still out of place. Another player, Suki, also encountered coaches who stood in the way of her progress:

> I still had one more chance, which was [name of school], one of the Assistant Coaches came to watch me for one of the [tournament] games and . . . a lot of family came to watch me and a lot of my past coaches . . . which was a huge thing for me seeing as all these adversities were here and now I'm able to show you where I got even when you guys were pushing me down kind of thing. He sat me the whole game. . . . I lost a scholarship, I lost MVP . . . we also lost that

game.... So I lost a lot that game. I didn't get to play and show off... which was humiliating for me. (Personal communication, June 15, 2016)

Suki's narrative exemplifies how much power coaches have in either facilitating or hindering a player's progress through the system. What is supposed to be a meritocratic institution where the best players will always rise to the top is a myth that downplays the constrained power that players have in determining their own futures.

These narratives about gatekeeping point to a larger issue of justice and who gets to count in a society or culture. Nancy Fraser (2009a) contends that in a world of global movement and interaction we must pivot discussions of justice away from "*What* counts as a bonafide matter of justice" to ask, "*Who* counts as a bonafide subject of justice?" (p. 5). She advocates for a three-dimensional theory of justice that addresses inequalities of distribution (economic), recognition (cultural), and representation (political). Citizens can lack the economic resources to participate with their peers, which Fraser labels a form of distributive injustice or maldistribution, or citizens can be excluded for their lack of cultural value and "requisite standing" needed to make a claim of inequality; this is referred to as misrecognition.

From a hockey standpoint, the narratives above articulate Fraser's principle of misrecognition in that not every player is seen to have equal cultural value. By concentrating on the political dimension of representation Fraser (2009a) asserts, "it tells us not only who can make claims for redistribution and recognition, but also how such claims are to be mooted and adjudicated" (p. 17). Misrepresentation functions by denying "some people the possibility of participating on par with others in social interactions" (p. 18). The absence of official racial segregation in hockey gives the illusion that participation is equal, but what happens in the game forces us to question *who* is equal because "we cannot assume that we already know who counts" (Fraser, 2009b, p. 283). Simply being on the ice with one's peers does not mean that all experiences are equal or that each body is equally valued, as the previous chapters have demonstrated. As a result, the assumption that Kiran would not continue her hockey career past a certain point or the inability for Suki, Brian, or Raj to make a claim of racism (because there is no space to assert such an injustice) facilitates the erasure of their experiences. In essence, they are made to not count and have no recourse for such injustices.

It would be easy to dismiss these examples of gatekeeping as part of the subjective nature of hockey: Players get cut all the time; maybe these South Asian players are just legends in their own minds. What makes the racialized character of these experiences more difficult to reject is how they are situated in broader accounts of racial slurs and challenges to their belonging noted by nearly all the players interviewed in this study. The injustice lies in the inability to speak openly about one's perceptions for fear of still not being heard or simply dismissed. Still, despite the numerous hurdles that make participation in hockey for racialized Canadians difficult, the vast majority of my participants were confident or hopeful that change was inevitable; all that is required is hard work and patience.

Assumptions about Diversity: Flaws in Logic

When I asked participants to offer recommendations for making hockey more diverse and representative of broader Canadian society, the dominant answer was time. There was an assumption that as time passed, and racialized immigrants became more assimilated, those children would rise up through the system. Hockey parent Kevin explained:

> I think it's a generational thing. In all walks of life, every example, every industry some of the smartest brightest people in the world aren't white or Caucasian or the elitist. They are from all over the world and I think it's a matter of time somebody does dominate that isn't white in the NHL. You know this doesn't bode well for your study but why should it be a question? Nowadays do we sit there and go wonder when the next really good South Asian heart surgeon is coming or when is the next great fighter pilot is coming? The Minister of Defense in this country is a Sikh. . . . So does it matter? No. It is coming? Absolutely. (Personal communication, November 21, 2016)

When I asked Dev, 31, his thoughts about future diversity he echoed something similar to Kevin, suggesting that we are already witnessing the leading edge of tomorrow; however, when pressed to offer examples of this forthcoming diversity he wasn't able to name anyone:

DEV: I think it's really starting to. . . . Before it seemed like it was very much a political process, like you kind of had to know people in order to advance but now it seems like everyone is getting their fair shot. You're seeing it in the NHL. You're seeing it in the minor leagues as well too.

CS: Who are those people you are seeing?

DEV: There's minor leaguers in Edmonton that are of Indian descent.

CS: Jujhar [Khaira]?

DEV: Yeah. You start seeing them. You start hearing names. It's getting there. I'm sure. (Personal communication, August 12, 2016)

I am still unsure as to which other South Asian prospects Dev was thinking of, but he seemed very certain that change was on the way. Similar assumptions surrounded Tiger Woods and the Williams sisters in their respective sports that a large influx of racialized participants in golf and tennis was inevitable (but this wave of diversity has yet to come to fruition). Unfortunately, Dev's assurance comes with little precedent.

In sports, there is one prime example that debunks the myth that diversity fixes itself with generational change: the institution of Title IX in the United States. In 1972, the Education Amendments Act (Title IX) made it illegal to discriminate against anyone on the basis of their sex "under any education program or activity receiving Federal financial assistance" (NCAA, 2014). This significantly opened up athletic opportunities for women in U.S. colleges. The logical assumption was that the next generation of women athletes would end up being future coaches, athletic administrators, and so on; the future would filter up and equality would be established forever. Yet, the Tucker Center for Research on Girls & Women in Sport reported a dramatic decline in women coaches in the 40 years following Title IX, despite women's sports participation being at an all-time high (Lavoi, 2013). In 1974, more than 90% of "college female athletes were coached by women, but today the number is around 43%" (Acosta & Carpenter, 2012 as cited in Lavoi, 2013, p. 1). Lavoi (2013) explains that even though Title IX opened up participation for women, the accompanying employment opportunities were available to anyone and the majority of those jobs went to men. Consequently, we need to question not only what opportunities are available, but *which* people are deemed ideal for those positions. The case of Title IX and U.S. college athletics demonstrates that increasing opportunities for women to participate did not alter the socialized preference to place men in those gatekeeping roles.

Likewise, almost 70% of the players in the National Football League (NFL) are Black, but those responsible for the league remain older white men. Recognizing the lack of diversity in the NFL's back offices and coaching ranks, the league instituted the Rooney Rule in 2003 (requiring teams to interview minority candidates for upper-level positions) as a form of affirmative action to stimulate more diversity amongst coaches (Sando, 2016). ESPN reported in 2016 that the Rooney Rule has been wholly ineffective, with little changing in hiring practices since 1997 (Sando, 2016). The path to becoming a head coach often starts through the NFL coordinator position, but because the Rooney Rule does not apply to coordinator positions, "minorities are at an inherent disadvantage for head coaching positions" (Sando, 2016, para. 5) and upward mobility. This is not to say that there is an orchestrated effort to keep racialized people out of gatekeeper positions, but when teams look for the best people, whether as players or in administrative roles, "those best people are all suspiciously similar" (Carleton & Morrison, 2016, para. 7). Thus, while the white-dominated governance of professional sports may not be intentional, the existing structures work to reproduce yesterday's discrimination in tomorrow's game.

The other problem with assuming that diversity moves upwards is that most national sporting systems no longer work as a pyramid, where the grassroots levels feed the high-performance system. Donnelly and Kidd (2015) pinpoint the move away from a pyramid sporting model to the Cold War when the Soviet system of early talent identification demonstrated tangible results, most notably at the 1972 Summit Series (an 8-game series between Canada and the USSR) when the Soviet hockey team shocked the Canadians in a too-close-for-comfort battle. The draw of the problematic, yet effective Soviet sporting system meant that resources would no longer be "squandered" on a broad base of athletes in the hope that some of them would eventually become successful. Instead . . . there were two systems: a poorly funded grassroots system; and a relatively well-funded high-performance system that drew young athletes at a very early age from the grass-roots system and exposed them to intensive training and competition, employing the best available resources" (p. 61).

Since 2002, *Canadian Sport Policy* has discursively reproduced the distinction between sport participation and sport excellence, with international success in ice hockey as a driving motivation for this delineation (Donnelly & Kidd, 2015, p. 62). It has become common practice for NHL agents to recruit players as young as 13–14 years old (Campbell, 2017). The effects of this bifurcated sporting system will be further discussed in the following chapter, but here it is important to recognize that South Asian presence in the minor hockey system does not necessarily represent the future of hockey.

Initiatives such as *Hockey is for Everyone* month and the Rooney Rule are all attempts to acknowledge and address a problem; regrettably, they treat inequality as a numbers issue instead of as issues of power, privilege, and access. Time certainly plays a role, but we must be careful not to become complacent when seeing increased diversity at the grassroots levels because what happens on the ice, the field, or the court does not dictate the future of the game; the future of the game is, in large part, decided in board rooms and in offices. Angela Davis reminds us that we should not accept "diversity as a synonym for justice. Diversity is a corporate strategy. It's a strategy designed to ensure that the institution functions in the same way, except now that you have some brown and black faces" (Eckert, 2015, para. 12). Meritocratic assumptions have been disproven on numerous occasions, yet many appear to cling to this particular expression of hope. I believe that much of the lack of reflexivity and passivity around this issue has to do with a tacit acceptance that these hurdles have become permanent fixtures; in turn, racialized players resign themselves to a life of working harder than everyone else for the same opportunities.

Meritocratic and Resilient Subjects

Along with the assumption that the passing of time facilitates equality and diversity, working harder than everyone else was also cited as a way to address discrimination. Elite players suggested that if a South Asian player and a white player of equal ability were up for the same spot, the edge would often be given to the white player. On this point, elite player, Billy, claimed, "They're not going to take the minority over the other kid because it's just the way it is with anything. I believe that and, not in a bad way, but I think that's just how it is. I think that's why it's difficult for some of us to get to the next point but that just means we have to work twice as hard and that's up to us to do that" (personal communication, July 20, 2016).

Previous research has documented the desire for racialized people to work harder for the same opportunities as a response to discrimination (Lamont, Welburn, & Fleming, 2013). Work ethic, then, is not so much a cultural trait as it is a means of survival. Still, if resilience requires hardship as an instigator, we need to ask ourselves *which* groups *get* to be resilient? Or perhaps more accurately: which groups *have* to be resilient in order to be equal?

The concept of resilience originates from physical sciences and is used to describe a material that has the ability to bend or bounce back when stressed (Norris, Stevens, Pfefferbaum, Wyche, & Pfefferbaum, 2008). Beyond fields such as mathematics and physics, the concept of resilience "is fundamentally a metaphor" when applied to social systems (Norris et al., 2008). It has become a popular research area and buzz term in the fields of psychology, education, economics, and disaster communications, so widely used that Klein, Nicholls, and Thomella contended in 2003, "the definition of resilience has become so broad as to render it almost meaningless. . . . Resilience has become an umbrella concept for a range of system attributes that are deemed desirable" (as cited in Tierney, 2015, p. 1331). With regard to sport, resilience appears in sport psychology literature as a way to understand and/or enhance performance (e.g., Galli & Gonzalez, 2015; Morgan, Fletcher, & Sarkar, 2013; Sarkar & Fletcher, 2014).

The fundamental problem with the concept of resilience when used to explain or theorize social systems is that it "presupposes a social order that is continually at risk of disruption" (Tierney, 2015, p. 1332) or hardship. Julien Reid (2012) articulates this specific implication through his deconstruction of the global transition from a discourse of security to one of sustainable development. Reid explains that post–Cold War international relations were heavily premised upon the notion of security, which informed how subjects were governed and how the accompanying policies and practices were implemented. As neoliberalism gained prominence, strategies of governmentality changed accordingly; no longer would the state be responsible for the security of its citizens; instead, citizens would be encouraged to be resilient in the face of danger, disruption, and uncertainty:

> The account of the world envisaged and constituted by development agencies concerned with building resilient subjects is one which presupposes the disastrousness of the world, and likewise one which interpellates a subject that is permanently called upon to bear the disaster—a subject for whom bearing disaster is a required practice without which he or she cannot grow and prosper in the world. This may be what is politically most at stake in the discourse of resilience. The resilient subject is a subject which must permanently struggle to accommodate itself to the world. (Reid, 2013, p. 355)

Equating natural disasters with racism as an obstacle to one's hockey career would be a false equivalence, but the notion of a subject who has learned to "accommodate itself to the world" can be applied to many areas. Thus, when the media, as an example, offers stories of human resilience as fodder for inspiration, these narratives contribute to pacifying citizens into accepting misfortune as life's guarantee while also conflating systemic inequality with bad luck. Perhaps this is why human-interest stories have become central to Western media discourses (e.g., Ellen Degeneres spotlighting underprivileged citizens who find the capacity to perform good deeds; adoration for competition show winners who overcome trauma and obstacles to achieve individual success; regular citizens who make tremendous sacrifices for strangers after terrorist attacks or natural disasters); not only do they make for feel-good stories, they also reinforce resilience as a valued characteristic. Rarely, however, do we question why bad luck, trauma, and disaster are so common.

Discourses of resilience are especially prevalent in the world of sports, where assumed meritocracy is part of the draw. To illustrate, when *Hockey Night Punjabi* interviewed Sudharshan Maharaj (the goaltending coach for the Anaheim Ducks and one of two South Asians in the NHL coaching system), the advice he provided for young South Asian hockey players was, "There are going to be obstacles. No question that there will be comments, there will be things that will work against you sometimes that you think are completely unfair, and in some cases, are, but the reality is if you love the game enough and you really are willing to put in the work ... and if you put in the dedication of your parents, you'll do fine" (*Hockey Night Punjabi*, 2017).

Maharaj concedes that racism exists but that hard work and dedication can help overcome this obstacle, an obstacle that is not present for all players. Participants are expected to change themselves to fit into an inequitable system so they can be recognized as "good" citizens. Robin James (2015) argues that "good" women and racialized citizens are those who actively commit to "overcoming their damage" (p. 84) rather than exposing their damage as a problem created by the system itself—"resilience discourses '[naturalize]' damage" (p. 83). Even though Maharaj's comments are meant to inspire tomorrow's youth, they also help naturalize racism in the game.

Moreover, we must differentiate between hard work with the goal of excellence versus hard work for equal opportunities. The social and cultural capital of South Asian players, along with other model minorities, has little currency in hockey culture at this point; therefore, the only tangible agency that individuals are able to exercise comes in the form of work ethic. Hard work is essential for any player who wants to succeed in sport; yet, this is not hard work for the sake of excellence but hard work with the intent of avoiding dismissal. Resilience, then, is not so much something that individuals or groups conjure as much as it is something externally imposed.

Players tend to internalize this discourse of resilience. Looking back at Raj's narrative of not being named MVP, he shrugged off this instance as "part of life." Billy also expressed a lack of options when facing a deck stacked against him: "It would be nice to maybe get some leeway once and awhile and get that break because I think a lot of it has to do with who you know and what you have. Like I say to myself all the time, that's the way it is, and you've just got to push yourself that much harder" (personal communication July 20, 2016). Even one of the *Hockey Night Punjabi* commentators interviewed in this study asserted that, as racialized people, "we have to be good and we have to be better than good" (personal communication, 2016) to receive opportunities that have traditionally been held by white Canadians.

There is nothing wrong with the desire to work hard; nonetheless, to privilege resilience as a response to racism simultaneously thwarts activism because resilient subjects learn to bear and accept the status quo (R. James, 2015; J. Reid, 2013). As Lamont et al.'s (2013) research observed, there is a dominant belief that working *through* racism is the best response available for racialized people. This articulation of liberal ideology teaches marginalized populations "to take responsibility for themselves" (J. Reid, 2013, p. 357). Or, as Sara Ahmed (2017) writes, resilience is a conservative technology of governance where "you encourage bodies to strengthen so they will not succumb to pressure; so they can keep taking it; so they can take more of it" (p. 189). And, if one were to snap under the additional pressure placed on them to *overcome* racism, the racialized body becomes a site of violence when they "lose it." The violence is framed as originating from those who snap, as opposed to those who apply the pressure (Sara Ahmed, 2017). Objects that bounce back from stress tend not to bear traces of the stressor. Racism reproduces itself by keeping racialized people silent and grooming them to accept more racism. By fostering self-reliant individuals, we erase the need to change an inequitable system because just as one's successes can be attributed to effort, so too can one's failures. Still, it leaves many players wondering what their hockey career could have been.

Hoping for generational change is also indicative of resilience discourses because there was, overall, little urgency to see any systemic changes made to hockey. The optimism that things will naturally evolve over time could be read as evidence of neoliberal pacification since these participants, or subjects, have been governed into a state of contentment. Optimism for the future can, unfortunately, create grounds for inaction (Solnit, 2014); however, in the next chapter I will elucidate a segment of South Asians players who are offering a form of resistance through ethnically segregated hockey programs.

It should also be pointed out that Indigenous conceptions of resilience tend to invoke collectivity and resistance in ways that challenge neoliberal ideology (Kirmayer, Dandeneau, Marshall, Phillips, & Williamson, 2011). For example, the Inuit "concept of *niriunniq*" (an Inuktitut word) which loosely translates as "hope," implores the understanding that there are many things beyond the control of any one individual. It is a sociological and cosmological interpretation of how the world operates. For the Mi'kmaq Peoples of the Atlantic Canadian regions, restorative justice and reconciliation inform their cultural conceptualizations of resilience. And, for the Mohawk communities located in the Quebec, Ontario, and upstate New York areas, emboldening their cultural and linguistic practices are seen as ways to reclaim control from colonial histories. Adapting is certainly part of the overall practice of resilience, but the solutions are found through collective action and identity confirmation, rather than through individual will. Moreover, Indigenous groups center colonization as the reason for their communal resilience. They offer an interconnected path forward without erasing the history that made their resilience necessary. Resilient subjects may bounce back from unseen forces, but resistant subjects need something against which to push back. This act of pushing back makes those previously unseen forces visible.

Understanding intersections between economic and cultural capital is particularly helpful in understanding internal boundaries to citizenship because it highlights that not all forms of capital can be accumulated and that within multi-ethnic nation-states we must be cognizant of how different forms of capital and identities articulate with each other. Bourdieu (1984) notes that culture is purposefully inequitable so as to "separate the barbarians from the elect" (p. 250). This statement becomes even more salient with growing concerns over immigration, and in particular what kind of racialized people are allowed into *which* spaces; "who becomes the *right people* when diversity, culture, and commerce are linked together" (Teelucksingh, 2006, p. 2). The relationship between forms of capital and the notion of resilience is also an insidious one. So long as individual will and choice are privileged over institutionalized forms of justice, resilience itself becomes a form of capital (R. James, 2015). It makes other forms of capital seem irrelevant because a lack of economic, cultural, and/or social capital could arguably all be overcome with enough resilience. This is how exceptions to the rule become alibis against institutional marginalization, because there is no need to ensure equal access to forms of capital if the most significant type of capital can be produced from within. We are then left with a battle between those who advocate for a better system versus those who advocate for better people.

7

Racialized Money and
White Fragility

Class and Resentment
in Hockey

> Our national winter sport has become
> terrifyingly expensive, dangerously
> elitist, and is slowly but surely hacking
> away at the roots of what made the
> possibility of greatness accessible, albeit
> at greater or lesser odds, to any kid with
> talent and a dream.
> Now it takes money and plenty of it.
> —C. Cole, 2015, para. 9

Connections between class, race, gender, and hockey participation among
South Asian groups in Canada run far deeper than the perceived barriers to
participation outlined in the previous chapter and require more detailed
analysis. In 2016, *The Hamilton Spectator* published independent demographic research on Ontario Hockey League (OHL) players based on postal
codes that revealed a significant portion of its players come from "a small and
exclusive sliver of society where incomes, housing values and post-secondary
education rates are abnormally high and poverty levels are extremely low"
(Pecoskie, 2016, para. 10). The amount of criticism that hockey has received

for being economically inaccessible continues to dominate discussions in the media and at the rink, and there are frequent stories in Canadian news media about declining rates of participation in the game; however, the focus on the economics of participation misses a significant part of the story. For example, in cities such as Vancouver and Toronto racialized Canadians help maintain minor hockey registration numbers, which means that we cannot speak about racialized Canadians as a monolithic group that necessarily represents the lower socioeconomic strata of our society. As Stuart Hall (1996) observed more than two decades ago, "The problem here is not whether economic structures are relevant to racial divisions but how the two are theoretically connected" (p. 308).

Model Minorities

The term *model minority* was first introduced by sociologist William Pettersen in 1966 when he wrote about the success of Japanese immigrants for *The New York Times* (Pettersen, 1966). Since then, the term has grown to include Asians of all ethnicities. Broadly speaking, model minorities are defined as a group of racialized people who have migrated to a new homeland and, through hard work, dedication, and education, have managed to secure a relative level of financial security and social mobility by stereotypically working in professional sectors such as finance and technology. Put more bluntly, to be a model minority involves "a capitulation to the ideology of white superiority, trepidation about forging alliances across class, ethnic, or religious boundaries, and a willingness to be used as a silent symbol in the rollback of social-justice initiatives like welfare and affirmative action" (Vaidhyanathan, 2000, para. 16). As immigrants who are perceived to be different but valuable, model minorities have successfully complicated race relations in settler nations by widening the racial hierarchy between whites and Indigenous groups in Canada and whites and Blacks in the United States. Thobani (2007) explains, in the Canadian context, that racialized Canadians contribute to the ongoing colonization of Indigenous groups because they exist in a liminal position between white settlers and Indigenous communities "marked for physical and/or cultural elimination," meaning "these migrants become implicated, whether wittingly or otherwise, in the dispossession of Aboriginal peoples" (p. 16). Nayar's (2012) study of Punjabis in northern British Columbia elucidates this tension between racialized immigrants and Indigenous communities when, during the 1960s and 1970s, Punjabi workers in the mills and canneries were socially constructed as reliable and hardworking employees in contrast to the discursively produced "lazy Natives" (p. 153).

In the American context, Prashad (2000) argues that the success of Asians has become a *weapon* in the war against Black America. The position of model minorities is not one that is fully fluid; it is very much fixed because certain groups are never allowed to become model minorities (Chou & Feagin, 2015). Prashad illustrates this point by highlighting that African-born migrants had higher education rates than Asians, Central Americans, and the American-born population in the 1990 U.S. census: "46 per cent of the African-born migrants [came] to the United States with a B.A." compared to only 20% of U.S.-born citizens holding bachelor's degrees at the time (p. 171). Despite these statistics, Black Americans were unable to alter their racialized construction as a group that is uneducated, unmotivated, and, in Du Bois' (1993) words, a problem to be solved in the white imagination.

A Canadian example of how model minorities can be used as a weapon was illustrated by Jonathan Kay of *The National Post* in 2013 in an article titled, "Urban-bound Aboriginals Pose Canada's Biggest Integration Challenge, Not Immigrants." Kay started his piece by highlighting *Hockey Night Punjabi* and its commentators as individuals who "perfectly symbolize Canada," calling our "diverse, tolerant, hockey-mad land of immigrants" a stereotype that is "perfectly accurate" (Kay, 2013, para. 3–4). The problem is not the promotion of *Hockey Night Punjabi* but rather how he uses some Canadians as a viable reason to forcibly assimilate others. Kay explains: "Many of the immigrants coming to Canada, however, long after their voyage, are city-dwellers who already are familiar with retail capitalism, digital technology, the daily crush of strangers, and the frenzied pace of urban life. In cultural terms, Mumbai and Hong Kong are closer to Toronto than Attawapiskat or Yellow Quill [First Nations]" (para. 9). This statement exemplifies how Canadian Indigenous Peoples are forced to stay on the bottom rung of the racial hierarchy in Canada through the construction and privileging of model minorities. The ability (and willingness) of racialized citizens and immigrants to assimilate into a neoliberal capitalist society reproduces Indigenous cultures as Other and a problem to be solved.

The existence of the model minority construct also reproduces meritocratic ideals as proof that institutional racism is no match for hard work (read: resilience) because what differentiates a model minority from just a minority is that they never complain about the hurdles they may encounter; they become the model through docility. According to Al-Solaylee (2016) and Kymlicka (2013), the myth of the model minority was born out of a need to suppress the civil rights movement; that is to say, civil rights activists were told to look to Asian immigrants as proof that people of color could exist and succeed in America without disturbing power relations. Notably, Al-Solaylee argues that the existence of a "buffer group" between whites and Blacks and/or Indigenous Peoples is made possible by the inflections of neoliberalism on racial discrimination. In market-driven societies that privilege individual liberties and entrepreneurism, "the elevation of brown (and Chinese) people as full participants in the market economy is cited as evidence that the system is color-blind, that racism no longer exists" (p. 47).

Aihwa Ong's (1999) work on transnational movement and "flexible citizenship" is useful for understanding the connection between immigration, race, and claims to belonging within capitalist frameworks. She encourages scholars to "consider the reciprocal construction of practice, gender, ethnicity, 'race,' class, and nation in processes of capital accumulation" (p. 5). In this way, transnationalism is conceived of as not only flows of movement but something that makes certain tensions and social orders possible.

Postwar Canadian immigration laws were written to attract a very specific type of foreign laborer and potential citizen (Abu-Laban, 1998). Especially noticeable during the immigration reforms of the 1960s, the connection between *which* immigrants were deemed acceptable by the Canadian government for the Canadian economy became increasingly intertwined with Lester B. Pearson's 1966 White Paper on immigration that outlined, "immigration policy must be consistent with national economic policy in general" (as cited in Abu-Laban, 1998, p. 74). Similarly, Prashad (2000) articulates the reality of immigration controls as "state engineering" (p. vii). The Canadian Business Immigration Program officially began in 1978 with potential applicants categorized as either "entrepreneurs" or "self-employed," joined in 1986 by the "investor" category, requiring "the immigrant to own capital which would be invested in Canada" (Wong, 1993, p. 174). The investor immigrant quickly became one of the highest priorities for the Canadian government, facilitated by expedited processing.[1] *MacLean's* magazine sums up the Immigrant Investor Program as two decades of selling passports for the "cheap" price of $800,000 (Gillis, Sorensen, & Macdonald, 2016); therefore, when Canadians complain about the amount of real estate being bought by foreign money and the influx of racialized immigrants, it is integral to understand the legislation that has made such transnational movement (of both capital and people) possible, as well as the macroeconomic decisions that manifest as racialized tension in cities such as Vancouver (e.g., Gillis et al., 2016; McElroy, 2016). This anti-immigrant sentiment can be summarized as wanting racialized labor and capital but not the lives of racialized people (Prashad, 2000).

South Asians were fairly insignificant in the business class of immigrants during the 1970s because of the low value of the Indian rupee; however, around 1999 there was an increase in the number of Indian business class immigrants (Walton-Roberts, 2003). South Asians are not implicated in the foreign real estate discussion with the same vitriol that is often directed at Chinese immigrants/investors (although they are included in the problem of multigenerational "Monster homes" [G. S. Johal, 2007]), but it is imperative to understand that the underlying mechanisms that make these tensions possible in the housing market parallel developments in the hockey landscape.

Ian Young, Vancouver correspondent for the *South China Morning Post*, has attempted to quell some of the racism that accompanies the foreign money injected into Vancouver's housing market by explaining, "What defines those people in terms of their behavior here in Vancouver . . . is not their 'Chineseness,' it's their 'millionaireness'" (Gillis et al., 2016, para. 28). In other words, we should not confuse issues of race with those of class. Still, if Anderson (1983) was correct in his assertion that "the dreams of racism actually have their origin in ideologies of class, rather than those of the nation" (p. 149), the flexible attitude adopted by Canada and other nations toward citizenship and immigration based on the desire for economic growth has set the stage for ongoing, and perhaps escalating, racial tension for the foreseeable future.

Asian American/Canadian advocacy groups and scholars caution against such generalized racial representations (Leung, 2013) because there is a great disparity of wealth that exists amongst those assumed to be model minorities. Indian American families tend to earn higher than the national average, whereas Bangladeshi families are below the national average: "Asian Americans earn more than whites on average, but they also have higher rates of poverty. . . . Such disparities are completely invisible according to the usual way we consider racial differences, which focuses on averages, not levels of inequality" (Guo, 2016, para. 3–4).

Similar patterns exist in Canada, with South Asian Canadians more likely to be low-income (23% of South Asians compared to 16% of the general population), have lower overall incomes, and higher rates of unemployment when compared to the general populace (Statistics Canada, 2007). Therefore, even though a more nuanced discussion about access to hockey is needed, the middle- and upper-class positions of the research participants included in this study should not skew the broader reality of Canadian demographics. The model minority myth erases the heterogeneity of Asians and distracts us from more complex discussions about the implications of racialized class mobility.

Sport is not exempt from the model minority myth, with professional basketball player Jeremy Lin serving as a prime example. Lin is a California-born, Harvard-educated, Taiwanese American who was never drafted by the National Basketball Association (NBA) but instead paid his dues in the NBA's development league. In 2012, the New York Knicks acquired Lin and a three-week "Cinderella story" (Benjamin, 2015), better known as "Linsanity," ensued. Lin's rise to fame was notably couched in American notions of meritocracy, citing his "grit, discipline, and integrity" as central to his success, with little to no discussions about anti-Asian racism (Yep, 2012, p. 134). In the documentary about his journey to the NBA, *Linsanity*, Lin himself mused that if he were a Black athlete he would no doubt have received multiple scholarship offers considering he led his high school team to a state championship in his senior year (Leong, 2013).

Lin provides a current example of the unpreparedness of Canadian and American (sports) media (and fans) to discuss race outside of the Black–white dichotomy. ESPN twice made the comment "Chink in the armor" after Lin-sanity started to subside and Madison Square Garden Photoshopped an image of Lin's disembodied head floating above an open fortune cookie that read "The Knick's Good Fortune" (Freeman, 2012). The model minority myth makes it difficult to grapple with racialized people in contexts that have not been (re)produced by the white imagination. The result of this confusion ranges from bullying to tasteless humor and hate speech to resentment.

In *The Karma of Brown Folk*, Prashad (2000) explores the consciousness involved in being prescribed as a social solution to the problem of Blacks in America, and observes that the success of South Asians (marked by capital accumulation) often ignores the fact that the state handpicked certain South Asians over others. South Asian success becomes a tool for white supremacy to be deployed in multiple fashions. As a result, racialized immigrants in set-tler societies often find themselves wanting to assimilate into the whitestream but are still met with discrimination and racism. We are long overdue in rec-ognizing the "harmful invisibility" of Asian experiences in North America (Chou & Feagin, 2015, p. 4).

In my view, this is where hockey can help tell part of the untold story of racialized Canadians because, as Tim Hortons, Scotiabank, and Molson Cana-dian commercials tell us: To participate in hockey is to participate in Canada (albeit a problematic construction itself). Therefore, if racialized Canadians have chosen to integrate through hockey, why would they be met with anything but open arms? The remainder of this chapter focuses on who is allowed to buy and spend the symbolic capital that has traditionally been designated for white Canadians.

Throwing Money at Hockey

Eleven of the players, parents, and coaches interviewed in this study came from hockey families—families where more than one child (if not all children) participated in the sport and therefore embody a certain level of economic mobility. Of the parents interviewed, four were self-employed and the other two worked in professional occupations. The players cited similar employment circumstances, with six of them having self-employed parents. This resonates with Agrawal and Lovell's (2010) observations that nearly 20% of affluent Cana-dians with Indian heritage are entrepreneurs.

According to *The Globe and Mail*, the average cost to enroll a child in hockey was CAD $3,000 in 2011–2012 (Mirtle, 2013). Approximately $1,200 of that cost went to registration fees and ice time costs, $900 for travel expenses, and upwards of $600 for equipment. As children progress through the system, it is not uncommon for parents to pay almost $4,000 per season/ per child between the ages of 11 and 17.

For those able to choose the elite hockey academy route, the fees easily top $10,000 per season. Hockey academies merge sport and scholarship into a singular program, enabling aspiring athletes to focus equally on their athletic and academic skills. They also help groom hopeful youth into the lifestyle of a professional athlete. In the Lower Mainland of British Columbia there are five hockey academies that compete in the Canadian Sport School Hockey League (CSSHL): Yale, Delta, West Vancouver, Burnaby Winter Club, and St. George's private school. Registration fees range from $12,500 (for Yale's under-16 team), to a "projected" $16,000 at Burnaby Winter Club, all the way up to $28,000 to $29,000 for the West Vancouver academy (depending on the payment option chosen). West Vancouver Hockey Academy also charges a $125 tryout fee and if players are billeted they must pay an additional $700 directly to the billet family each month (Hockey Canada Sports School, 2016/2017).[2] Delta Academy notes that out-of-province players must pay an additional $8,000 for the "Out of Province Education Fee," payable to the school district (Delta Hockey Academy, 2016). The draw of these academies is famous alumni who have made it to the NHL or major junior leagues, with Jonathan Toews and Sidney Crosby as prime examples of academy products. The Burnaby Winter Club Hockey Academy Information Package (Burnaby Winter Club, n.d.) states clearly on the second page: "8 of the top 10 B.C. players (99's) taken in the WHL draft chose to play at an Academy in 2014–15," and of the 10 Surrey/Delta selections for the 2015 WHL Bantam Draft, all but one was associated with an academy (Kupchuk, 2015). There are also other hockey programs, such as the North Shore Winter Club (NSWC), that are not officially academies but are "run like a hockey academy"; in other words, they train students around the clock, which explains why NSWC fondly refers to its own program as "The Factory" (Penton, 2015).

Accordingly, it is important to situate my participants as middle- and upper-class Canadians who, in many ways, help reproduce the model minority myth through the ability to enroll multiple children in the hockey system, academy or otherwise. In the last chapter, cost was cited as a barrier to participation; still, even though it was not necessarily a barrier to *their* participation, it was recognized as a potential barrier for others. Interestingly, the issue of class did not really come to the forefront in any meaningful way until I began speaking to parents who currently have children competing at the Atom and Pee Wee levels (ages 9–12).

Kevin, a 46-year-old father of three, emigrated from India to Vancouver at the age of 5. His father had emigrated to Canada a few years earlier than the family during the 1970s influx. Kevin's son is his only child involved in hockey (his other children participate in another sport), and he served on the board of his son's hockey association for 2 years. He never played ice hockey himself and spoke about how his parents were "too busy building a life in Canada as immigrants" (personal communication, November 21, 2016) for him to receive enough exposure as a child to develop the desire to participate in hockey. He arrived for our interview wearing a three-piece-suit and carrying a business attaché case in hand. During our conversation, he mentioned being a long-time supporter of a local charity event that costs $500 per plate to attend; yet, Kevin also detailed typical immigrant frugality when discussing the equipment-buying process.

I asked Kevin what his experience has been like as a South Asian hockey parent, to which he replied:

> From my experience it's been great, I think the challenge you see sometimes is South Asians are well to do and giving people, generally speaking. I think for some families on your team the socio-economic gap is starting to be more prevalent because, this may be a generalization but it's an observation of mine, Indians will just throw money at it. "Oh, he needs this? Okay, we'll go get it." Then you see other people, "Oh, we have to pay how much in team fees? We'll have to do this and that?" So, it's a little tougher and I think you see some resentment that way. (Personal communication, November 21, 2016)

Kevin raises a vital point about (perceived) resentment, and this reiterates the importance of including parent voices in this project because, even though many players are beneficiaries of socioeconomic advantages, players did not necessarily recognize or acknowledge them.

Still, as Hall and his colleagues suggest, if "race is the modality through which class is lived" (S. Hall, 1996, p. 55), this is not necessarily surprising. Similarly, we should not be surprised by degrees of resentment and resistance from others that can echo "white fragility" (explained in the next section). In this regard, it is useful to consider Ong's (1999) attempt to understand how Marx's work on class struggle and Foucault's theory of governmentality can be combined in subject formation: How do strategies of capitalism intersect with modes of governmentality and culture? And, more specific to this study, how do strategies of capitalism intersect with the policing of cultural boundaries? The hockey rink in twenty-first century Canada becomes one of many transnational settings where we can explore hierarchies of cultural distinction and "assess the symbolic status of locals, and more critically, that of newcomers, no matter how cosmopolitan they are in practice" (Ong, 1999, p. 90). Arguably, white Canadians are just now learning how to make sense of racialized Canadians with not only disposable income but legitimate wealth and lives of luxury (Walton-Roberts & Pratt, 2005). Subsequently, there is a "perceived mismatch between the distinction of their symbolic capital and their racial identity" (Ong, 1999, p. 91) that, for the most part, continues to be a representation of low-income South Asians grinding to establish themselves and master the English language.

When I asked Kevin about potential barriers to participation, like many other respondents, he mentioned language first. However, his answer quickly segued into another statement about class and resentment:

> I think a lot of South Asians, I don't know if shy away is the right word, but they just don't come forward to be part of the social hockey circle. If you have fundraisers at pubs, they would rather say, "Okay, here's $100, I don't want to go." And other parents would go "What?" And that almost the other way turns to resentment from non–South Asians because, that example from earlier, just throw money at it. I would rather give $100 because I won't be comfortable in this social setting, whether it's a pub, a restaurant, a fundraiser and you have to sell 50/50 tickets at the game or something. (Personal communication, November 21, 2016)

Interestingly, Kevin's response started off as a critique of South Asians being reluctant to integrate into hockey circles because of poor English rather than the English majority not wanting to include newcomers. But, as he points out, the ability to buy one's way out of an uncomfortable situation can create unintended consequences. It also illustrates Ong's (1999) claim that "it is primarily economic capital that is being converted into all other forms of capital, not the other way around" (p. 90). And, unless the host society decides that (a) racialized wealth is acceptable and (b) the demonstration of such wealth accumulation is an acceptable social practice, the reaction of resentment may be read as a symptom of white fragility.

White Fragility

Robin DiAngelo (2011) explains that white North Americans operate in an "insulated environment of racial protection" (p. 54), enabling them to move through space and life without having to acknowledge whiteness as a privileged structure of racial hierarchy. Because of this insulation, many white people are unable to "tolerate racial stress," a state that DiAngelo terms "white fragility": "White Fragility is a state in which even a minimum amount of racial stress becomes intolerable, triggering a range of defensive moves. These moves include the outward display of emotions such as anger, fear, and guilt, and behaviors such as argumentation, silence, and leaving the stress-induced situation. These behaviors, in turn, function to reinstate white racial equilibrium. Racial stress results from an interruption to what is racially familiar" (p. 57).

Two interruptions that DiAngelo (2011) identifies as pertinent for this discussion of white racial insulation include challenges to white authority and white centrality. DiAngelo contends that when white people are faced with racialized people in leadership positions (i.e., as coaches or in administrative positions) or in nonstereotypical roles (i.e., as a wealthy hockey parent), many are "often at a loss to respond in constructive ways" because they have never been forced to develop the skills necessary for "engagement across racial divides" (p. 57).

An example of this inability to engage across racial divides comes from another hockey parent, Randy, who also held a position in his son's association: "I'm on the board and there was an issue with a vote and one of the other board members said to the person affected by the decision, 'Oh, well the brown guys stuck together.' I was like, you don't need to say that. It would be like me saying 'All the white people voted this way'" (personal communication, November 15, 2016).

For DiAngelo (2011), white fragility is conceptualized as a product of Bourdieu's habitus, "a response or 'condition' produced and reproduced by the continual social and material advantages of the white structural position" (p. 58). By extension, we can read the response "the brown guys stuck together" as an inability to engage with racialized people in a leadership and/or management setting where their opinions are, theoretically, weighted equally with their white counterparts. It is an interruption of what has been racially familiar for generations of white Canadians. As Randy points out, the same assumption could be made of the white board members and the way they voted; however, it seems an unfair/illogical statement to make because the normativity of white supremacy enables white people to embody objective subjects that exist outside of culture—"white people are just people" (DiAngelo, 2011, p. 59); hence, their votes lack racial identity.

Conversely, racialized people, within the confines of whiteness, are always subjects of their race and therefore can only speak about the racialized experience (Dyer, 1997); the speaker (the who) becomes central rather than the issue (the what) (Sara Ahmed, 2017). This reaction can also be framed under the experience of amplification, whereby one or two bodies "become amplified in imagination as four or five, especially if they work together" (Puwar, 2006, p. 79); therefore, solidarity amongst bodies out of place could be interpreted as a "potential troublemaking bloc" (p. 79). In this way, "a single body can be seen to be taking up more physical space than it actually occupies" (Puwar, 2004, p. 49), but more importantly, more space than it is assumed to deserve.

We must acknowledge that the hockey rink has historically been a racially and gender segregated space. A statement made about Herb Carnegie, arguably the best Black player the NHL never let play, exemplifies this spatial exclusion. Conn Smythe, then owner of the Toronto Maple Leafs during the 1940s and early 1950s, reportedly said that he would sign Carnegie tomorrow for the Maple Leafs if someone could turn him white (Carnegie, 1997). Thus, the rink was first segregated through literal racial segregation and subsequently through class segregation. DiAngelo (2011) highlights that growing up in segregated environments creates an inability to understand the perspectives of racialized people:

> White people are taught not to feel any loss over the absence of people of color in their lives and in fact, this absence is what defines their schools and neighborhoods as "good;" whites come to understand that a "good school" or "good neighborhood" is coded language for "white" (Johnson & Shapiro, 2003). The quality of white space being in large part measured via the absence of people of color (and Blacks in particular) is a profound message indeed.... This dynamic of gain rather than loss via racial segregation may be the most powerful aspect of white racial socialization of all. (pp. 58–59)

Comparably, while I believe many parents of any race would comment that diverse environments are beneficial for their children, it would probably be less noticeable to a team of all-white players that they were operating in the absence of racial diversity and be able to articulate a sense of loss (read: something missing). In fact, when Venus and Serena Williams started having an impact on professional women's tennis, questions of "Are they good for tennis?" and are "all Williams'" finals good for the women's tour circulated as fair discussion topics. Venus Williams responded by pointing out that such a question had never been posed in the sport before (Douglas, 2005, p. 266); that is to say, while all-Black finals are stressed as potentially *too* diverse, there is nothing missing from an all-white final.

This segregation essentially ensures that white interests and perspectives remain central, meaning that empathizing with different perspectives is rarely necessary. Randy's example of other board members assuming that "the brown people stuck together" illustrates a manifestation of this discomfort through what Omi and Winant (1986) term a racial disequilibrium, where such comments attempt to restore white privilege by, at the minimum, reproducing the Otherness of racialized people.

Furthermore, hockey academies add another wrinkle in the presumed meritocracy of hockey because, even if minor hockey numbers are starting to reflect the demographics of their areas, the questions of *who* is able to attend an academy and who makes it *out* of these academies represents a more accurate look at the future of hockey at the elite levels. The academy serves as another filter or hurdle that is becoming more popular/desired just as racialized Canadians have started to figure out the minor hockey landscape. The fact that academies are (a) considerably more expensive than minor hockey programs, (b) limited in number, and (c) more selective in nature helps ensure that color does not filter upwards, at least not easily. This development could be equated with the rise of gated communities as a response to increasing immigration and class mobility (Low, 2008; Vesselinov, 2008). Low (2008) observes that the symbolic power of gated communities "rests on its ability to order personal and social experience" (p. 45) but, as a result, intensifies social segregation, racism, and the politics of space. The movement toward private spaces over public ones symbolizes class segregation in transnational spaces (Arat-Koc, 2010). White flight from urban areas to the suburbs exemplifies the racial privilege of being able to create spaces that are constructed as psychologically, emotionally, and physically safe. As DiAngelo (2016) highlights, "White flight is the primary reason that racial integration has not been achieved; the majority of whites, in both the expression of their beliefs and the practice of their lives, do not want to integrate with [people of color]" (p. 189).[3] This is not to say that hockey academies premeditate segregation, rather that this new development has created (or perhaps reproduces) an additional hurdle that aids in either consciously or unconsciously filtering racialized Canadians out of the elite levels of the game—the level where public memory and the ability to represent the nation are at stake.

Correspondingly, Ong's (1999) work observes that affluent Asian immigrants who arrive to a new country with economic and social capital traditionally associated with white supremacy "confound the expectation of an orderly ethnic succession" (p. 100), calling into question the proper location or stratification of racialized citizens in the existing hierarchy. Kevin elucidated this fact in our interview: "I'll be frank with you, when we were growing up it was elitist white people [playing hockey] because we couldn't afford it and now the tables have turned. Because somebody has cheated, lied, or milked the system? No! It's because the South Asian community has worked their asses off for the last 30–40 years, 18–20 hours a day and built something and now they can throw money at it just like 20 years ago other aspects of society could do it, and still do it" (personal communication, November 21, 2016).

The ability to "throw money at problems" signifies, to many immigrants, arrival and a form of equality because they are performing wealth the way that it has been enacted by white supremacy. In the previous chapter, I noted how Kevin talked about parents having to drop their kids off at the rink to go to their manual labor jobs, and here he describes the result of that generation's withdrawn participation from hockey culture. Still, social mobility represents a deviation from normalized race relations in which South Asians have long been associated with manual labor (Nayar, 2012). The ability to participate in whiteness through economic mobility represents a symbolic economy—an economy where "images of an affluent, Western consumer lifestyle" have become the benchmark of success (Bonnett, 2004, p. 34). There is arguably a disconnect between brown bodies usually marked as tools for capital accumulation versus brown bodies as symbolic of accumulated capital.

Class plays an important role in this discussion of barriers to participation because financial capital enables participation as well as the creation of new opportunities. A few of my research participants talked about a desire for South Asian–specific training groups, which is the direct result of the ability to convert economic capital into other forms of capital.

Brown-Out Hockey: Capitalism at Its Best?

There were mixed views on South Asian–specific hockey programs, such as powerskating camps and coaching sessions. Sara, a second-year hockey parent, voiced a preference for diverse teams, saying, "I don't see the purpose of having an all-Indian team. I don't know, just because they are all Indian to be on one team, doesn't make any sense to me" (personal communication, October 10, 2016). Kari, 56, also preferred a "mixed group" of players (personal communication, January 16, 2017). We can see that racialized people are able to articulate a sense of loss if there is a lack of racial diversity in certain spaces. Coach and former player Brian expressed a strong dislike for the trend toward ethnically segregated hockey groups:

> I think it's almost, the tables are almost turning and it's one of the aspects I don't want to be a part of where you are getting East Indian guys that are now, maybe they were first generation guys that dealt with [racism] and I went one way with it and they went the other way with it and it still bothers them. Maybe I got to play a little better hockey than they did and now they are only selecting East Indian players. . . . It's more so the Indian community creating that segregation. You see it in spring hockey now too, they're making, I've had people approach me and my brother and go "You know a great way you guys can make tons of money? Open up an Indo-Canadian hockey school because without a doubt everybody would just go there." And I kind of looked at him and said if I'm starting a hockey academy I want to develop hockey players, not just one race of hockey players, right?
>
> It's great to empower these kids but you're empowering them the wrong way, you're getting them all together and you're getting them to play hockey for the wrong motives. Not for the competition of it, not because we all wear the same jersey color, where it's not a religion and a culture versus the other team and I don't think that's right. (Personal communication, September 11, 2016)

Discursively, Brian implies that there can be incorrect reasons to play hockey and incorrect methods for empowerment. There is a common saying in sports that "you play for the logo on the front of the jersey, not the name on the back of it," in essence privileging group success over individual rewards. Hence, by creating South Asian–specific hockey groups, in Brian's eyes, South Asians are paying too much attention to interests that serve their racial identity as opposed to their hockey identity, assuming that these two can be disentangled.

Counter to these opinions, Thangaraj's (2015) study of South Asian basketball leagues in the United States highlights the agency that exists in creating ethnically segregated spaces. He describes South Asian–specific sporting spaces as "browning out," whereby the sporting arena serves as a point of integration for heritage and citizenship: "The process of browning out involves weaving in South Asian American sporting histories alongside the already present athletic histories, awards, and celebrations at the gym. These historical markers do not erase other histories but effect an integration that makes South Asian American athletic identities a normal part of this urban American landscape" (p. 81).

According to Thangaraj, brown-out spaces "offer respite from racialized marginalization in mainstream, multiracial basketball circuits" (p. 4). Specifically, with respect to masculinity and cultural citizenship, these ethnic spaces enable "players [to] inscribe meanings to their brown bodies that are not available in other realms of society" (p. 5). Players in the South Asian–only basketball leagues explained that participating in mainstream leagues meant that they would be subject to racial comments and challenges to both their citizenship and masculinity. Brown-out spaces represent "spatialized struggles between groups to *claim* space" (Teelucksingh, 2006, p. 8).

The South Asian American basketball players in Thangaraj's (2015) study held Vancouver in high regard based on the assumption that it represents a utopic space where basketball and culture have successfully been interwoven. For South Asian American basketball players, "Vancouver's South Asian community is seen as a vision of what South Asian America can (and shall) be" (p. 209), but unfortunately elides the racism that exists within Vancouver. Vancouver becomes an additional player in the intersection of race, sport, and identity because of its mythological position as a multicultural utopia contrasted against the reality of institutionalized racism and everyday racial tensions. Race riots in the early 1900s, appropriation of Asian Canadian properties during World War II, and, more recently, white flight into suburbs such as Tsawwassen and South Surrey counter images of Vancouver as a multicultural mosaic.

Sonia, 26, reflected that when she was younger she would not have engaged with "brown out" spaces because she never wanted to be recognized as non-white; however, as she has matured and is better able to articulate her struggles with racialization, South Asian–specific hockey groups offer a certain appeal. For those who willingly identify as different, "the body, as emblematic of the state, presents an important gendered and sexualized forum in which to tease out the particularities of citizenship and national representations" (Thangaraj, 2015, p. 7). Therefore, brown-out spaces enable racialized bodies to not only challenge dominant discourses about their bodies but also share in a collective experience of difference.

Connecting brown-out spaces back to class struggle, Kevin's words again help to inform part of the desire to create these brown-out hockey spaces:

> I think it's coming because I don't think it's a racial thing, I think it's an economic thing. Personally, that's my opinion. If you have the resources to do something for your child and it's not available, you create your own opportunity. . . . Does it look

superficially [bad] on the surface? Yeah, it does, of course it does.... But as far as practicing and creating your own academies, the resources aren't there then you have to go do something yourself.... We always find solutions. If the solution is we can't get our kid into this academy or that academy for whatever reason then we'll make our own and hire the best people. Is that any different than any other business anywhere else? Is that any different from Starbucks versus Tim Hortons? Is that any different from Rogers versus Telus? Those are big companies but point being if there's a need and you can't get an adequate solution you build you own solution. That's true entrepreneurial spirit if you think about it. That's capitalism at its best. (Personal communication, November 21, 2016)

It is curious that Kevin believes the motivation for creating brown-out spaces is not based on racial similarity because the desire to create more opportunity for everyone is quite different from attempting to claim space in what is perceived as justice or equality. He acknowledges that the perception of brown-out hockey looks bad on the South Asian community, just as donating money to a team fundraiser elicits a different response compared to a donation of time and effort. His thoughts led us to discuss parallels between the Vancouver housing market and its accompanying racial tensions. Kevin's perspective is also reflective of the Punjabi-operated sawmills that were created during the early 1900s in British Columbia (Nayar, 2012). Discrimination and a lack of opportunities fostered a culture of resilience through innovation. According to Kymlicka (2013), the ideal neoliberal interpretation of multiculturalism is "not a tolerant national citizen who is concerned for the disadvantaged in her own society but a cosmopolitan actor who can compete effectively across state boundaries" (p. 111). The model minority is then proven to be self-reliant, and capitalism is positioned as an equalizer instead of a system of oppression.

Greg, a 47-year-old parent of three, two of whom play hockey (a daughter and a son), also referenced conflicts that arise from changes in balances of power and a perceived mismatch between race and class:

That's because the majority of individuals like status quo; they don't like change. And, when they see minorities doing better that's jealousy kicking in. Jealousy brings in racial tension and every other kind of tension you can imagine and that's what it is. And in sports, I can honestly say, once other cultures start getting into sports in a big way you watch the changes.... There will be more and more racial tension because of jealousy. Built in jealousy. "How did so and so make it? He's brown! He should be a taxi driver or a have a pizza shop or whatever." (Personal communication, November 21, 2016)

This feeling of jealousy or resentment may be perception more than reality (much like racism, resentment is difficult to prove); however, there is a history of white resentment and hostility toward South Asian claims to space and belonging in Vancouver, with the development of Sikh temples and the expansion of the City of Surrey as prominent examples (G. S. Johal, 2007). When I asked Greg about hurdles specific to the participation of South Asians he answered:

GREG: Yeah, while Caucasians still run it there will be. Always. Until there is more of an even balance from the boards all the way through coaching, all the way down, you will see it. What's happening now is South Asians and East Asians are doing their own thing. They're doing their own organizations; they're doing their own sports. They feel, the reason they're doing that is because, they're not given a fair chance at the other part. It's the truth.

CS: Where do you see that divergence going? Will it feed back into the same system?

GREG: Nope. It's going to turn into its own.

Of the 36 minor hockey associations in the Pacific Coast Amateur Hockey Association, South Asians hold 4.2% of executive positions despite South Asians representing 20% of the population demographics in the Fraser South area (e.g., Langley, Surrey, New Westminster), 6% in Fraser North (e.g., Coquitlam, Belcarra, Maple Ridge), almost 11% in Fraser East (e.g., Chilliwack, Abbotsford, Mission), and 5.6% in the City of Vancouver (Foster, Keller, McKee, & Ostry, 2011). Bourdieu (1984) believed that markers of cultural capital, such as education, degrees, property, and citizenship, are more valued by the host society than wealth as forms of assimilation. Conversely, from a structural standpoint, the nation-state sees wealth as the most important factor in selecting its potential citizens/residents; as a result, we have a clash of interests and values in places where racialized Canadians are trying to *be* Canadian but still do not *look* Canadian. Both Kevin and Greg identified the effects of this breach of "spatial and symbolic borders that have disciplined" (Ong, 1999, p. 100) racialized Canadians, keeping them on the margins of Canadian society. Transnational movement has blurred what used to be distinct lines of division between rank and space.

The desire to create racially exclusive brown-out spaces serves as a form of cultural citizenship because it enables South Asians to write onto the hockey landscape. Segregated environments (whether by gender, sexuality, race, etc.) arguably provide safe spaces for free(er) expression, a common baseline experience for discussion, and a site for empowerment through difference (Aly, 2017). It can be exhausting to constantly navigate identities, exclusion, and expectations on a daily basis; therefore, minoritized spaces can offer a respite. Moreover, while the existence of one or two South Asians on the ice at any given time may not challenge the whiteness of hockey, seeing an entire group of South Asians training should start to raise questions about the future of hockey and why they are training in a racially exclusive group. As participants have identified, it will likely be perceived as self-segregation, and in a way, it is; however, what makes it possible is the confluence of inequality and the ability to do something about that inequality. Even though coach Brian expressed a dislike of brown-out spaces, he did acknowledge, "If you see a team of all East Indian players, I think you should ask questions. If you have a team where there's no Indian players, you should also ask questions [especially in areas where there is a large South Asian population]" (personal communication, September 11, 2016).

Brown-out hockey spaces are a new development and require more research into the motivations behind their creation and the implications of such spaces. Granted, those who resist the trend toward brown-out spaces reproduce the model minority myth because participating in such a space highlights difference, and if there is one thing the model minority is expected to be it is "like everyone else." On the other hand, participating in ethnically segregated spaces may confirm suspicions from certain Canadians that *these* Canadians are not really Canadians after all because they have not properly assimilated into mainstream offerings. This seems like a lose–lose situation for racialized Canadians seeking any belonging through hockey, because marginalization may result in further exclusion. Again, we have to question *which* Canadians hockey brings together and under what circumstances. Moreover, how beneficial is the re-creation of hockey systems that have proven themselves to be problematic and inequitable? And, to take it one step further, how beneficial is it to be recognized by a nation-state that was founded on oppression and dispossession?

C.L.R. James (1969) wrote in *Beyond a Boundary*, his autobiographical discussion about cricket and class in the West Indies, "he [the West Indian cricket player] never forgets that his liberation exists only within the boundaries of the game, and then only for the gamers. . . . Sport is not sanctuary from the real world because sport is part of the real world, and the liberation and the oppression are inextricably bound" (p. xviii).

Through an examination of class and race at the rink, the myth of hockey's meritocratic nature is exposed while we simultaneously test the limits of Canadian acceptance. Whether brown-out hockey spaces are needed or simply wanted by some illustrates how much work needs to be done with respect to understanding hockey's relationship with racialized participants and claims to spatial representation.

Furthermore, model minorities exist in a paradox where they are expected to have sufficient wealth in order to avoid burdening the state but not be so wealthy that they are able to wield influence and power. Drawing parallels to Ong's work from the late 1990s, the pivotal issue underpinning the tensions that can be felt at the ice rink, and beyond, is that the presence of wealthy racialized Canadians and immigrants challenges white Canadians' "understanding of themselves as privileged [Canadian] natives who should take no back seat to foreigners, especially Asians" (p. 101). In connection to this feeling of resentment, the key to understanding white fragility is not so much focusing on its existence but unpacking how it can derail opportunities for meaningful discussions about racism and racialized experiences. The fragility of white privilege works to silence claims about racism and thus emboldens the existence of it.

Last, it is important that we continue to explore how cost affects participation in hockey, but we must do so with a more detailed approach. *The Globe and Mail*'s 2013 article that referenced the increasing costs of hockey participation was titled, "The Great Offside: How Canadian Hockey Is Becoming a Game Strictly for the Rich" (Mirtle, 2013). Knowing that despite rising costs some racialized Canadians are still able to play and pay their way to the elite levels of the game, perhaps "The Great Offside" is not so much that hockey weeds out certain Canadians from participation (since it always has) but that it no longer weeds out the correct (read: appropriate) Canadians from participation. Mirtle (2013) writes in "The Great Offside," "a sport that was once a true meritocracy is increasingly one where money talks"; yet, hockey has never been a sport based solely on merit—access and opportunity have always trumped skill, especially for those marked as Other.

8

Taking Stock

Public Memory and the
Retelling of Hockey in Canada

> History is about the past. Memory is
> about how we use the past for the
> present.
> —Rieff as cited in Lamar, 2016, para. 10

Returning to the power that hockey holds in Canadian cultural mythology, Barthes (1972) posits that myths appear natural, not because they hide anything but because they are "deprived of memory" (p. 232). If, according to French historian Ernest Renan (1992), nations are founded on rich memories, but forgetting is also an essential factor in nation building, *who* gets to decide *which* stories we collectively forget, and which are canonized into the national story? Which Canadian memories have we been deprived of in the servicing of these particular mythologies? This last chapter challenges the white-washed history of hockey as one aspect of institutionalized and systemic racism that may seem like a minor issue but in fact contributes to and reproduces whiteness as both normative and superior.

At the end of our interview, I asked *Hockey Night Punjabi* broadcaster Harnarayan Singh if there was anything else that he would like to talk about. He mused:

It's funny, like my basement has become the Punjabi Hockey Hall of Fame because there was a weekend that I was away, and my wife surprised me and made this whole, kind of the history of the show and all kinds of artifacts and put it all together on this wall . . . there's some really cool stuff in there. You know, it would be cool to eventually have some of our artifacts at the Hockey Hall of Fame. I think we're a part of the hockey family and I think, most of, especially in Canada, most of the hockey world knows who we are and what we're doing and things like that. So now the next step is kind of integrating ourselves amongst the normal hockey world right. (Personal communication, April 18, 2016)

Since our interview, one of Singh's "Bonino! Bonino! Bonino!" T-shirts was included in the Canadian History Museum's "Hockey" 2017 exhibit, which is a good start for recognizing the significance of the broadcast. But, more importantly, Singh was referencing a desire to be included in the shared Canadian hockey memory and recognized as someone who helped shape and grow the game. Margalit (2002) distinguishes a "common memory" from a "shared memory" by emphasizing that common memories are based on one unifying experience, whereas shared memories are a form of communication—it is a calibrated and voluntary process. For Margalit, memory "travels from person to person through institutions, such as archives, and through communal mnemonic devices, such as monuments and the names of streets" (p. 54). In Canada, one major mnemonic device that contributes to the shared memory of hockey is the Hockey Hall of Fame (HHOF).

According to Geiger (2008), the concept of a "hall of fame" dates back to approximately 42 B.C.E. when Augustus created the Gallery of Heroes in his Forum (*Forum Augustum*).[1] Augustus was not the first person in antiquity to use statues and inscriptions to commemorate those deemed worthy of memory—the practice was common in other Mediterranean civilizations too; however, the assemblage of select individuals into a program, of sorts, was instrumental for future Western conceptions of public memory: "A group was conceived, closed in relation to the past and open-ended in the relation to the future: it had been decided once and for all who these *summi viri* [highest] were, no addition of past heroes was permitted and clear directives were given to the Princeps' heirs concerning the inclusion of those who were to prove themselves worthy in the future"[2] (p. 7).

Augustus's selections for the Forum became "the official list of the state and the nation" (p. 7) and to be excluded from this selection process was, in many ways, more significant than being one of the chosen few. Geiger clarifies, "If non-inclusion in Anthologies, or Selected Works, often passes a death-sentence (even if unintentional) over works of literature, non-inclusion in a

FIG. 8.1 Harnarayan Singh at Hometown Hockey, Surrey, 2017.

normative list of persons often amounts to almost instant oblivion" (p. 8). This inaugural hall of fame set a precedent whereby the heroes of a nation, state, or peoples would be "chosen for them albeit not chosen by them" (p. 8). Arguably, the main purpose of the Gallery of Heroes was to enhance the memory of the Roman people while also predetermining what the future would look like. The comparison to Augustus's Gallery may seem distant, but I think it notable that Canada is currently home to 39 sport museums and/or halls of fame (Phillips, 2012).

The modern sports hall of fame and museum have carried on this tradition by immortalizing specific past accomplishments, while concurrently, as Geiger (2008) points out, relegating others to oblivion. Paralympic sporting heritage provides us with a useful example of the consequences of exclusion. Brittain, Ramshaw, and Gammon (2013) observe that, despite being the second largest multi-sporting event in the world (behind the Olympic Games), the Paralympic Games have been woefully underrepresented in both sporting and social heritage. The exclusion of Paralympic athletes from any organized form of collective memory has resulted in many athletes (and their families) throwing their physical artifacts away (such as trophies, medals, and equipment) because they are perceived as socially worthless. By extension, the disabled are then reproduced as having little value and not worthy of remembrance. Women's hockey in Canada has also faced similar circumstances. Following the closure of the CWHL, the league was forced to auction off its league trophies (i.e., most valuable player, highest scorer, coach of the year) as part of its fiduciary responsibilities and to help pay off remaining debts (McGran, 2019). These artifacts exist in a space where they have extraordinary sentimental and cultural value but little social or market value. Hence, to commemorate specific groups of athletes does more than historicize a sport; it can serve as an act of advocacy and activism for marginalized athletes more generally as recognition of their humanity.

The politics of recognition become salient far beyond access to and participation in sport because marginalization can carry on in the form of canonization or obscurity. Furthermore, when segregation and racial discrimination on the playing field are memorialized as the way it was, the act of exclusion fortuitously disappears. The history of racial exclusion becomes as obvious as the glass that encloses these historical exhibits but is equally as inconspicuous.

Hockey Hall of Fame

Singh's narrative above discursively reproduced the HHOF as symbolic of the "normal hockey world." It is there where hockey players, coaches, managers, and officials are gifted with "eternal life" and hence value to the nation and to the sport. The HHOF was born on September 19, 1943, with its first class of members inducted two years later in 1945, and the original physical building (at the Canadian National Exhibition grounds) opened in Toronto on August 26, 1961 (Hockey Hall of Fame, 2017a). It moved to its current location at Brookfield Place in downtown Toronto in 1993. The HHOF accepts inductees in three categories: players, builders (coaches, managers, or any other people who have had a "significant off-ice role" (Hockey Hall of Fame, 2017b), and referees/linesmen. A maximum of four male and two female inductees are allowed in the player category each year, and candidates must receive at least 75% of the votes from the 18-person Selection Committee. The HHOF outlines that the Selection Committee "be generally, but not necessarily exclusively, composed of former hockey players, former coaches of hockey teams, former referees or linesmen for hockey leagues or associations, current or former senior executives of hockey teams or hockey leagues or associations and present or former members of the media who cover or covered the game of hockey" (Hockey Hall of Fame, 2017a).

These criteria mean that, to date, women and racialized people have had limited representation on the Selection Committee, which helps explain why there have been only five women inducted thus far and only four racialized players in total.[3] After much campaigning, Willie O'Ree, the first Black player the NHL allowed into the league, was inducted into the Builder category in 2018 (Hockey Hall of Fame, 2018), but the late Herb Carnegie remains excluded from the hall. Carnegie's exclusion from the NHL carries over into his inability to "fulfil the conditions necessary to become a hockey legend—at least a hockey legend as adjudged by the dominant benchmarks of NHL success and/or Hall of Fame induction" (Norman, 2012). This is an example of how racism carries forward by denying one's existence in the past. Moreover, critics have pointed out that it is the *Hockey* Hall of Fame and not the NHL Hall of Fame (Nelson, 2017), meaning that trailblazers and formidable contributions should (in theory) play more of a role in the public memory of the sport.

Bruce Kidd (1996) asserts halls of fame "play a strategic role in the public remembering and interpretation of sports" (p. 328), but the Hockey Hall "is a disappointing example of effective 'public history'" (p. 331). Ken Campbell pinpointed part of what Kidd was referring to in *The Hockey News* in 2012:

> It's made up of 18 NHL-establishment white guys, not a single one of whom is under the age of 50. And the ones who carry the most weight among them are the same people who had to be dragged into the 21st century to allow women to be inducted. Just listen to them when they call the inductees, basically congratulating them for becoming one of their little insular group.[4] (para. 3)

As a result, gatekeeping in hockey (as in all sports), does not end when one decides to hang up the skates because selection committees curate social memory (J. E. Johnson, Giannoulakis, Tracy, & Ridley, 2016; Parsons & Stern, 2012). To be memorialized is, no doubt, a great privilege; yet, the ability to decide who is and who is not immortalized is seemingly the greater privilege. Similar to how Augustus's directives were meant to avoid re-interpretations of greatness by future generations (Geiger, 2008), so too are the choices made by sports hall of fame committees. Halls of fame solidify, regulate, and standardize the values and ambitions of that institution; and, because hockey is Canada's game, the HHOF subsequently does the same for the Canadian nation. These committees and their selections have the ability to challenge the history of racism in sports by offering a more inclusive retelling but inclusion and equality are conscious efforts, rarely do they happen naturally.

Phillips (2012) categorizes sports museums/halls of fame into four general groups: academic, corporate, community, and vernacular. The HHOF is delineated as a corporate museum for the following reasons: It employs more marketing and public relations type staff than museum professionals; public education is not a high priority; it uses its platform to influence public opinion, serving as a form of advertising; and it relies heavily on collective nostalgia as a way to defect/minimize controversial, marginalized, and/or contested histories. Nostalgia is key to the (re)production of sport as a cultural artifact. Nostalgia references "an emotional component"; it is "a preference (general liking, positive attitude, or favorable affect) towards objects (people, places, experiences or things) from when one was younger or from times about which one has learned vicariously, perhaps through socialization of the media" (Fairley as cited in J. E. Johnson et al., 2016, pp. 310–311). Thus, nostalgia is a social construct, and we learn what things, which people, and which spaces are deserving of emotional investment.

The Role of Media

Media are crucial in fostering nostalgia and the production of public memory (Jackson & Ponic, 2001). Due to Canada's struggle to cement a national identity unique from America and Britain, and establish political and cultural legitimacy as a white settler nation, the nexus between Canada's hockey heroes and the media has been integral in narrating and defining the nation's past, present, and future (Jackson & Ponic, 2011). Joanne Garde-Hansen (2011) asserts that "our engagement with history has become almost entirely mediated" (p. 1) through its symbiotic relationship with the media. Her book, *Media and Memory*, develops the "idea that media compels an end to history and the beginning of memory" (p. 3). In other words, media frames our perceptions about certain events, people, and places by marking particular instances worthy of collective remembrance, but always in a mediated form. Similar to Baudrillard's (1994) theory of hyperreality, collective memories (e.g., the death of Princess Diana) are, in a way, more real than the actual event because they have been repeatedly reconstructed for public consumption. Media, therefore, can foster a specific and unified memory that does not necessarily exist in reality.

Scholars such as P. Lee and Thomas (2012) and Reading (2011) approach public memory as a human right and a matter of justice that is inherent in the realization of other rights such as freedom of expression and access to education. Lee and Thomas (2012) refer to the "right to memory" as situated "with the purview of third-generation human rights" (p. 7) following civil and political rights (first generation), and social, economic, and cultural rights (second generation). The right to memory, along with communication rights, speaks to human dignity and identity as part of a functioning democratic society. The role of the media, then, is not only as a curator of history but also a defender of democratic accountability. Furthermore, with the development of participatory media, Reading (2011) contends that digitalization and global movement force us to reinterpret traditional forms of memory practices.

Similar to Singh, Bhupinder Hundal also spoke about the potential legacy of the *Hockey Night Punjabi* broadcast as the true arbiter of the program's social impact; however, Hundal's reflection was not so much about physical artifacts as it was a hope that the show opens a door to Canadian media that cannot be shut:

> So, while it may not be me, I think our responsibility is to use the opportunity that we have to educate so that a five-year-old kid maybe has that opportunity that perhaps we didn't have, and that's kind of the responsibility we all have

moving forward. This is where I think the broadcast, talking about the legacy perspective, that's where it actually matters, is how we open the doors not only for future players but open the door for future broadcasters and how we help propel them in their career.[5] (Personal communication, April 28, 2016)

He also expressed that the more the broadcast is able to tell "stories about South Asians in the game," the more impactful the broadcast can be through its parallel but alternative narrative. Arguably, one component of a free and credible press is the inclusion of diverse stories and opinions beyond dominant narratives. In this way, we may be able to read *Hockey Night Punjabi* as a defender of a more *inclusive* public memory and democratic accessibility, while *Hockey Night in Canada* serves as the curator of hockey history. The tension in their parallel movements symbolizes the struggle over public memory as a marker of legitimacy and citizenship.

The mythologies of hockey and the HHOF are powerful because they exist in plain sight—their obviousness, ubiquity, and proximity are precisely what deflect criticism. It does, however, make one wonder if hockey is as vital to national unity as the sport and its pundits purport. And is it possible to separate the myth from the actual sport? Why write out the contributions of Indigenous, Black, and Asian Canadians that help strengthen the mythological relationship between hockey and multiculturalism? On the other hand, scholars who advocate that public memory is a right generally do so on behalf of war, genocide, and/or the overt destruction of communities. Thus, it seems almost trivial to write anyone out of a sporting history—that is, unless seemingly trivial edits to the national narrative open the door for larger or more egregious erasures.

Canada's struggle with Indigenous reconciliation is instructive of what happens when a nation edits certain people from its historical narrative. In 2008, the Canadian government offered an official apology for its role in instituting residential schools and in 2015 the Truth and Reconciliation Commission was published. The document amplifies the voices of survivors and their experiences, which have, by and large, been edited from the Canadian education system and broader discussions of history. Ninety-four Calls to Action accompany the commission's report and five of them are specifically directed at sport. Call No. 87 places specific responsibility on sport halls of fame to "provide public education that tells the national story of Aboriginal athletes in history" (Truth and Reconciliation Commission of Canada, 2015b, p. 10). In other words, because sport has been used throughout history as a tool of oppression, colonization, and marginalization, incomplete sporting histories are also incomplete national histories; we are "not willing to get over histories that are not over" (Sara Ahmed, 2017, p. 262). These specific erasures to hockey's history have allowed colonialism and institutionalized racism to live in perpetuity without being marked as such. These Calls to Action are first and foremost designed to reclaim Indigenous contributions and experiences, but they also open the door for other racialized histories to be reclaimed in the process. This means that attempts at diversifying the sport are misguided because hockey's history is already multicultural and racialized. Hence, working toward anti-racism actually means returning hockey to its multicultural roots.

It is also critical to note that the privatized nature of *HNIC*, *Hockey Night Punjabi*, and the HHOF places limits on the right to campaign for a more inclusive rewriting of history. Once the rights to *HNIC* were bought by Rogers Communications from the CBC, it no longer belonged publicly to the citizens of Canada in the same way. This is not to say that things were all that different or more transparent (Worthington, 2011) when the program was broadcast on the CBC, but at least citizens could lodge a grievance on the basis of public broadcasting as a public good (Scherer & Whitson, 2009). In contrast, the HHOF belongs to a litany of corporate sponsors including the NHL, Imperial Oil Limited, PepsiCo Canada, Tim Hortons, Molson Coors Canada, and Reebok-CCM Hockey, to name a few. If public memory, in this instance, is written by corporations instead of citizens, how do we ensure that the people's heroes and the people's stories are not relegated to oblivion? How do we move toward a more democratic and inclusive form of public memory that includes as many citizens and versions of Canada as possible?

Writing In: DIY Citizenship

If there is no will to remember certain people, events, or artifacts (Parsons & Stern, 2012), it is difficult to challenge the dominant narrative. The obvious answer is to alter the institutional barriers by campaigning for more diverse selection committees and revamping selection criteria. However, because institutions such as the HHOF are private entities, public shaming and campaigning can be blunted by simple organizational stubbornness. As a result, the development of do-it-yourself (DIY) heritage institutions offers one instructive solution to *accompany* institutional change.

The h(er)story of DIY culture stems from the transition from second-wave to third-wave feminism (Kempson, 2015). As feminism grew from a collective (albeit exclusive) movement into a more consumption-oriented, individualized, and fragmented movement, DIY culture developed within this chasm. Feminist zines (independently created, nonprofit, amateur publications) are the most noticeable aspect of DIY subcultures (Chidgey, 2014; Kempson, 2015). Zines predominantly articulate marginalized stories, whether they are resistive in nature or simply an expression of the self (Kempson, 2015). The linchpin of DIY feminism is that it encourages active, politically engaged citizenship from everyone. Using this ethos of grassroots and community agency, DIY institutions seek to democratize the notion of heritage by creating institutions of memory that exist beyond national archives (Baker, 2016).

DIY institutions, a term coined by Baker (2016) in specific reference to popular music culture, identifies "a group of popular music archives, museums and halls of fame that were founded by enthusiasts, run largely by volunteers and which exist outside the frame of authorized projects of national collecting and display" (p. 173). These repositories are created as a response to a community need; they "self-authorize" that which is worthy of commemoration. What Singh described as his personal basement hall of fame is how many DIY institutions begin, as individual collections. Baker asserts that these repositories broaden our interpretation of history, offer sites for research, and are "important in epistemological terms because the parameters of the archival record are determined by the community of volunteers and enthusiasts . . . whereas national institutions tend to have selective collection practices which work to reinforce existing musical canons" (p. 183). They give specific communities control over how the past should be remembered; in this way, DIY citizens write in what has been written out. Memory, then, becomes a subversive act—an act of citizenship, reconciliation, and justice.

These DIY institutions reflect a broader ethos of DIY citizenship by "hacking" (i.e., providing a work around) traditional interpretations of citizenship (Ratto & Boler, 2014). Self-organized activities that offer access to support, instruction, and information are political acts that challenge existing structures by inciting questions about ownership and accountability (Ratto & Boler, 2014). DIY citizens make "themselves as they go along" (Hartley, 1999 as cited in Ratto & Boler, 2014, p. 5). For Ratto and Boler (2014), DIY citizenship "sits at the intersection of a series of tensions: between consumers and citizens, between experts and novices, between individuals and communities, and between politics as performed by" (p. 5) traditional governments and those of grassroots democracies. The power and potential of DIY citizenship lies in the invitation to question how things are now and if they ought to continue in the same fashion for the future. As a form of cultural activism, DIY citizenship can be seen as an outlet of cultural citizenship because culture and citizenship are seen as co-constitutive and part of larger political processes.

Just as cultural citizenship works outside of the boundaries of political citizenship, DIY activism/citizenship seeks to create alternatives for the here and now where buy-in from institutional powers is unnecessary (Chidgey, 2014). One of the benefits of social marginalization is that little can be taken away when there is nothing to lose. As Hurley (2007) points out, "marginality and power are *productive* and often require thinking in specific contexts rather than just generally. The marginal are not always powerless" (p. 179). Both interpretations of citizenship demand authorship along with the taking and making of space. Counter to the passive hope discussed in chapter 6 about waiting for generational change, DIY citizenship is inherently participatory and encourages the sharing of skills, knowledge, and resources to "create the things we want to see" (Chidgey, 2014, p. 104). In my opinion, DIY citizenship can be encompassed under the umbrella of cultural citizenship, with the main distinction being that DIY citizenship is more overt about its activism; DIY citizenship offers a method to achieve and exercise cultural citizenship.

The HHOF needs to incorporate stories of minoritized contributions into the curated history of the game if it wants to continue growing the sport. The HHOF's attempt to put diversity on display as part of the NHL's 100th anniversary highlights the general absence of diversity. The exhibit explains: "Many young hockey players, regardless of their ethnicity, gender or sexual orientation dream of someday playing professionally. However, due to the exclusion of many marginalized peoples from the NHL, this was not an option until four pioneers broke through the barriers that kept them from playing at hockey's highest level."

The description then goes on to highlight Larry Kwong, Fred Sasakamoose, Willie O'Ree, and Manon Rheaume as leaders for racial and gender progress (there is noticeably no leader to speak of with regard to LGBTQ+ equality in professional hockey). The hall represents racism as a relic of the past, stating "hurdles of race and ethnicity remained in place for decades" but that today players like "Carey Price and P. K. Subban continue to inspire the next generation of minority youth" ... to realize that their success is "only dependent on their desire and their talent." Drawing this back to Fosty and Fosty's (2008) critique that because there are no monuments dedicated to the Colored Hockey League of the Maritimes and racialized contributions have largely been excluded from the HHOF, the erasure of these contributions challenges the visibility and legitimacy of racialized citizens. It also means that we miss out on the opportunity to celebrate hockey's (and Canada's) racial heroes.

In an attempt to address this erasure, in 2017, I approached the South Asian Studies Institute at the University of the Fraser Valley to create a museum exhibit dedicated to telling the stories of racialized contributions in hockey's history. Inspired by the research conducted in this study, but more inclusive of all racialized experiences, the exhibit titled, "We Are Hockey,"[6] launched on March 29, 2019, at the Sikh Heritage Museum in Abbotsford, British Columbia. The exhibit centers the journeys of racialized people and "challenges singularly racial perspectives on the meaning of Hockey as Canada's national sport while negotiating the often ambivalent, yet very relevant interrogations of race, ethnicity and the privilege and power of settler communities" (Sandhra, 2019, para. 1). This hack is not meant to absolve mainstream hockey institutions of their responsibility to include diverse narratives knowing that "those people" are featured elsewhere; instead, this DIY institution demonstrates that there is a desire and value in reforming racially homogeneous public memories.

DIY citizenship offers a way to galvanize communities in the face of feeling helpless and what may seem like something immutable (hopefully spurring them on to additional political acts). Collective hope exists in stark contrast to passive individual optimism; it creates space and energy for possibilities and alternatives and is an impetus for social betterment. Promoting alternative, community, or DIY spaces for public memory enables traditionally marginalized groups to scribble onto the national narrative in search of inclusion, justice, and equality for all.

Conclusion

A Commitment to the Future

> Hope does not only or always point
> toward the future, but carries us through
> when the terrain is difficult, when the
> path we follow makes it harder to
> proceed. Hope is behind us when we
> have to work for something to be
> possible.
> —Sara Ahmed, 2017, p. 2

On February 23, 2019, Jonathan Diaby, a 24-year-old Black semi-professional player in Quebec's Ligue Nord-Américaine de Hockey, left during the second period of a game in tears because of the racist taunts he and his family were facing. Fans hurled the N-word at them. They compared Diaby to a baboon. They touched his father's hair. They compared Diaby's hair to a mop. When the taunting escalated the arena security guards asked Diaby's family and friends to move seats so that people "could have a quiet game" (CBC News, 2019). Diaby wanted to leave the game after the first period but his coach convinced him to stay. The second period was even worse than the first. In Diaby's (2019) own words, "it was the first time that hockey has ever made me cry." He questioned whether or not it is worth the racism to continue playing the sport he loves. In his op-ed for the CBC, Diaby (2019) pointed to his artistry as a rap musician as perhaps his best outlet for dealing with the racism he has faced as a Black Canadian because he "[has] lots to say" (para. 42). Thus, while hockey represents an escape for many, it can be the cause of pain for others and it is important to recognize the spectrum of experiences.

Hockey may be the game of the Canadian state, but can it ever really be the game of the Canadian people? I contend that as long as racism in hockey lives only in the past tense and we continue to privilege stories of perseverance over those of exclusion, hockey will never truly be the game of Canada's people. Diaby's experience is a prime example of how we deal with racism in Canada. We ask the subjects of abuse (notice I did not use the word *victim* here) to endure more. We ask the subjects of abuse to acquiesce to the racists. We do not ask the racists to stop or leave. The game continues in Diaby's absence. We follow up by denouncing hate as un-Canadian (and un-hockey), which is what Jean-François Laplante, the commissioner of the league, did (Bruemmer, 2019). We chalk it up as a bad day but far from representative of life in Canada. Returning to Ahmed's critique of evidence, we need to ask ourselves how many incidents of racism in Canada's game are enough to be considered representative of racialized experiences? In the weeks surrounding Diaby's incident, an Indigenous minor hockey team received racist taunts at a tournament in Neepawa, Manitoba (Monkman, 2018); a 13-year-old Black player, Divyne Apollon II, was taunted with monkey chants in Maryland and was eventually ejected from the game for fighting because neither the coaches nor referees stopped the taunts (Feingold, 2019); and Vimal Sukumaran was the recipient of "inappropriate language" during an NCAA game but no punishment was levied because officials were unable to determine who made the remark (Shah, 2019b). Racism exists on both sides of the Canada–U.S. border, at all levels of the game, and is experienced by all non-white groups. Diaby held nothing back when he wrote, "let's not lie to ourselves: racism is everywhere, all the time" (Diaby, 2019, para. 20).

People have asked me if I have seen any changes to hockey culture while conducting this research. Honestly, I haven't seen much significant change. What I have noticed is the NHL increasingly working with (or perhaps surveilling/co-opting) grassroots initiatives that challenge hockey's normative whiteness. For example, Black Girl Hockey Club was created in 2018 and quickly received support from the Washington Capitals (Gulitti, 2018). However, a few months after the Capitals hosted a Black Girl Hockey Club event, the vast majority of the team also accepted their White House invitation to celebrate their 2018 Stanley Cup win with President Trump (Gulitti, 2019), which sent conflicting messages about racial equity because of the administration's history of racially divisive policies and rhetoric. It is these kinds of contradictory decisions that separate diversity initiatives from anti-racism initiatives and make very clear that men's professional hockey is not yet ready or willing to set a precedent for the rest of hockey culture to follow suit.

In the NHL's Policy Brief on the changing demographics of hockey, racism is not mentioned once in the four-page document (NHL, 2018). It does, however, argue that "to remain relevant and to accelerate the growth of the sport, hockey must embrace the ongoing diversity explosion" (p. 4). The phrase "diversity explosion" appears three times in the policy brief. The rhetoric of inclusion and diversity is responsible for the narratives shared in this book because we continue to invite minoritized participants into institutions that are wholly unprepared for their presence. We do this because, as the NHL outlines in its policy brief, the future of the sport depends on these traditionally marginalized markets. In other words, hockey *needs* all of the people it has historically relegated to the sidelines: racialized people, Indigenous Peoples, queer communities, women, and disabled participants. Embracing the "diversity explosion" will do nothing to address issues of power, privilege, and access— the pillars required for racial justice. Fostering anti-racism means that power can no longer be hoarded amongst "old school" gatekeepers. This is not just a grassroots, entry-level issue; top-level management must change itself to reflect the participants hockey thinks it deserves. The privilege of having white male contributions stand in as the universal national (or sporting) narrative must be challenged. And, handing out free equipment and holding learn-to-play sessions to enhance access, while an important part of the process, should be recognized as the least we can do. We should not be patting ourselves on the back for incorporating more minoritized youth into a culture that has demonstrated itself to be sexist, homonegative, racist, and elitist unless we are ready and willing to overturn the people, practices, and policies that made it that way.

That being said, I did witness one noteworthy change over the five years of this project. When I first observed how people reacted to *Hockey Night Punjabi* via Twitter (Szto, 2016), approximately half of the reactions were negative in nature. But on June 4, 2017, Bhupinder Hundal highlighted a racist tweet about the show that stated, "Are you kidding me they [South Asians] don't care about hockey" and 119 people responded in support of the show, 529 retweeted Hundal's response, and 1,600 liked his response (Hundal, 2017). The support was overwhelmingly from non–South Asians expressing their appreciation for the show. This is not to say that I believe racism has declined in the past five years because of the broadcast but that the success of *Hockey Night Punjabi* has given Canadian hockey fans something they can speak up about and defend. In five years' time, I witnessed laughter at the show and its commentators evolve into increasing mainstream attention, original programming, and crossover segments. *Hockey Night Punjabi* is evidence that multiple storylines can co-exist for the benefit of hockey and Canadian multiculturalism.

Shifting Labor

Multiculturalism and hockey have only begun to negotiate each other's existence, and discussions about race and racism continue to be necessary *because* hockey is not yet diverse, nor for everyone. While conducting this research, I encountered some reluctance from hockey parents who told me "no one wants to talk about that," referring to racism in hockey. This reaction could be the result of a relatively small hockey community and a fear that others could take retribution against those who speak out. It could be because such experiences are traumatic and do not want to be relived. Or it might feel like showing a lack of gratitude to a nation that apparently does not suffer from widespread racism. The fact is we do not know the reason, but there are clearly more stories out there.

There was a quote provided by elite player Kiran that resonated with me throughout this project. It was the simple idea that no one had ever asked her about her sporting experience because we have assumed for far too long that sporting experiences are relatively similar. It seemed momentous for her to be able to express and share her experiences that had, in a sense, been held captive:

> It's something I've never been asked about and, when you . . . asked me if I would do this interview I looked at my mom and I was like, "Wow, no one has ever asked me about this." I guess it kinda is something that is hard to do, hard to survive in a sport world where you are kinda on your own. . . . I was just really surprised that no one's ever asked me about it. No one ever asked me if it was okay. No one really approached me and [was] like, "Hey are these people bugging you?," "Are you okay?" just because I have such a happy, passive personality, people just assume that I'm okay. (Personal communication, April 28, 2016)

The narratives in this book offer some insight into why that assumption is problematic and potentially harmful. It seems that we have been filling in answers for questions that have never been asked. Therefore, we must continue to tell "hockey history through its minoritarian elements" in order to expand "the cultural files of the game and the potential for new subject formations that are not limited by the standard account" (Genosko, 1999, p. 145). We must actively work to tell the stories and contributions of racialized hockey participants both as a form of resistance and as an act of citizenship. Simply declaring multiculturalism as a value does not make racism disappear. As Sara Ahmed expresses in the quote that opens this chapter, action is impossible without the hope that a better tomorrow is possible (and/or necessary). While optimism and fairy tale endings have their place, it is those who find the present uninhabitable (not the ones who wait for better days) that are able to drive social change for the generations that follow.

It is also important to acknowledge that the purpose of making whiteness and white supremacy visible in hockey culture is not to retract the privileges that exist for those who benefit from whiteness, rather anti-racism work seeks to extend such normative privileges to everyone. White hockey players never have to question their racial belonging in the game, whereas the belonging of racialized Canadians remains a constant negotiation, both on and off the ice. In practice, a multicultural Canada would be one where all citizens have the privilege of moving through spaces without their racialized appearance preceding them because racial hierarchies do not exist.

White people are the solution to racism. In chapter 1, I framed this analysis as one about whiteness and South Asian experiences in equal measure. It was a white player who taunted Suki on the ice. It was her white teammates who bore witness to her targeting. It was a white coach who left Brian behind at the hotel. They were white parents who accused the "brown guys" on the board of voting as a bloc. It was a white security guard who asked Jonathan Diaby's family to move to another spot in the arena. It is a white selection committee that chooses what hockey's history looks like. But it also took white allies to help launch and sustain the *Hockey Night Punjabi* broadcast. It was a white mother who co-founded the Players Against Hate (2019) initiative after her son's teammate, Divyne Apollon II, was subjected to racist abuse during a game. It was a white coach who helped Kiran advance her career. It was a white man who gave Willie O'Ree his shot in the NHL.

Racism is often framed as an issue for racialized people to solve even though the solution has very little to do with how hard racialized people work, how talented they are, or who they know. As Toni Morrison (1985) declared: "The function, the very serious function of racism is distraction. It keeps you from doing your work. It keeps you explaining, over and over again, your reason for being. . . . None of this is necessary. There will always be one more thing."

"One more thing" is what keeps racialized folks docile and optimistic. Racialized people can absolutely help perpetuate systems of oppression and discrimination, but the responsibility of dismantling systemic racism is overwhelmingly a project for white allies. NBA player Kyle Korver recently penned an eloquent piece for *The Player's Tribune* addressing his white privilege acknowledging that: "No matter how passionately I commit to being an ally, and no matter how unwavering my support is for NBA and WNBA players of color . . . I'm still in this conversation from the privileged perspective of *opting in* to it. Which of course means that on the flip side, I could just as easily *opt out* of it. Every day, I'm given that choice—I'm granted that privilege—based on the color of my skin" (original emphasis, Korver, 2019).

Lack of racial discrimination represents a small part of white privilege. As Korver points out, it's also the privilege of not having to constantly think about one's race or the ability to avoid racism altogether if one chooses not to engage. The work of tearing down the walls created by racism have disproportionately fallen on the shoulders of racialized people, and it is time that there be a shift in labor.

We need to understand that racism isn't about an insult here or there, or one or two bigots sprinkled in various boardrooms. It is about how we organize our society in a way that benefits some to the detriment of others. And, from this society we create sporting systems that are part and parcel of those existing structures and logics. Systemic racism is the result of decisions that all of us make each and every day to either support inequitable systems or to actively resist them. Not being a racist, or not saying racist things, is not the same as being *anti-racist*. Until hockey culture adopts this perspective, hockey will not be for everyone.

Writing the Wrong

> Writing thru race stages the eruption of cultural difference, or "other" scenes within the liberal nation, without claiming the privilege to alone represent that scene. Writing thru race haunts the nation with its other which it cannot possess. Instead, the nation is possessed; history calls forth its debts otherwise.
> —Abdel-Shehid, 2000, p. 76

Hockey is the only sport where players change on the fly, which means that players can be substituted without a stoppage in play. This is one of the aspects of the game that makes hockey extremely dynamic because players must constantly adjust to new teammates, opponents, and conditions. Ironically, even though the game expects adaptability from its players, the institution seems to have a hard time adjusting to all the new players entering the game and letting go of the previous generations. History does not stop time for us to gather ourselves and re-assess; consequently, this anti-racism work must be done on the fly.

By giving voice to South Asian hockey players, parents, coaches, and broadcasters with regard to hockey in Canada, I have attempted to heed Abdel-Shehid's (2000) request to write "hockey thru race" (p. 76). By writing thru race we are able to think "beyond myth" and think about race, and in this case brown-ness, differently (Abdel-Shehid, 2000, p. 78). This study helps amplify the contributions of South Asian Canadians to the national culture and challenges the systemic dismissal of so-called bodies out of place.

It has been 20 years since Abdel-Shehid (2000) implored Canadians to write in all the Canadians who speak and live a different Canada, to counter the dominant narrative of "what this land is like, and who [lives] here" (p. 82); yet, both hockey and the academy have done very little to address this debt. Another way to understand writing thru race is through the words of Nigerian American author Teju Cole (2014): "Writing as writing. Writing as rioting. Writing as righting. On the best day, all three." Canadians have been called upon to write the wrong, and the response has been far too slow. This study is a small contribution toward a more inclusive national narrative; a narrative that welcomes multiple authors to the writing desk. It is an attempt to add some grit to the glossy veneer of Canadian multiculturalism.

No longer should marginalized citizens be content with the ability to participate; it is time we demand space on the ice, behind the bench, in the board rooms, and in the broadcasting booths to co-create Canada's game. Racism does not have to be part of the future narrative of hockey but, as I quoted Walter Beach in chapter 1, until racism is no longer accepted as a normal and expected experience for those marked as different, we have no choice but to draw attention to these practices of inequality. Hockey was never just a white man's game; it is time we restore hockey to its truly multicultural roots by telling a more complex story about hockey in Canada.

Appendix A

Qualitative Methodology

This project draws from the methodological frameworks of postcolonial feminism, critical race theory, and intersectionality to make sense of contemporary racism in Canada. A postcolonial perspective is necessary for Canadian scholarship because the nation was founded on colonization and the dispossession/exploitation of racialized persons. As Sara Ahmed (2000) explains in *Strange Encounters*, postcolonialism is

> about the complexity of the relationship between the past and the present, between the histories of European colonization and contemporary forms of globalization. That complexity cannot be reduced by either a notion that the present has broken from the past . . . or that the present is simply continuous with the past. . . . To this extent, post-coloniality allows us to investigate how colonial encounters are both determining, and yet not fully determining, of social and material existence. (p. 11)

A postcolonial lens highlights the fact that nations such as Canada are not so much *post*-colonial as they are struggling to reach de-colonization. At the heart of postcolonial analyses are questions about power, voice, and agency: Who gets to speak? Who listens? When do they listen? What makes this possible?

For Canada specifically, postcolonial analyses that "interrogate, decolonize, and [re-route]/[root]—the founding assumptions and practice of universal citizenship" helps to "[unsettle]" the story that we tell ourselves about our Canadian selves (Fleischmann, Van Styvendale, & McCarroll, 2011, p. xiv). Citizenship and postcolonialism are closely connected projects that work to alienate or assimilate, ostracize or equalize. As Canada recently celebrated its sesquicentennial birthday, many Canadians, led by Indigenous groups, wondered why we were celebrating "the beginning of an abusive relationship" (Canadian Press, 2017a)—a relationship that continues to this day. This study operates on the premise that Canada continues to feel the effects of colonization and that racialized Canadians are very much part of this ongoing history and relationship.

Critical race theory (CRT), as an ontological standpoint and a movement, foregrounds racism as an institutional system that is built into society and is intimately intertwined with other social relations; it normalizes racial hierarchy (Crenshaw, 2011). As such, CRT overtly challenges neoliberal beliefs such as individualism, meritocracy, and color-blindness (Gardiner & Welch, 2001; Nebeker, 1998). Evolving out of legal studies, it attempts to offer counter-narratives by racialized people as a form of resistance (and social justice) but also to re-center the logic of race and the processes of racialization as integral to how we govern and experience the cultures we inhabit (Hylton, 2009). Moving us away from ideas of incrementalism and linear progress, CRT challenges the foundations of liberalism (Delgado & Stefancic, 2001). Dr. Cornel West describes CRT as such:

> But like all bold attempts to reinterpret and remake the world to reveal silenced suffering and to relieve social misery, Critical Race Theorists, put forward novel readings of a hidden past that disclose the flagrant shortcomings of the treacherous present in the light of unrealized—though not unrealizable— possibilities for human freedom and equality. (As cited in Crenshaw, Gotanda, Peller, & Kendall, 1995, pp. xi—xii)

CRT, then, works to expose erasures and through this process provides an analysis of possibilities.

The downside to amplifying racialized voices, however, is that these "highly valued" (Hylton, 2009, p. 33) voices can become essentialized voices used to represent a universal experience. Or, as bell hooks (1990) warns, "voice" can be appropriated so that the original author is no longer needed to tell the story. With this in mind, Hylton (2009) writes, specifically regarding sport, that we should not view racialized voices as items to be collected in order to address a "deficit"; rather, "voice" becomes an "asset, a form of community memory and a source of empowerment and strength" (p. 5). The work of amplifying voices is not the end goal—it becomes the starting point of our work.

Similarly, intersectionality is also recognized as a starting point, "the point from which we must proceed if we are to offer an account of how power works" (Sara Ahmed, 2017, p. 5). McClintock (1995) argues that in order for one to understand colonialism and postcolonialism, one must acknowledge that issues of race, gender, and class are not experienced within distinct silos; they are, instead, constituted through tension and conflict with each other.

Introduced in the late 1980s (Crenshaw, 1989), intersectionality focuses "attention on the vexed dynamics of difference and the solidarities of sameness in the context of antidiscrimination and social movement politics" (S. Cho, Crenshaw, & McCall, 2013, p. 787). Adopting an intersectional stance enabled me to question (quite specifically) *which* men and *which* women are privileged and/or oppressed through Canadian hockey culture and under what circumstances certain identities come to the forefront. For example, notions of masculinities were important in chapter 5 as gender was observed to work in tandem with race when dealing with racism. And chapters 6 and 7 emphasized the intersection of class and race with respect to access to social capital and the acceptance of demonstrable wealth, respectively, by racialized Canadians.

Ultimately, this project was one of sense-making. It sought to make sense of the paradoxical relationship between South Asian interest/participation in hockey and the broader tensions directed toward racialized citizens in contemporary Canada; to make sense of the role that hockey may play in one's national belonging; and to make sense of the ways in which certain peoples come to be memorialized and represented in the national narrative while others are simply forgotten.

Participant Observation

Developed in the nineteenth century, ethnography involves long-term, time-consuming, intensive participation and observation of select people. The interpretive practice of ethnography represents part of the epistemological transition away from the empiricist tradition toward interpretive approaches that privilege the realm of the subject. Scholars such as Clifford (1988) and Geertz (1988) have adopted the interpretive turn with the epistemology that cultures are unique and each creates its own perspectives, morals, and values. Since the 1980s, however, ethnographic practices have changed from the interpretivist approach in a number of ways. First, rather than understanding cultures as monolithic and existing in silos, the interpretation of culture has become more contextual but still situated within a world nexus. Second, ethnographies tend to be more topic or issue centered instead of focusing on a group of people (Sands, 2002). Third, globalization has become a critical factor for ethnographers in the way that it has dissolved boundaries, transformed the movement of capital and people, contested national sovereignty, and renegotiated social structures. Thus, as Norman Denzin (1997) posits, the practice of ethnography has had to change because the world it intends to study has changed: "We do not own the field notes we make about those we study. We do not have an undisputed warrant to study anyone or anything. . . . The writer can no longer presume to be able to present an objective, noncontested account of the other's experiences. . . . Ethnography is a moral, allegorical, and therapeutic project. Ethnography is more than a record of human experience. The ethnography writes tiny moral tales" (pp. xii—xiv).

Ethnography adopted a critical turn by incorporating postcolonial approaches in an attempt to restructure the balance of power. Clifford (1988) suggests that even though the "new" ethnographic turn cannot fully escape the inherent dichotomy involved in writing about Others, ethnographers "can at least struggle self-consciously to avoid portraying abstract, ahistorical 'others'" (p. 23). In this way, ethnography represents a work of struggle—a struggle with authority, of plurality, and of de-colonization.

Clifford (1988) encourages ethnographic researchers to "quote regularly and at length from informants" as a way to "break up monophonic authority" (p. 50). With this in mind, I attempted to include narratives at length where pertinent and to let the participants' words carry the discussion as much as possible, but even trying to amplify voices with as much context and original text still faces the problem that "quotations are always staged by the quoter and tend to serve merely as examples or confirming testimonies" (Clifford, 1988, p. 50). In turn, it is always important to read participant data as partial and contextual.

"Ethnography is separated from other qualitative social science research methods by its emphasis on intensive, focused, and time-consuming participation and observation of the life of the people being studied" (Sands, 2002, p. 21); yet, sport has long been ignored as a viable means for exploring human behavior. The "ethnographic" portion of this study was used to complement interview data and media analyses. I use scare quotes around ethnographic because many factors limited the ability for this study to be a "true" ethnography. The nature of hockey and hockey teams makes it difficult to study any group as a collective. As Robidoux (2001) observed in his ethnographic research of an American Hockey League team, his presence in the locker room (even as a white male) was interpreted as espionage. Thus, for me to observe an entire hockey team but only amplify the experiences of one or two players would have made for an extremely unnatural environment. If "brown out" hockey spaces continue to grow, ethnographic studies of these groups could result in observations akin to Stanley Thangaraj's work on South Asian basketball leagues; however, these ethnically segregated spaces do not enable researchers to observe interactions with and among non–South Asian Canadians, which was really the purpose of this study—how does Canada interact with, respond to, and receive South Asians in hockey spaces?

As a result, my participant observations were fragmented in nature. I attended 10 local hockey games and four events where the *Hockey Night Punjabi* team publicly advertised their attendance. The hockey games I attended ranged from Atom to Junior B and university level with South Asian players on the roster. Counter to popular claims, I failed to witness any significant diversity at the minor hockey level.

The notion of a "participant–observer" carries with it a number of assumptions: (a) that cultural truths exist and are privileged through experience and participation, (b) these "truths" are discernible, (c) that the "Other" exists within clear boundaries (Alexander, 2004). Still, it is important to acknowledge that while I was observing those marked as "Other" at hockey rinks, I was simultaneously marked as "Other," illustrated by my field observation notes in chapter 3. S. Johal (2002) posits that when everyday experiences are aggregated into a "substantial body of isolated bits of evidence" (p. 231) the issue grows from one of individual concern into one that should be highlighted as a problem of society. In this way, ethnographic work is ideally suited for researching the "everydayness" of citizenship struggles. By using participant observation, I was able to provide a small glimpse into the interactions and experiences that occur around the nexus of race and Canadian hockey culture and unpack daily claims made by racialized bodies regarding citizenship and belonging. Scholars of race have been encouraged to adopt the perspective of the daily struggle, arguing that it is not in the extreme cases of hatred where we learn about racism because both race and racism are produced and reproduced in the routine everyday workings of life (Knowles, 2010). Citizenship becomes something that racialized citizens need to reclaim in daily interactions.

I attended four events where *Hockey Night Punjabi* publicly advertised its presence: Hometown Hockey–New Westminster 2016; Hometown Hockey–Vancouver January 2017 (2 days); the 2017 Vancouver Vaisakhi celebration—an annual event commemorating the New Year and the harvest season, especially significant to those who identify as Punjabi (Kang, 2002); and Hometown Hockey–Surrey December 2017 (2 days). At the Hometown Hockey event in 2016, the broadcast team was featured on television with Ron MacLean but had no designated autograph booth. I observed from afar watching South Asian families approach some of the commentators, shake hands, and engage in a casual conversation. I did not witness any non–South Asians approach the broadcast team. It was at this event that I first met the team, introduced myself, and informed them about my research. Even though it was raining, there were a number of South Asian families in attendance, with children running around in their New Westminster minor hockey association jerseys.

At the 2017 Hometown Hockey–Vancouver event, the broadcast team was invited to a private event in the Vancouver CBC building with Ron MacLean, but they had no formal role or station at the Hometown Hockey event. The *Hockey Night Punjabi* team was scheduled for Sunday, but I also attended Hometown Hockey on Saturday as a sort of "control test" to see if there would be noticeably more South Asians in attendance on Sunday. I was surprised that there was no observable difference in demographics between Saturday and Sunday. The most significant racialized group in attendance were East Asians. On Sunday, I explored the event with the broadcast team, gathering free merchandise and chatting about the progress of my project. I had expected more people to recognize the team in 2017 after the social media popularity that they experienced during the 2016 playoffs, but very few people recognized them. Again, there was no physical space for the broadcast team to station themselves.

At the Vancouver Vaisakhi festival the team had a station set up for fans to come find them and take photos. The OMNI television booth was handing out popcorn and corporate head scarves. The Vancouver Canucks had a booth set up next to the OMNI booth, but no players were sent to represent the organization. I watched as South Asian children took photos with the Canucks photo props and collected hockey cards. Many Sikh families came over to have their photos taken with the *Hockey Night Punjabi* team and have a brief chat.[1]

I witnessed the greatest integration of the *Hockey Night Punjabi* crew with "mainstream" hockey culture at the Hometown Hockey–Surrey event in December 2017. The Punjabi broadcast team was included on the official schedule with an autograph session, and their presence and work were heavily promoted by the Hometown Hockey social media accounts. They did not receive an official autograph booth and were somewhat hidden away in an indoor space, but they shot intermission segments with Randip Janda and Bhupinder Hundal on location during their own Saturday night broadcast, Hundal hosted the "hot stove" interview with Vancouver Canucks alumni Dave Babych and Kirk McLean (a job that has been reserved for Hometown Hockey host Tara Slone), and Singh, Hundal, and Janda were featured with Ron MacLean during the Sunday evening primetime broadcast. What was noticeably different from previous Hometown Hockey events was the diversity of fans who approached the broadcast team. Fans of every age, race, and gender approached the crew to take photos and ask them for autographs. They were recognized as local celebrities in their own right. Surrey easily drew the most diverse fan base of any Hometown Hockey event that I attended.

Unlike Burdsey's (2007) and Thangaraj's (2015) studies where they were able to complement their in-depth interviews with participant observations and "enjoy stories" through interaction (Burdsey, 2007, p. 6), my observations were strictly that—observational. Whenever I attended a hockey game or event, I carried with me an uneasy feeling of not belonging. Despite the fact that I eat, sleep, and breathe the game, these environments, while not overtly unwelcoming to an Asian woman in her 30s without a child in tow, are not exactly welcoming either. I kept my hockey blogging credential in my figurative back pocket just in case anyone asked what I was doing there, because explaining my research about racism in hockey felt wrong. Wrong in the sense that it would likely add to my outsider status or be outright dismissed as an attempt to stir up trouble.

My own apprehension around discussing the topic of my research and moving about in these spaces further animates the power of "Canadiansplaining" as a tool of dismissal and abjection. "We learn about materiality from such dismissals" (Sara Ahmed, 2017b, p. 6) and these experiences generate "sweaty concepts" (p. 12). Sweaty concepts can be explained as "one that comes out of a description of a body that is not at home in the world. . . . Sweat is bodily; we might sweat more during more strenuous and muscular activity. A sweaty concept might come out of a bodily experience that is trying" (Sara Ahmed, 2017, p. 13). Therefore, we sweat because we are uncomfortable and/or because we are putting effort into something that resists us. Hence, the struggle to name racism that developed during interviews was also evident in the participant observation portion. I also reflected that if I were a single male, without a child, carrying a camera, attending some of these events, I would probably draw a different kind of (suspicious) attention; however, white men can generally move in and out of hockey spaces largely without question and unnoticed.

Recruitment

I started by going through local rosters for various hockey teams to identify potential participants. I put out an open call to local associations through Twitter and, if potential participants had a public Twitter account, I invited them to participate and contact me via email. Six participants were recruited via Twitter. The majority of participants were contacted through mutual contacts (16) or coaches/associations (3). I also posted an open call for participants on The Hockey Community discussion boards and sent out an e-blast to the Burnaby 8 Rinks Adult Safe Hockey League (ASHL), all of which resulted in only one interview. I had originally envisioned the recruitment process to be a snowball sampling, with one participant offering the name of another potential participant. This happened on six occasions where I was successfully referred to another participant; however, because most of the participants never played with other South Asians, my sampling resulted in a very fragmented recruiting process. In total, 26 interviews were conducted between February 2016 and January 2017: five with members from the *Hockey Night Punjabi* broadcast, eight with hockey parents, and 14 with players, almost half of whom also have coached or currently coach (there was an overlap between hockey players and parents). Twenty-six interviews were deemed "sufficient" for this project because there were decreasing amounts of "new data" and individual narratives demonstrated repeated patterns of experience.

The Interview Schedule and Data Analysis

Semi-structured interviews were arranged for public locations and at the participants' convenience. They lasted anywhere from 30–90 minutes, largely dependent on how much detail each participant was willing to provide about their experiences and how many experiences they wanted to share. Each interview began by going over the consent form and asking if the participant(s) had any questions before we began. I then started by asking participants to introduce themselves and we would have a general discussion about their interest in hockey to ease the participant into more specific questions. Interviews were tape recorded and later transcribed. Participants had the option to review their transcripts, but none obliged. They were also informed that they could skip questions, return to questions, and/or retract statements/comments at any time during or after the interview.

All but five of the interviews were conducted one on one. Suki and Kulbir chose to be interviewed together as father and daughter, and Shane, Prav, and Ryan also chose to be interviewed as a small group. It was definitely more difficult to elicit individualized responses in a group setting; however, this is how these participants felt most comfortable discussing the subject matter. This group dynamic was also factored into the weight that I gave some of the responses, for example, if a participant merely stated that they agreed with a previous person's answer.

I transcribed all of the interviews using Google's Transcribe application. I then used Nvivo to help organize my inductive coding into nine emergent themes: difference, gatekeeping, hate speech/chirping, *Hockey Night in Canada/Punjabi*, hockey as a unifier, hurdles, joking about race, reluctance to name racism, and self-identification. The categories of "difference" and "hurdles" provided the largest data sets, with 113 and 106 references from 20 and 21 different participants, respectively.

Appendix B

Participant Information

Appendix B provides general demographic information about interview participants, excluding the *Hockey Night Punjabi* representatives.

Pseudonym	Age	Competition level	Self-identification
Ryan	16	Competitive	Canadian; Indian
Prav	20	Recreational	Canadian; Indian
Shane	20	Competitive	Canadian; Indian
Sunny	20	Elite	East Indian
Billy	20	Elite	East Indian
Suki	21	Elite	Canadian; Indian
Kiran	22	Elite	Canadian; Punjabi; Sikh
Amit	24	Recreational	Mainly Fijian
Gurp	25	Recreational	Brown
Brian	25	Elite	Hockey player; East Indian
Sonia	26	Competitive	Indian; South Asian; Punjabi
Dev	31	Recreational	East Indian
Gary	39	Recreational	Canadian; East Indian
Sara	Early 40s	Recreational	Canadian; South Asian; Indo Canadian
Randy	43	Competitive	East Indian
Kevin	46	Competitive	Canadian; Sikh; Punjabi
Greg	47	Competitive	Human being
Raj	50	Elite	East Indian; Indian
Harry	52	Competitive	
Kari	56	Competitive	
Kulbir	50s	Elite	Canadian; Punjabi; Indo Canadian

NOTE: *Elite* designation includes professional, semi-professional, minor pro (AHL, Europe, ECHL, UHL, CHL, WPHL), NCAA Division I, Major Junior (QMHJL, OHL, WHL, USHL); Women's (or Girls) AAA, AA, CIS, NCAA. *Competitive* designation includes Rep AAA, AA, or A. *Recreational* designation includes house leagues or introductory organized hockey.

Appendix C

British Columbia Competitive Hockey Structure

Category	Age	Alternative name	Notes
Hockey 1 & 2	5–6	Initiation/Mini Mite	
Hockey 3 & 4	7–8	Novice/Mite	
Atom	9–10	Squirt	Start of rep system for top players AAA, AA, A, or B rep teams.
Peewee	11–12		
Bantam	13–14		Second-year bantam players are eligible for Major Junior drafts.
Midget	15–17	Minor Midget	
Major Midget	15–17	Midget AAA	
Juvenile	18–20		
Junior B	16–20	Junior AA/ Tier III	Considered feeder system for Junior A and sometimes for Major Junior Leagues (WHL, OHL, QMJHL).
Junior A	16–20	Junior AAA/ Tier II	One level below CHL. Also feeds American and Canadian university systems.
Major Junior	N/A	Tier I	Highest level of junior hockey: WHL, OHL, QMJHL. Most popular route for those attempting to make the NHL.

Acknowledgments

First, I would like to acknowledge that my work is made possible by the Black, Indigenous, and racialized scholars and activists who are cited in these pages. Thank you for forging a path where others may follow.

To my supervising committee of Richard Gruneau, Katherine Reilly, and Wendy Chan, thank you for your insights, mentorship, and guidance. It was a privilege to work with and learn from each of you. Also thank you to Ann Travers, David J. Leonard, Douglas Hartmann, Aarti Ratna, and Stanley Thangaraj for your support, feedback, and positivity through various stages of the publishing process.

I am forever indebted to my "brain trust" for their unwavering support and friendship: Brett Pardy, Vincci Li, Layla Cameron, Nicolien van Luijk, Sarah Gray, Lyndsay Hayhurst, Mark Norman, Kyoung-yim Kim, and Estee Fresco.

Thank you to my friends and family, who don't always understand what I am working on but support me regardless.

Funding for this project has been generously provided by the Social Sciences and Humanities Research Council (SSHRC), Sport Canada, the Dr. Hari Sharma Foundation for South Asian Advancement, and the Simons Foundation.

Notes

Introduction

1 Drawing from Kimberle Crenshaw's (1991) interpretation of Black as a cultural group, I capitalize minoritized group names such as Black, Asian, and Indigenous, whereas white will not be capitalized because "whites do not constitute a specific cultural group" (p. 1244). Similarly, brown will not be capitalized because it refers to various cultural groups that are distinct but share similarities within the white imagination. The idea of a brown identity is still being negotiated by its members.

2 Indigenous Peoples is an all-encompassing term for the Aboriginal groups in Canada and references their international legal rights under the United Nations Declaration on the Rights of Indigenous Peoples. The Aboriginal groups in Canada include the First Nations, Inuit, and Métis.

3 The Punjabi Sikh demographic represents the starting point for analysis because of Breakaway and HNIC Punjabi; however, given the heterogeneity and fluidity of ethnicity, race, and the geographical region of South Asia, this project is not limited to analysis of the Punjabi Sikh voices or experiences.

Chapter 1   Myth Busting

1 Latinx is increasingly being used in academic literature as the gender-inclusive term (Monzó, 2016).

2 Canadian women are also ensconced in this imagined way of life because the achievements of women hockey players are constantly compared to those of the men (HappyCaraT, 2016); and, despite the two-decade dominance of the Canadian Women's Olympic team, the NHL remains the benchmark of success. There is no equivalent concept of "good ol' Canadian girls," except to adhere to the values established for men.

3 South Asians and West Asians (Iranian, Armenian, Afghans, and Turkish) are grouped geographically by Statistics Canada, whereas Filipinos, Chinese, Japanese, and Koreans are delineated as individual groups.

Chapter 2   Narratives from the Screen

1   *La Soiree du Hockey*, the French sister broadcast to HNIC ran from 1937–2004.
2   On March 24, 2019, Sportsnet and the Indigenous broadcaster APTN aired an NHL game in Cree for the first time ever (Sportsnet, 2019).
3   Don Cherry was fired on November 11, 2019, after an on-air rant that suggested racialized immigrants disrespect military veterans and Canadian traditions by not wearing poppies, a symbol of remembrance in Canada (Allen, 2019).

Chapter 4   Racist Taunts or Just Chirping?

1   As an example, the Malaysian soccer team was recently fined US$30,000 by the Asian Football Confederation when Malaysian fans chanted "Brunei dogs should just be killed" at the Singapore/Brunei team (Nair, 2017).

Chapter 5   South Asian Masculinities and Femininities

1   Shinny is a colloquial term used for pick-up hockey. It often requires far less protective equipment than is required by organized hockey.

Chapter 6   Hockey Hurdles and Resilient Subjects

1   As an example, the 2017 tryout fee for the Langley Rivermen, a Junior A team in the BCHL, was $175 per player.
2   Powerskating is a term used for on-ice training that focuses on stickhandling, skating technique, and conditioning. It is distinct from regular team practices.
3   Demarcated as anyone listed with "coach" in their official title, including strength and conditioning coaches.
4   Racialization of gatekeepers determined by surnames, team photos, and publicly available self-identification information.
5   Determined from the public information made available by each 2016–2017 team.

Chapter 7   Racialized Money and White Fragility

1   The Immigrant Investor Program ended in 2014.
2   Temporary housing provided for players, usually within a local family's home.
3   In 2014, the *National Post* published a piece detailing how British Columbians have found race-based housing covenants from the 1940s that explicitly prohibited housing sales to "Asiatics" (the practice was ended in 1955; Hopper, 2014). Even as recent as the 1990s, there is evidence of rental agreements stating that no renters shall be of "negro or oriental blood or extraction" (Hopper, 2014, para. 10).

Chapter 8   Taking Stock

1   For example, the Greeks had an affinity for creating inventories of the best in particular fields, including statues for Olympic victors in PanHellenic athletic contests (Gruneau, 2017). According to Geiger (2008), a major difference, however, was that the *Forum Augustum* was curated to guide spectators through in a particular path but also to encourage visitors "to arrive at specific conclusions" (p. 19).

2 Princeps is the head of state under the Roman Empire.

3 Angela James, dubbed the "Wayne Gretzky" of women's hockey, is a biracial Canadian woman and was the first to be inducted into the HHOF in 2010, along with American Cammi Granato. Geraldine Heaney (CAN) was inducted in 2013, Angela Ruggiero (USA) in 2015, and Jayna Hefford (CAN) in 2018. Grant Fuhr (biracial), Brian Trottier (Metis), and Willie O'Ree are the only racialized men in the HHOF.

4 Cassie Campbell-Pascal was added to the selection committee in 2018 as the youngest member at 46 years old and is the only woman. Luc Robitaille is currently the youngest male member on the Selection Committee at 53 years old. James (Jim) Gregory (83) is the oldest member.

5 The broadcast hired Mantar Bhandal, a 21-year-old South Asian broadcasting graduate from the British Columbia Institute of Technology at the start of the 2017–2018 season. This hire was significantly dictated by the competitive advantage that *Hockey Night Punjabi* can provide to young South Asian broadcasters.

6 Exhibit sponsored by Rogers, Cross Connect Media, and Simon Fraser University's School of Communication. The Vancouver Canucks, OMNI TV, and Sportsnet also represent community partnerships.

Appendix A

1 I was not at the Surrey Vaisakhi festival the following weekend, but I was told by the broadcast team that so many South Asian fans wanted to take photos with the Canucks' mascot, Fin, that they had to hide him for a break and provide him with some food and water. It was supposedly the first time that there seemed like no end in sight of fans wanting to meet the mascot. This is an example of the South Asian hockey fandom that exists in the Lower Mainland.

References

Abdel-Shehid, G. (2000). Writing hockey thru race: Rethinking Black hockey in Canada. In R. Walcott (Ed.), *Rude: Contemporary Black Canadian cultural criticism* (pp. 70–86). Toronto, Canada: Insomniac.

Abdel-Shehid, G., & Kalman-Lamb, N. (2015). Multiculturalism, gender and *Bend It Like Beckham*. *Social Inclusion, 3*(3), 142–152. https://doi.org/10.17645/si.v3i3.135

Abraham, N., & Shryock, A. (2000). *Arab Detroit: From margin to mainstream.* Detroit, MI: Wayne State University Press.

Abu-Laban, Y. (1998). Keeping 'em out: Gender, race, and class biases in Canadian immigration policy. In V. Strong-Boag, S. Grace, A. Eisenberg, & J. Anderson (Eds.), *Painting the maple: Essays on race, gender, and the construction of Canada* (pp. 69–82). Vancouver, Canada: UBC Press.

Adams, C. (2008). "Queens of the Ice Lanes": The Preston Rivulettes and women's hockey in Canada, 1931–1940. *Sport History Review, 38*, 1–29. https://doi.org/10.1123/shr.39.1.1

———. (2014). Troubling bodies: "The Canadian girl," the ice rink, and the Banff winter carnival. *Journal of Canadian Studies; Toronto, 48*(3), 200–223. https://doi.org/10.3138/jcs.48.3.200

Adams, M. L. (2006). The game of whose lives? Gender, race, and entitlement in Canada's "national" game. In D. Whitson & R. Gruneau (Eds.), *Artificial ice: Hockey, culture, and commerce* (pp. 71–84). Toronto, Canada: Broadview Press.

Agergaard, S., & Sørensen, J. K. (2009). The dream of social mobility: Ethnic minority players in Danish football clubs. *Soccer & Society, 10*(6), 766–780. https://doi.org/10.1080/14660970903239966

Agrawal, S. K., & Lovell, A. (2010). High-income Indian immigrants in Canada. *South Asian Diaspora, 2*(2), 143–163. https://doi.org/10.1080/19438192.2010.491295

Ahluwalia, M. K., & Pellettiere, L. (2010). Sikh men post-9/11: Misidentification, discrimination and coping. *Asian American Journal of Psychology, 1*(4), 303–314. http://dx.doi.org/10.1037/a0022156

Ahluwalia, M. K., & Zaman, N. K. (2009). Counseling Muslims and Sikhs in a Post-9/11 world. In J. G. Ponterotto, M. Casas, L. A. Suzuki, & C. Alexander (Eds.), *Handbook of multicultural counseling* (3rd ed., pp. 467–478). Thousand Oaks, CA: Sage.

Ahmad, M. (2011). Homeland insecurities: Racial violence the day after September 11. *Race/Ethnicity: Multidisciplinary Global Contexts, 4*(3), 337–350.

Ahmed, S. [Sara] (2000). *Strange encounters: Embodied Others in post-coloniality.* London, UK & New York, NY: Routledge.

———. (2012). *On being included.* Durham, NC & London, UK: Duke University Press.

———. (2016, July 12). Evidence. *Feminist Killjoys.* Retrieved from https://feministkilljoys.com/2016/07/12/evidence/Ahmed, S. [Sara] (2017). *Living a feminist life.* Durham, NC: Duke University Press.

Ahmed, S. [Shireen] (2017, February 17). I never thought the U.S. president would have an impact on my daughter's ability to play soccer. *Today's Parent.* Retrieved from http://www.todaysparent.com/blogs/on-our-minds/i-never-thought-the-u-s-president-would-have-an-impact-on-my-daughters-ability-to-play-soccer/

Aldama, F. L. (2005). *Brown on brown: Chicano/a representations of gender, sexuality, and ethnicity.* Austin: University of Texas Press.

Alexander, C. (2004). Writing race: Ethnography and the imagination of the Asian gang. In M. Bulmer & J. Solomos (Eds.), *Researching race and racism* (pp. 134–149). London, UK: Routledge.

Allain, K. (2010). Kid Crosby or golden boy: Sidney Crosby, Canadian national identity, and the policing of hockey masculinity. *International Review for the Sociology of Sport, 46*(1), 3–22. https://doi.org/10.1177/1012690210376294

———. (2015). "A good Canadian boy": Crisis masculinity, Canadian national identity, and nostalgic longings in Don Cherry's Coach's Corner. *International Journal of Canadian Studies, 52,* 107–132. https://doi.org/10.3138/ijcs.52.107

———. (2016). "The mad Russian": Representations of Alexander Ovechkin and the creation of Canadian national identity. *Sociology of Sport Journal, 33*(2), 156–168. https://doi.org/http://dx.doi.org/10.1123/ssj.2015-0082

Allen, K. (2019, November 11). Hockey Night in Canada analyst Don Cherry fired after making racist comment on air. *USA Today.* Retrieved from https://www.usatoday.com/story/sports/nhl/2019/11/11/don-cherry-fired-racist-anti-immigrant-comment/2566800001/

Al-Solaylee, K. (2016). *Brown: What being brown in the world means today (to everyone).* Toronto, Canada: Harper Collins.

Aly. (2017, January 10). You can't sit with us: The importance of minority-only safe spaces. *Affinity.* Retrieved from http://affinitymagazine.us/2017/01/10/you-cant-sit-with-us-the-importance-of-minority-only-safe-spaces/

Anderson, B. (1983). *Imagined communities: Reflections on the origin and spread of nationalism.* London, UK: Verso.

Andone, D. (2018, December 23). A varsity wrestler was told to cut his dreadlocks or forfeit the match. Now the attorney general is investigating. *CNN.* Retrieved from https://www.cnn.com/2018/12/22/us/wrestler-dreadlocks-new-jersey-investigation/index.html

Andrew-Gee, E. (2015, March 14). 19th-century Toronto Irish immigrants a lesson in upward mobility. *Toronto Star.* Retrieved from https://www.thestar.com/news/gta/2015/03/14/19th-century-toronto-irish-immigrants-a-lesson-in-upward-mobility.html

Arat-Koc, S. (2010). New whiteness(es), beyond the colour line? Assessing the contradictions and complexities of "whiteness" in the (geo)political economy of capitalist globalism. In S. Razack, S. Thobani, & M. Smith (Eds.), *States of race:*

Critical race feminism for the 21st century (pp. 147–168). Toronto, Canada: Between the Lines.

ASHL. (2016). *Adult Safe Hockey League 2016–17 rule book*. Retrieved from http://ashl.adultrechockey.ca/files/ASHL_Rulebook1617_Final_ENG.pdf

Avelar, I., & Dunn, C. (2011). *Brazilian popular music and citizenship*. Durham, NC: Duke University Press. Retrieved from http://public.eblib.com/choice /publicfullrecord.aspx?p=1172252

Bahdi, R. (2003). No exit: Racial profiling and Canada's war against terrorism. *Osgood Hall Law Journal, 41*(2/3), 293–317.

Baird, M., & Major, M. (2013, July 1). Did Serena Williams's angry outburst really threaten the entire game of tennis? *Vanity Fair*. Retrieved from http://www .vanityfair.com/news/daily-news/2013/07/angry-outburst-tennis-serena-williams

Baker, S. (2016). Do-it-yourself institutions of popular music heritage: The preservation of music's material past in community archives, museums and halls of fame. *Archives and Records, 37*(2), 170–187. https://doi.org/10.1080/23257962.2015.1106933

Bannerji, H. (1997). Geography lessons: On being an insider/outsider to the Canadian nation. In L. Roman & L. Eyre (Eds.), *Dangerous territories: Struggles for difference and equality in education*. London, UK & New York, NY: Routledge.

Barnett, H. L., Keel, P. K., & Conoscenti, L. M. (2001). Body type preferences in Asian and Caucasian college Students. *Sex Roles, 45*(11–12), 867–878. https://doi .org/10.1023/A:1015600705749

Barthes, R. (1972). *Mythologies*. New York: Editions du Seuil.

———. (2007). *What is sport?* New Haven, CT, and London, UK: Yale University Press.

Barton, D., Hamilton, M., & Ivanic, R. (2005). *Situated literacies: Theorising reading and writing in context*. New York, NY: Routledge.

Basran, G. S., & Bolaria, B. S. (2003). *The Sikhs in Canada: Migration, race, class, and gender*. New Delhi, India: Oxford University Press.

Bathe, C. (2016, May 26). The most exciting goal calls of the Stanley Cup playoffs aren't in English or French. *Fox News*. Retrieved from http://www.foxsports.com /nhl/story/hockey-night-punjabi-stanley-cup-final-penguins-sharks-san-jose-nhl -tampa-bay-canada-052616

Baudrillard, J. (1994). *Simulacra and simulation*. Ann Arbor: University of Michigan Press.

Beeby, D. (2010, November 29). Massive failure rates follow new, tougher Canadian citizenship tests. *Toronto Star*. Retrieved from https://www.thestar.com/news /canada/2010/11/29/massive_failure_rates_follow_new_tougher_canadian _citizenship_tests.html

Benjamin, J. (2015, July 13). Three years later, Linsanity is officially dead. *Forbes*. Retrieved from http://www.forbes.com/sites/joshbenjamin/2015/07/13/three-years -later-linsanity-is-officially-dead/

Bennett, P. W. (2018). Re-imagining the creation: Popular mythology, the Mi'kmaq, and the origins of Canadian hockey. In J. Ellison & J. Anderson (Eds.), *Hockey: Challenging Canada's game* (pp. 45–60). Ottawa, ON: Canadian Museum of History and the University of Ottawa Press.

Berg, C. (1951). *The unconscious significance of hair*. London, UK: Allen and Unwin.

Bhavnani, K. K. (1993). Tracing the contours. *Women's Studies International Forum, 16*(2), 95–104. https://doi.org/10.1016/0277-5395(93)90001-P

Bissinger, H. G. (1990). *Fight night lights*. Reading, MA: Addison-Wesley.

Bissoondath, N. (1994). *Selling illusions: The cult of multiculturalism in Canada.* Toronto, Canada: Penguin Books.

Boei, W. (2009, January 23). Just what constitutes the "lower mainland?" *Vancouver Sun.* Retrieved from http://www.vancouversun.com/Just+what+constitutes+Lower+Mainland/1207993/story.html

Boele van Hensbroek, P. (2012). Cultural citizenship as a normative notion for activist practices. In J. Vega & P. Boele van Hensbroek (Eds.), *Cultural citizenship in political theory* (pp. 73–86). New York, NY: Routledge.

Bohaker, H., & Iacovetta, F. (2009). Making Aboriginal people "immigrants too": A comparison of citizenship programs for newcomers and Indigenous peoples in postwar Canada, 1940s–1960s. *The Canadian Historical Review, 90*(3), 427–461. https://doi.org/10.3138/chr.90.3.427

Bonilla-Silva, E. (2017). *Racism without racists: Color-blind racism and the persistence of racial inequality in America.* Lanham, MD: Rowman & Littlefield.

Bonnett, A. (2004). *The idea of the West: Culture, politics, and history.* New York, NY: Palgrave Macmillan.

Bourdieu, P. (1984). *Distinction: A social critique of the judgement of taste.* Cambridge, MA: Harvard University Press.

———. (1986). The forms of capital. In J. G. Richardson (Ed.), *Handbook of theory and research for the sociology of education* (pp. 241–258). New York, NY: Greenwood.

———. (1990). *The logic of practice.* Cambridge, MA: Polity.

Bourdieu, P., & Wacquant, L. (2002). *An invitation to reflexive sociology.* Chicago, IL: University of Chicago Press.

Boyer, P., Cardinal, L., & Headon, D. J. (2004). *From subjects to citizens: A hundred years of citizenship in Australia and Canada.* Ottawa, Canada: University of Ottawa Press.

Brah, A. (1996). *Cartographies of diaspora: Contesting identities.* London, UK: Routledge.

Bramadat, P., & Seljak, D. (2009). *Religion and ethnicity in Canada.* Toronto, Canada: University of Toronto Press.

Brittain, I., Ramshaw, G., & Gammon, S. (2013). The marginalisation of paralympic heritage. *International Journal of Heritage Studies, 19*(2), 171–185. https://doi.org/10.1080/13527258.2012.681679

Bromberger, C. (2008). Hair: From the West to the Middle East through the Mediterranean. *The Journal of American Folklore, 121*(482), 379–399. doi:10.2307/20487626

Brown, A. (2002). Performing "truth": Black speech acts. *African American Review, 36*(2), 213–225. https://doi.org/10.2307/1512256

Bruemmer, R. (2019, February 27). League apologizes for racist taunts directed at hockey player, family. *Montreal Gazette.* Retrieved from https://montrealgazette.com/news/local-news/league-apologizes-for-racist-taunts-directed-at-hockey-player-family

Burdsey, D. (2007). *British Asians and football: Culture, identity, exclusion.* London, UK: Routledge.

Burnaby Winter Club. (n.d.). *Burnaby Winter Club Hockey Academy information package.* Retrieved from http://assets.ngin.com/attachments/document/0110/4887/BWC_Hockey_Academy_Info_Package_15-16_Final.pdf

Butler, J. (1988). Performative acts and gender constitution: An essay in phenomenology and feminist theory. *Theatre Journal, 40*(4), 519–531. doi:10.2307/3207893

Campbell, K. (2012, June 26). Choosing Mats Sundin over Brendan Shanahan makes little sense. *The Hockey News*. Retrieved from http://www.thehockeynews.com/news/article/choosing-mats-sundin-over-brendan-shanahan-makes-little-sense

———. (2017, February 19). Have agents gone too far in chasing pre-teen hockey prospects? *The Hockey News*. Retrieved from http://www.thehockeynews.com/news/article/have-agents-gone-too-far-in-chasing-pre-teen-hockey-prospects

Canadian Press. (2013a, November 26). CBC loses control of "Hockey Night in Canada" to Rogers in blockbuster deal. *The Hockey News*. Retrieved from http://www.thehockeynews.com/news/article/cbc-loses-control-of-hockey-night-in-canada-to-rogers-in-blockbuster-deal

———. (2017a, June 13). Many Indigenous people see little reason to celebrate Canada's 150th birthday. *Toronto Star*. Retrieved from https://www.thestar.com/news/canada/2017/06/13/many-indigenous-people-see-little-reason-to-celebrate-canadas-150th-birthday.html

———. (2017b, October 28). Justin Trudeau says few symbols bring Canada together like Stanley Cup. *CBC*. Retrieved from http://www.cbc.ca/sports/hockey/nhl/justin-trudeau-stanley-cup-monument-ottawa-unveiling-1.4377294

Canessa, A. (2007). Who is Indigenous? Self-identification, indigeneity, and claims to justice in contemporary Bolivia. *Urban Anthropology and Studies of Cultural Systems and World Economic Development*, *36*(3), 195–237. https://www.jstor.org/stable/40553604

Caplan, G. (2010, July 23). Honour killings in Canada: Even worse than we believe. *Globe and Mail*. Retrieved from https://www.theglobeandmail.com/news/politics/second-reading/honour-killings-in-canada-even-worse-than-we-believe/article1314263/

Carleton, R. A., & Morrison, K. (2016, November 22). MLB's ongoing search for front office diversity. *Baseball Prospectus*. Retrieved from http://www.baseballprospectus.com/article.php?articleid=30742

Carnegie, H. (1997). *A fly in a pail of milk: The Herb Carnegie story*. Oakville, Canada: Mosaic Press.

Carpenter, L. (2016, September 15). Jaime Jarrín: The remarkable story of the Latino Vin Scully. *The Guardian*. Retrieved from http://www.theguardian.com/sport/2016/sep/15/jaime-jarrin-los-angeles-dodgers-announcer-vin-scully

Carrington, B. (2008). "What's the footballer doing here?" Racialized performativity, reflexivity, and identity. *Cultural Studies ↔ Critical Methodologies*, *8*(4), 423–452. https://doi.org/10.1177/1532708608321574

———. (2010). *Race, sport and politics: The sporting black diaspora*. Thousand Oaks, CA: Sage.

CBC. (2013, February 20). An ugly message: Gurdeep Ahluwalia and Nabil Karim targeted by racist tweets while hosting 'SportsCentre.' *CBC*. Retrieved from http://www.cbc.ca/strombo/news/an-ugly-message-gurdeep-ahluwalia-and-nabil-karim-targeted-by-racist-tweets

———. (2017, May 11). The turban that rocked the RCMP: How Balteg Singh Dhillon challenged the RCMP—and won. Retrieved from https://www.cbc.ca/2017/canadathestoryofus/the-turban-that-rocked-the-rcmp-how-baltej-singh-dhillon-challenged-the-rcmp-and-won-1.4110271

CBC News. (2019, February 26). Quebec hockey player and his family taunted by racist fans. Retrieved from https://www.cbc.ca/news/canada/montreal/quebec-hockey-player-and-his-family-taunted-by-racist-fans-1.5034645

CBS Pittsburgh. (2016, June 17). Hockey Night Punjabi crew truly appreciative of reception from Pens fans. *CBS*. Retrieved from http://pittsburgh.cbslocal.com/2016 /06/17/hockey-night-punjabi-crew-truly-appreciative-of-reception-from-pens-fans/

CBC Sports. (2008, December 2). BC Hockey allows religious exemption from helmet policy for coaches. Retrieved from https://www.cbc.ca/sports/hockey/bc-hockey -allows-religious-exemption-from-helmet-policy-for-coaches-1.722590

Cheng, H. (2014). Disordered eating among Asian/Asian American women: Racial and cultural factors as correlates. *Counseling Psychologist, 42*, 821–851. https://doi .org/10.1177/0011000014535472

Cheng, H., McDermott, R. C., Wong, Y. J., & La, S. (2016). Drive for muscularity in Asian American men: Sociocultural and racial/ethnic factors as correlates. *Psychology of Men & Masculinity, 17*(3), 215–227. https://doi.org/10.1037 /men0000019

Chicago Blackhawks. (2016, September 21). Blackhawks to broadcast 14 games on Univision Chicago. *NHL*. Retrieved from https://www.nhl.com/blackhawks /news/univision-to-broadcast-14-games/c-282009998

Chidgey, R. (2014). Developing communities of resistance? Maker pedagogies, do-it-yourself feminism, and DIY citizenship. In M. Ratto & M. Boler (Eds.), *DIY citizenship: Critical making and social media* (pp. 101–113). Cambridge, MA: MIT Press.

Cho, L. (2011). Affecting citizenship: The materiality of melancholia. In A. Fleischmann, N. Van Styvendale, & C. McCarroll (Eds.), *Narratives of citizenship: Indigenous and diasporic peoples unsettled* (pp. 107–128). Edmonton, Canada: University of Alberta Press.

Cho, S., Crenshaw, K. W., & McCall, L. (2013). Toward a field of intersectionality studies: Theory, applications, and praxis. *Signs, 38*(4), 785–810. https://doi.org/10 .1086/669608

Chou, R. S., & Feagin, J. R. (2015). *The myth of the model minority: Asian Americans facing racism*. Boulder, CO: Paradigm Publishers.

Chunn, D. E., Menzies, R. J., & Adamoski, R. L. (2002). *Contesting Canadian citizenship: Historical readings*. Toronto, Canada: Broadview Press.

Citizenship and Immigration Canada. (2012). *Discover Canada: The rights and responsibilities of citizenship*. Retrieved from http://www.cic.gc.ca/english/pdf/pub /discover.pdf

City of Surrey. (n.d.). Culture days in Surrey. Retrieved from http://www.surrey.ca /culture-recreation/12290.aspx

Clifford, J. (1988). *The predicament of culture: Twentieth-century ethnography, literature, and art*. Cambridge, MA: Harvard University Press.

Coakley, J., & White, A. (1992). Making decisions: Gender and sport participation among British adolescents. *Sociology of Sport Journal, 9*(1), 20–35. https://doi.org/10 .1123/ssj.9.1.20

Cole, C. (2015, December 19). An illness, possibly untreatable: Hockey in Canada has become terrifyingly expensive and dangerously elitist. *National Post*. Retrieved from http://news.nationalpost.com/sports/nhl/an-illness-possibly-untreatable -hockey-in-canada-has-become-terrifyingly-expensive-and-dangerously-elitist

Cole, T. (2014, April 11). Twitter post. Retrieved from https://twitter.com/tejucole /status/454646310994710528?lang=en

Colour Code Episode 4: "The angel complex." (2016). *Globe and Mail*. Retrieved from https://www.youtube.com/watch?v=quyHGHA2HeI

Conn, V. S., Chan, K., Banks, J., Ruppar, T. M., & Scharff, J. (2014). Cultural relevance of physical activity intervention research with underrepresented populations. *International Quarterly of Community Health Education, 34*(4), 391–414. https://doi.org/10.2190/IQ.34.4.g

Cooky, C. (2009). "Girls just aren't interested": The social construction of interest in girls' sport. *Sociological Perspective, 52*(2), 259–284. https://doi.org/10.1525/sop.2009.52.2.259

Coombes, A. E. (2003). *History after Apartheid: Visual culture and public memory in a Democratic South Africa.* Durham, NC & London, UK: Duke University Press.

Crenshaw, K. W. (1989). Demarginalizing the intersection of race and sex: A black feminist critique of antidiscrimination doctrine, feminist theory and antiracist politics. *University of Chicago Legal Forum*, 139–167.

———. (1991). Mapping the margins: Intersectionality, identity politics, and violence against women of color. *Stanford Law Review, 43*(6), 1241–1299.

———. (2011). Twenty years of critical race theory: Looking back to move forward. *Connecticut Law Review, 43*(5), 1253–1352.

Crenshaw, K., Gotanda, N., Peller, G., & Kendall, T. (1995). *Critical race theory: The key writings that formed the movement.* New York, NY: The New Press.

Daigle, C. (2016, September 5). Unlearning anti-Black racism 101: Stop Canadians-plaining. *Rabble.* Retrieved from http://rabble.ca/blogs/bloggers/views-expressed /2016/09/unlearning-anti-black-racism-101-stop-canadiansplaining

Danielsen, H., Jegerstedt, K., Muriaas, R. L., & Ytre-Arne, B. (2016). Gendered citizenship: The politics of recognition. In H. Danielsen, K. Jegerstedt, R. L. Muriaas & B. Ytre-Arne (Eds.), *Gendered citizenship and the politics of representation* (pp. 1–13). London, UK: Palgrave Macmillan.

de la Cretaz, B. (2018, August 31). The troubling reluctance of women's ice hockey to combat prejudice. *The Guardian.* Retrieved from https://www.theguardian.com /sport/2018/aug/31/womens-hockey-minnesota-whitecaps

De Fina, A. (2007). Code switching and ethnicity in a community of practice. *Language in Society, 36*(3), 371–392. https://doi.org/http://dx.doi.org/10.1017 /S0047404507070182

De Leeuw, S. (2017). Intimate colonialisms: The material and experiences places of British Columbia's residential schools. *The Canadian Geographer, 51*(3), 339–359. https://doi.org/10.1111/j.1541-0064.2007.00183.x

Delgado, R., & Stefancic, J. (2001). *Critical race theory: An introduction.* New York, NY: NYU Press.

Delta Hockey Academy. (2016, February 3). Fees and transportation. Retrieved from https://deltahockeyacademy.com/feestransportation/

Denis, C. (1997). *We are not you: First Nations and Canadian modernity.* Peterborough, Canada: Broadview Press.

Denzin, N. (1997). *Interpretive ethnography: Ethnographic practice for the 21st century.* London, UK: Sage.

Dhinga, P. (2016). Indian Americans and the "brain sport" of spelling bees. In S. I. Thangaraj, C. R. Arnaldo Jr., & C. B. Chin (Eds.), *Asian American sports cultures* (pp. 127–151). New York, NY and London, UK: New York University Press.

Diaby, J. (2019, March 2). It's 1920 in Saint-Jérôme, Que. *CBC News.* Retrieved from https://www.cbc.ca/news/canada/montreal/jonathan-diaby-hockey-player-racism -1.5039698

DiAngelo, R. (2011). White fragility. *International Journal of Critical Pedagogy, 3*(3), 54–70.

DiAngelo, R. J. (2016). *What does it mean to be white?: Developing white racial literacy*. New York, NY: Peter Lang.

DiCarlo, D. (2016). Playing like a girl? The negotiation of gender and sexual identity among female ice hockey athletes on male teams. *Sport in Society, 19*(8–9), 1363–1373. https://doi.org/10.1080/17430437.2015.1096260

Dimanno, R. (2010, March 14). Can't Canada just leave hockey alone? *Toronto Star*. Retrieved from https://www.thestar.com/news/insight/2010/03/14/cant_canada _just_leave_hockey_alone.html

Dixon, N. (2007). Trash talking, respect for opponents and good competition. *Sport, Ethics and Philosophy, 1*(1), 96–106. https://doi.org/10.1080/1751132060 1143025

Doherty, A., & Taylor, T. (2007). Sport and physical recreation in the settlement of immigrant youth. *Leisure/Loisir, 31*(1), 27–55. https://doi.org/10.1080/14927713 .2007.9651372

Donnelly, P., & Kidd, B. (2015). Two solitudes: Grass-roots sport and high-performance sport in Canada. In R. Bailey & M. Talbot (Eds.), *Elite sport and sport-for-all: Bridging the two cultures?* (pp. 57–71). London, UK & New York, NY: Routledge.

Dormer, D. (2016, November 30). Sikh play-by-play announcer makes English debut in NHL broadcast tonight. *CBC*. Retrieved from http://www.cbc.ca/news/canada /calgary/harnarayan-singh-english-punjabi-nhl-commentator-1.3875319

Douglas, D. D. (2002). To be young, gifted, black and female: A meditation on the cultural politics at play in representations of Venus and Serena Williams. *Sociology of Sport Online, 5*(2), 1–16.

———. (2005). Venus, Serena, and the Women's Tennis Association: When and where "race" enters. *Sociology of Sport Journal, 22*(3), 255–281. https://doi.org/10.1123/ssj.22 .3.255

Dowbiggin, B. (2013, March 15). Racist tweets about TSN hosts reveal Canada's nasty side. *Globe and Mail*. Retrieved from https://www.theglobeandmail.com/sports /more-sports/racist-tweets-about-tsn-hosts-reveal-canadas-nasty-side /article9845192/

Du Bois, W. E. B. (1993). *The souls of black folk*. New York: Knopf. (Original work published in 1903).

Dumont, L. (1980). *Homo hierarchicus: The caste system and its implications*. Chicago, IL: University of Chicago Press.

Dweck, J. (2010, July 10). Whence the mullet? The history of Iran's forbidden haircut. *Slate*. Retrieved from https://slate.com/news-and-politics/2010/07/the-history-of -the-mullet-iran-s-forbidden-haircut.html

Dyer, R. (1997). *White*. New York, NY: Routledge.

Eaton, J. (2012, June). Gender equity in Canadian ice hockey: The legal struggle. Retrieved from /core/journals/legal-information-management/article/gender-equity-in-canadian-ice-hockey-the-legal-struggle/67A2E7C644D0BCDC78A675 371796BAC6

Eckert, M. (2015, February 23). Civil rights leader Angela Davis speaks at Bovard. Retrieved from http://dailytrojan.com/2015/02/23/civil-rights-leader-angela-davis -speaks-at-bovard/

ecozens. (2013, May 29). What's in a (nick)name. *Stanley Cup of Chowder*. Retrieved from https://www.stanleycupofchowder.com/2013/5/29/4376782/whats-in-a-nick -name-sidney-crosby

Elghawaby, A. (2014, May 21). No turbans on TV: Have news anchors failed democracy? *Huffington Post*. Retrieved from http://www.huffingtonpost.ca/amira-elghawaby/diversity-in-canadian-media_b_5007568.html

Essed, P. (1991). *Understanding everyday racism: An interdisciplinary theory*. Newbury Park, CA: Sage.

Everett-Green, R. (2014, February 28). 200 years a slave: The dark history of captivity in Canada. *Globe and Mail*. Retrieved from https://www.theglobeandmail.com/globe-debate/200-years-a-slave-the-dark-history-of-captivity-in-canada/article17178374/

Eveslage, S., & Delaney, K. (1998). Talkin' trash at Hardwick High: A case study of insult talk on a boys' basketball team. *International Review for the Sociology of Sport, 33*(3), 239–253. https://doi.org/10.1177/101269098033003002

Farber, M. (2010, February 4). Michael Farber: Canadian Prime Minister Harper on national game. *Sports Illustrated*. Retrieved from https://www.si.com/more-sports/2010/02/04/stephen-harper

Feingold, L. (2019, January 9). Team rallies around Black hockey player after he receives racist taunts. *NPR*. Retrieved from https://www.npr.org/2019/01/09/683501433/father-and-son-who-are-african-americans-discuss-racism-in-youth-hockey

Field, R. (2014). Toques and turbans, sticks and show tunes. *Amodern*. Retrieved from http://amodern.net/article/toques-and-turbans/

The First Shift. (n.d.). Inspiration. Retrieved from http://www.thefirstshift.ca/inspiration/

Fleischmann, A. N. M., Van Styvendale, N., & McCarroll, C. (2011). *Narratives of citizenship: Indigenous and diasporic peoples unsettle the nation-state*. Edmonton, Canada: University of Alberta Press.

Fleming, D. (2017, June 30). Burns and Thornton share the secrets to beard maintenance. *ESPN*. Retrieved from http://www.espn.com/nhl/story/_/page/bodyburnsthornton/san-jose-sharks-brent-burns-joe-thornton-hockey-bods-body-issue-2017

Fleming, S. (1995). *"Home and away": Sport and South Asian male youth*. Brookfield, VT: Avebury.

Fletcher, T. (2014). "Does he look like a Paki?" An exploration of "whiteness," positionality and reflexivity in inter-racial sports research. *Qualitative Research in Sport, Exercise and Health, 6*(2), 244–260. https://doi.org/10.1080/2159676X.2013.796487

Fordham University. (1997). Sojourner Truth: "Ain't I a woman?," December 1851. *Modern History Sourcebook*. Retrieved from https://sourcebooks.fordham.edu/mod/sojtruth-woman.asp

Forman, M. (2000). "Represent": Race, space and place in rap music. *Popular Music, 19*(1), 65–90. https://www.jstor.org/stable/853712

Forsyth, J., & Giles, A. (2013). *Aboriginal Peoples and sport in Canada: Historical foundations and contemporary issues* (edited by Janice Forsyth & Audrey R. Giles). Vancouver, BC: UBC Press.

Foster, L. T., Keller, C. P., McKee, B., & Ostry, A. (2011). *British Columbia atlas of wellness*. Victoria, Canada: University of Victoria. Retrieved from http://www.geog.uvic.ca/wellness/wellness2011/

Fosty, D., & Fosty, G. (2008). *Black ice: The lost history of the Colored Hockey League of the Maritimes, 1895–1925*. Halifax, Canada: Nimbus.

Foucault, M. (1977). *Discipline and punish*. London, UK: Penguin.

Fox, L. (2015, July 13). Shot callers: Q&A with hockey voice Jim Hughson. *Sportsnet*. Retrieved from http://www.sportsnet.ca/hockey/nhl/jim-hughson-play-by-play -commentator-hockey-night-in-canada-stanley-cup/

Frankenburg, R. (1993). *The social construction of whiteness: White women race matters*. London, UK: Routledge.

Franks, S. (2016, August 18). Women hit the headlines in sport: Why aren't there more writing about it? *The Guardian*. Retrieved from https://www.theguardian.com /media/2016/aug/18/women-sport-rio-olympics-female-sports-journalists

Fraser, N. (2009a). *Scales of justice: Reimagining political space in a globalizing world*. New York, NY: Columbia University Press.

———. (2009b). Who counts? Dilemmas of justice in a postwestphalian world. *Antipode, 41*(1), 281–297. https://doi.org/10.1111/j.1467-8330.2009.00726.x

Freeman, H. (2012, February 21). Jeremy Lin row reveals deep-seated racism against Asian Americans. *The Guardian*. Retrieved from https://www.theguardian.com /commentisfree/cifamerica/2012/feb/21/jeremy-lin-racism-asian-americans

Freng, A., & Esbensen, F. A. (2007). Race and gang affiliation: An examination of multiple marginality. *Justice Quarterly, 24*(4), 600–628. https://doi.org/10.1080 /07418820701717136

Friesen, J. (1995). The changing public image of Doukhobors in Canada. *Canadian Ethnic Studies, 27*(3), 131–140.

Friesen, J., & Curry, B. (2009, November 12). The new Canada: A question of emphasis. *Globe and Mail*. Retrieved from https://www.theglobeandmail.com /news/politics/the-new-canada-a-question-of-emphasis/article1209099/

Frisby, W. (2011). Promising physical activity inclusion practices for Chinese immigrant women in Vancouver, Canada. *Quest, 63*(1), 135–147. https://doi.org/10.1080 /00336297.2011.10483671

Frisby, W., Thibault, L., & Cureton, K. (2014). Multiculturalism and federal sport policy in Canada. In I. Henry & L. M. Ko (Eds.), *International handbook for sport policy* (pp. 106–116). London, UK: Routledge.

Galli, N., & Gonzalez, S. P. (2015). Psychological resilience in sport: A review of the literature and implications for research and practice. *International Journal of Sport and Exercise Psychology, 13*(3), 243–257. https://doi.org/10.1080/1612197X.2014.946947

Gandbhir, G., & Foster, B. (2015, March 17). A conversation with my Black son. *The New York Times*. Retrieved from https://www.nytimes.com/2015/03/17/opinion/a -conversation-with-my-black-son.html

Garde-Hansen, J. (2011). *Media and memory*. Edinburgh, Scotland: Edinburgh University.

Gardiner, S., & Welch, R. (2001). Sport, racism and the limits of "colour-blind" law. In B. Carrington & I. McDonald (Eds.), *"Race," sport and British society* (pp. 133–149). London, UK: Routledge.

Garrioch, B. (2016, September 20). Number 11 sworn in as Canadian citizen. *Ottawa Citizen*. Retrieved from http://ottawacitizen.com/sports/hockey/nhl /senatorsextra/number-11-sworn-in-as-canadian-citizen

Gee, M. (2011, July 3). South Asian immigrants are transforming Toronto. *Globe and Mail*. Retrieved from https://www.theglobeandmail.com/news/toronto/south -asian-immigrants-are-transforming-toronto/article625650/

Geertz, C. (1988). *Works and lives: The anthropologist as author*. Stanford, CA: Stanford University Press.

Geiger, J. (2008). *The first hall of fame: A study of the statues in the Forum Augustum*. Boston, MA: Brill.

Genosko, G. (1999). Hockey and culture. In L. Luven & P. Walton (Eds.), *PopCan: Popular culture in Canada* (pp. 140–150). Scarborough, Canada: Prentice-Hall.

Georgiou, M. (2006). *Diaspora, identity and the media: Diasporic transnationalism and mediated spatialities*. Cresskill, NJ: Hampton Press.

Ghee, K. L. (1990). The psychological importance of self definition and labeling: Black versus African American. *Journal of Black Psychology, 17*(1), 75–93. https://doi.org /10.1177/00957984900171006

Ghosh, S. (2013). "Am I a South Asian, really?" Constructing "South Asians" in Canada and being South Asian in Toronto. *South Asian Diaspora, 5*(1), 35–55. https://doi.org/10.1080/19438192.2013.724913

———. (2014). A passage to Canada: The differential migrations of South Asian skilled workers to Toronto. *Journal of International Migration and Integration, 15*(4), 715–735. https://doi.org/10.1007/s12134-013-0298-0

Gilbert, H. (2003). Black and white and Re(a)d all over again: Indigenous minstrelsy in contemporary Canadian and Australian theatre. *Theatre Journal, 55*(4), 679–698.

Gillis, C., Sorensen, C., & Macdonald, N. (2016, May 9). China is buying Canada: Inside the new real estate frenzy. *Macleans*. Retrieved from https://www.macleans .ca/economy/economicanalysis/chinese-real-estate-investors-are-reshaping-the -market/

Gilroy, P. (2006). Multiculture in times of war: An inaugural lecture given at the London School of Economics. *Critical Quarterly, 48*(4), 27–45. https://doi.org/10 .1111/j.1467-8705.2006.00731.x

Glass, A. (2017, May 27). Jemele Hill: "Even if you think women don't belong—Guess what? We're not going anywhere." *Forbes*. Retrieved from http://www.forbes.com /sites/alanaglass/2017/05/25/jemele-hill-even-if-you-think-women-dont-belong -guess-what-were-not-going-anywhere/

Goff, P. A., Di Leone, B. A. L., & Kahn, K. B. (2012). Racism leads to pushups: How racial discrimination threatens subordinate men's masculinity. *Journal of Experimental Social Psychology, 48*(5), 1111–1116. https://doi.org/10.1016/j.jesp.2012.03.015

Goldberg, D. T. (2009). *The threat of race: Reflections on racial neoliberalism*. Malden, MA: Wiley-Blackwell.

Goldberg, D. T. (2015). *Are we all postracial yet?* Malden, MA: Polity Press.

Gongshow. (2019). *Our story*. Retrieved from https://www.gongshowgear.ca/pages/our -story

Gopal, S., & Moorti, S. (2008). Introduction: Travels of Hindi song and dance. In S. Gopal & S. Moorti (Eds.), *Global Bollywood: Travels of Hindi song and dance* (pp. 1–62). Minneapolis: University of Minnesota Press.

Goudge, P. (2003). *The whiteness of power: Racism in the third world development and aid*. London, UK: Lawrence and Wishart.

Government of Canada. (2019, February 24). *Ottawa Senators break NHL record with citizenship ceremony*. Retrieved from https://www.canada.ca/en/immigration -refugees-citizenship/news/2019/02/ottawa-senators-break-nhl-record-with -citizenship-ceremony.html

Grace, S., Strong-Boag, V., Anderson, J., & Eisenberg, A. (1998). *Painting the maple: Essays on race, gender, and the construction of Canada*. Vancouver, Canada: UBC Press.

Grammas, D. L., & Schwartz, J. P. (2009). Internalization of messages from society and perfectionism as predictors of male body image. *Body Image*, 6(1), 31–36. https://doi.org/10.1016/j.bodyim.2008.10.002

Grant, T. (2016, September 27). Canada's racial divide: Confronting racism in our own backyard. *The Globe and Mail*, p. A.8.

Grescoe, T. (1994/1995, Winter). Hot type. *Vancouver*, pp. 81–84.

Gretz, A. (2018, November 21). NHL's head coaching recycling bin is alive and well. *NBC Sports*. Retrieved from https://nhl.nbcsports.com/2018/11/21/nhls-head-coaching-recycling-bin-is-alive-and-well/

Griffith, T. (2015, January 27). Police probe opened in Rush racism incident. *Rapid City Journal*. Retrieved from http://rapidcityjournal.com/news/local/police-probe-opened-in-rush-racism-incident/article_9b65b4f5-9270-51bb-bafe-e1953d8cfdda.html

Gruneau, R. (1983). *Class, sport and social development*. Amherst: University of Massachusetts Press.

———. (1989). Making spectacle: A case study in television sports production. In L. Wenner (Ed.), *Media, sports, and society* (pp. 134–154.). London, UK: Sage.

———. (2016). Goodbye, Gordie Howe: Sport participation and class inequality in the "pay for play" society. In D. Taras & C. Waddell (Eds.), *How Canadians communicate V: Sports* (pp. 223–246). Edmonton, Canada: Athabasca University.

———. (2017). *Sport & modernity*. Malden, MA: Polity Press.

Gruneau, R., & Whitson, D. (1993). *Hockey Night in Canada: Sports, identities, and cultural politics*. Toronto, Canada: University of Toronto Press.

Gulitti, T. (2018, December 16). Capitals welcome Black Girl Hockey Club for inaugural outing. *NHL*. Retrieved from https://www.nhl.com/news/black-girl-hockey-club-meet-capitals-at-first-outing/c-302994340

Gulitti, T. (2019, March 25). Capitals put a wrap on Stanley Cup party with White House visit. *NHL*. Retrieved from https://www.nhl.com/news/capitals-visit-white-house-president-trump-with-stanley-cup/c-306122194

Gunaratnam, Y. (2003). *Researching race and ethnicity: Methods, knowledge, and power*. London, UK: Sage.

Guo, J. (2016, December 20). The staggering difference between rich Asian Americans and Poor Asian Americans. *The Washington Post*. Retrieved from https://www.washingtonpost.com/news/wonk/wp/2016/12/20/why-asian-americans-arent-as-rich-as-they-seem/?postshare=9741482346947256&tid=ss_tw&utm_term=.4b1ed176d86a

Gzowski, P. (2014). *The game of our lives*. Toronto, Canada: Heritage House.

Hall, M. A. (2002). *The girl and the game: A history of women's sport in Canada*. Toronto, ON: Broadview Press.

Hall, S. (1996). Race, articulation and societies structured in dominance. In H. A. Baker, M. Diawara, & R. H. Lindeborg (Eds.), *Black British cultural studies* (pp. 16–60). Chicago, IL: University of Chicago Press.

———. (2000). "The multicultural question." In B. Hesse (Ed.), *Un/settled multiculturalisms: Diasporas, entanglement, transruptions* (pp. 209–241). London, UK: Zed Books.

———. (2005). Thinking diaspora: Home thoughts from abroad. In G. Desai & S. Nair (Eds.), *Postcolonialisms: An anthology of cultural theory and criticism* (pp. 543–560). New Brunswick, NJ: Rutgers University Press.

Hammon, B. (2013). Playing the race card: White American's sense of victimization in response to affirmative action. *Texas Hispanic Journal of Law & Policy, 19*(1), 95–120.

HappyCaraT. (2016, September 8). Women do not need to compete against males to validate their achievements. *Arctic Ice*. Retrieved from https://www.arcticicehockey .com/2016/9/8/12837662/women-do-not-need-to-compete-against-males-to -validate-their-achievements

Harris, C. (2007). *Breaking the ice*. Toronto, Canada: Insomniac Press.

Hasbrook, C. A. (1986). The sport participation–social class relationship: Some recent youth sport participation data. *Sociology of Sport Journal, 3*(2), 154–159. https:// doi.org/10.1123/ssj.3.2.154

Hayden, Z. (2019, March 1). Editorial: White supremacy and bigotry disguised as feminism in women's hockey. *The Victory Press*. Retrieved from https://victorypress .org/2019/03/01/editorial-white-supremacy-and-bigotry-disguised-as-feminism-in -womens-hockey/

Helweg, A. W. (1987). India's Sikhs: Problems and prospects. *Journal of Contemporary Asia, 17*(2), 140–159. https://doi.org/10.1080/00472338780000131

Hill, J. H. (1998). Language, race, and white public space. *American Anthropologist, 100*(3), 680–689. https://doi.org/10.1525/aa.1998.100.3.680

Hill Collins, P. H., & Solomos, J. (Eds.). (2010). *The SAGE handbook of race and ethnic studies*. London, UK: Sage.

Hoch, P. (2004). White hero Black beast: Racism, sexism and the mask of masculinity. In P. F. Murphy (ed.), *Feminism and masculinities* (pp. 93–107). New York, NY: Oxford University Press.

Hockey Canada. (2018, December 10). Hockey Canada unveils roster for 2019 IIHF U18 women's world championship. Retrieved from https://www.hockeycanada.ca /en-ca/news/2018-19-nwu18t-roster-named-for-u18-wwc

Hockey Canada Sports School. (2016/2017). CSSHL hockey academy. Retrieved December 17, 2016, from http://westvancouverschools.ca/wp-content/uploads /2016/03/CSSHL-Parent-Information-Session-2016.pdf

Hockey Hall of Fame. (2017a). The history of the hockey hall of fame. Retrieved from https://www.hhof.com/htmlGeneralInfo/gi20300.shtml

———. (2017b). Selection committee by-laws. Retrieved from https://www.hhof.com /htmlinduct/indselect.shtml#members

———. (2018). Willie O'Ree—Builder category. Retrieved from https://www.hhof .com/htmlInduct/ind18Oree.shtml

Hockey Monkey. (2019). Bauer Supreme 1S senior ice hockey skates. Retrieved from https://www.hockeymonkey.com/bauer-hockey-skates-supreme-1s-sr.html

Hockey Night Punjabi. (2016a, December 2). Reminder: A camp to help find a match for Jasnoor Deol & Tegveer Minhas will be held tomorrow at the Ontario Khalsa Darbar (Dixie Gurdwara) pic.twitter.com/lXTvdvqSF4 [Tweet]. Retrieved September 28, 2017, from https://twitter.com/HkyNightPunjabi/status /815284841201573888

———. (2016b, June 12). Robin Bawa interview. Retrieved from https://www.facebook .com/HockeyNightPunjabi/videos/735251019911559/?hc_ref=ARSe -2XLV8CKSSqEv6uxonZu_YjUI9JMb-JqYtjVHFp-8A8XFFG_otoz2OtaAUgj5jM

———. (2017). *Sudarshan Maharaj interview*. Retrieved from https://www.facebook .com/pg/HockeyNightPunjabi/videos/?ref=page_internal

Holman, A. C. (2018). A flag of tendons: Hockey and Canadian history. In J. Ellison & J. Anderson (Eds.), *Hockey: Challenging Canada's game* (pp. 25–44). Ottawa, ON: Canadian Museum of History and the University of Ottawa Press.

hooks, bell. (1990). *Yearning: Race, gender and cultural politics.* Boston, MA: South End.

Hopper, T. (2014, May 16). B.C. property titles bear reminders of a time when race-based covenants kept neighbourhoods white. *National Post.* Retrieved from http://nationalpost.com/news/canada/b-c-property-titles-bear-reminders-of-a -time-when-race-based-covenants-kept-neighbourhoods-white

Hundal, B. (2017, June 4). Twitter post. Retrieved June 4, 2017, from https://twitter .com/BhupinderHundal/status/871531009845501953

Hurley, M. (2007). Who's on whose margins? In M. Pitts & A. Smith (Eds.), *Researching the margins: Strategies for ethical and rigorous research within marginalised communities* (pp. 160–189). Basingstoke, UK: Palgrave Macmillan.

Hylton, K. (2009). *"Race" and sport: Critical race theory.* New York, NY: Routledge.

Institute for Canadian Citizenship. (2014). *Playing together: New citizens, sports & belonging.* Retrieved from https://www.icc-icc.ca/site/pdfs/PlayingTogether _FullR%20Online_Final.pdf

Jackson, S. J., & Ponic, P. (2001). Pride and prejudice: Reflecting on sport heroes, national identity, and crisis in Canada. *Culture, Sport, Society, 4*(2), 43–62. https://doi.org/10.1080/713999819

James, C. L. R. (1969). *Beyond a boundary.* London, UK: Hutchinson.

James, R. (2015). *Resilience & melancholy: Pop music, feminism, neoliberalism.* Washington, USA: Zero Books.

James, V., & Gallagher, J. (2015). *Black ice: The Val James story.* Toronto, Canada: ECW Press.

Javed, N., & Rushowy, K. (2017, April 11). Mishandling of discrimination, dismantling of equity policy at heart of York board crisis. *Toronto Star.* Retrieved from https://www.scribd.com/embeds/344883412/content?access_key=key -14x2zy69z8ecwaowzhbu&jsapi=true&xdm_e=https://www.thestar.com&xdm_c =defaulto&xdm_p=1

Jeffries, M. P. (2011). *Thug life: Race, gender, and the meaning of hip-hop.* Chicago, IL: University of Chicago Press. Retrieved from http://site.ebrary.com/lib/alltitles /docDetail.action?docID=10448178

Johal, G. S. (2007). The racialization of space: Producing Surrey. In G. F. Johnson & R. Enomoto (Eds.), *Race, racialization and antiracism in Canada and beyond* (pp. 179–205). Toronto, Canada: University of Toronto Press.

Johal, S. (2002). *The sport of lions: The Punjabi-Sikh sporting experience.* University of Warwick, Warwick. Retrieved from http://wrap.warwick.ac.uk/2890/1/WRAP _THESIS_Johal_2002.pdf

Johnson, J., & Ali, A. E. (2016). Skating on thin ice? An interrogation of Canada's melting pastime. *World Leisure Journal, 0*(0), 1–13. https://doi.org/10.1080 /16078055.2016.1216889

Johnson, J. E., Giannoulakis, C., Tracy, D. R., & Ridley, M. J. (2016). An examination of institutional characteristics, selection committees, and induction criteria for college athletic halls of fame. *Journal of Heritage Tourism, 11*(4), 309–323. https:// doi.org/10.1080/1743873X.2015.1088857

Johnston, C. (2016a, June 1). Bonino, Penguins embrace HNIC Punjabi's "spectacular" goal call. *Sportsnet.* Retrieved from http://www.sportsnet.ca/hockey/nhl /bonino-penguins-embrace-hnic-punjabis-spectacular-goal-call/

———. (2016b, April 25). Tomalo! Meet the Florida Panthers' Spanish broadcast team. *Sportsnet*. Retrieved from http://www.sportsnet.ca/hockey/nhl/tomalo-meet-florida-panthers-spanish-broadcast-team/

Johnston, P. (2017, August 24). From south Vancouver driveway ball hockey to sports talk radio. *The Province*. Retrieved from http://theprovince.com/sports/hockey/nhl/vancouver-canucks/from-south-vancouver-driveway-ball-hockey-to-sports-talk-radio

Jones, J. (2015, October 31). Who are these enthusiastic guys broadcasting Carolina Panthers games in Spanish? *Charlotte Observer*. Retrieved from http://www.charlotteobserver.com/sports/nfl/carolina-panthers/article42088353.html

Joseph, J., Darnell, S., & Nakamura, Y. (2012). *Race and sport in Canada: Intersecting inequalities*. Toronto, Canada: Canadian Scholars' Press.

Kalaf, S. (2018, March 12). Minnesota high school hockey hair remains undefeated. *Deadspin*. Retrieved from https://deadspin.com/minnesota-high-school-hockey-hair-remains-undefeated-1823688588

Kalman-Lamb, N. (2018, June 21). The racist culture of Canadian hockey. *CounterPunch*. Retrieved from https://www.academia.edu/36487260/The_Racist_Culture_of_Canadian_Hockey

Kang, H. B. K. (2002). *A post-colonial Vaisakhi reading: Unveiling the Indo-Canadian Sikh identity through Canadian media*. Vancouver, Canada: Simon Fraser University.

Kaplan, E. (2019, May 7). The NHL's love affair with hair. *ESPN*. Retrieved from http://www.espn.com/nhl/story/_/id/26684893/the-nhl-love-affair-hair

Kaplan, W. (1993). *Belonging: The meaning and future of Canadian citizenship*. Montreal & Kingston, Canada: McGill-Queens University Press.

Kawai, Y. (2005). Stereotyping Asian Americans: The dialectic of the model minority and the yellow peril. *Howard Journal of Communications*, *16*(2), 109–130. https://doi.org/10.1080/10646170590948974

Kay, J. (2013, May 8). Jonathan Kay: Urban-bound Aboriginals pose Canada's biggest integration challenge, not immigrants. *National Post*. Retrieved from http://news.nationalpost.com/full-comment/jonathan-kay-aboriginals-pose-canadas-biggest-assimilation-challenge-not-immigrants

Kelly, N. R., Cotter, E. W., Tanofsky-Kraff, M., & Mazzeo, S. E. (2015). Racial variations in binge eating, body image concerns, and compulsive exercise among men. *Psychology of Men & Masculinity*, *16*(3), 326–336. https://doi.org/10.1037/a0037585

Kempson, M. (2015). "My version of feminism": Subjectivity, DIY and the feminist zine. *Social Movement Studies*, *14*(4), 459–472. https://doi.org/10.1080/14742837.2014.945157

Kerr-Dineen, L. (2017, February 20). Soccer player left the field in tears after suffering horrific racist abuse. *USA Today*. Retrieved from http://ftw.usatoday.com/2017/02/this-soccer-player-left-field-in-tears-after-horrific-monkey-chants-now-hes-speaking-out-against-racist-abuse

Keum, B. T., Wong, S. N., DeBlaere, C., & Brewster, M. E. (2015). Body image and Asian American men: Examination of the drive for muscularity scale. *Psychology of Men & Masculinity*, *16*(3), 284–293. https://doi.org/10.1037/a0038180

Kidd, B. (1996). The making of a hockey artifact: A review of the Hockey Hall of Fame. *Journal of Sport History*, *23*(3), 328–334. https://www.jstor.org/stable/43609607

Kim, C. J. (1999). The racial triangulation of Asian Americans. *Politics Society*, *27*(1), 105–138.

Kim, P. (2014, September 25). Hockey used to "Canadianize" new immigrants and help grow the sport. *Global News*. Retrieved from http://globalnews.ca/news/1583757/hockey-used-to-canadianize-new-immigrants-and-help-grow-the-sport/

King, C. R. (2006). Defacements/effacements: Anti-Asian (American) sentiment in sport. *Journal of Sport and Social Issues, 30*(4), 340–352. https://doi.org/10.1177/0193723506292965

Kirmayer, L. J., Dandeneau, S., Marshall, E., Phillips, M. K., & Williamson, K. J. (2011). Rethinking resilience from Indigenous perspectives. *The Canadian Journal of Psychiatry, 56*(2), 84–91. https://doi.org/10.1177/070674371105600203

Knapp, J. L. (1999). *Why kids drop out: A Duluth amateur hockey survey.* Unpublished manuscript retrieved through the Duluth Amateur Hockey Association. Duluth, MN.

Knowles, C. (2010). Theorizing race and ethnicity: Contemporary paradigms and perspectives. In P. Hill Collins & J. Solomos (Eds.), *The SAGE handbook of race and ethnic studies* (pp. 23–43). London, UK: Sage.

Korver, K. (2019, April 8). Privileged. *The Player's Tribune*. Retrieved from https://www.theplayerstribune.com/en-us/articles/kyle-korver-utah-jazz-nba

Koshy, S. (1998). Category crisis: South Asian Americans and questions of race and ethnicity. *Diaspora: A Journal of Transnational Studies, 7*(3), 285–320. doi:10.1353/dsp.1998.0013

Krebs, A. (2012). Hockey and the reproduction of colonialism in Canada. In J. Joseph, S. Darnell, & Y. Nakamura (Eds.), *Race and sport in Canada: Intersecting inequalities*. Toronto, Canada: Canadian Scholars' Press.

Kubrin, C. E. (2005). Gangstas, thugs, and hustlas: Identity and the code of the street in rap music. *Social Problems, 52*(3), 360–378. https://doi.org/10.1525/sp.2005.52.3.360

Kupchuk, R. (2015, May 11). Popowich, Burzan taken early in WHL draft. *Surrey News*. Retrieved from http://www.surreyleader.com/sports/303324511.html

Kymlicka, W. (2013). Neoliberal multiculturalism? In *Social resilience in the neoliberal era* (pp. 99–125). Cambridge, UK: Cambridge University Press.

Lamar IV, W. H. (2016, June 17). America is not ready to face the truth of racism. *The Undefeated*. Retrieved from https://theundefeated.com/features/america-is-not-ready-to-face-the-truth-of-racism/

Lamont, M., Welburn, J. S., & Fleming, C. M. (2013). Responses to discrimination and social resilience under neoliberalism: The United States compared. In P. A. Hall & M. Lamont (Eds.), *Social resilience in the neoliberal era* (pp. 129–157). Cambridge, UK: Cambridge University Press.

Landy, D., & MacLean, G. (eds.). (1996). *The Spivak reader*. Great Britain: Routledge.

La Rose, J. (2019, February 17). "Hate is just noise." *Hockey Canada*. Retrieved from https://www.hockeycanada.ca/en-ca/news/2018-19-nwt-nurse-overcomes-stereotypes.

Lavoi, N. M. (2013). *The decline of women coaches in collegiate athletics: A report on select NCAA Division-1 FBS institutions, 2012–2013*. Minneapolis, MN: Tucker Center for Research on Girls & Women in Sport. Retrieved from http://www.cehd.umn.edu/tuckercenter/library/docs/research/2012-13_Decline-of-Women-College-Coaches-Report_Dec-18.pdf

Lee, F. R. (1997, October 23). Young and in fear of the police: Parents teach children how to deal with officers' bias. *The New York Times*. Retrieved from http://www.nytimes.com/1997/10/23/nyregion/young-fear-police-parents-teach-children-deal-with-officers-bias.html

Lee, P., & Thomas, P. N. (2012). Introduction: Public media and the right to memory: Towards an encounter with justice. In P. Lee & P. N. Thomas (Eds.), *Public memory, public media, and the politics of justice* (pp. 1–22). New York, NY: Palgrave Macmillan.

Leonard, D. J. (2007). Innocent until proven innocent: In defense of Duke lacrosse and white power (and against menacing Black student-athletes, a Black stripper, activists, and the Jewish media). *Journal of Sport and Social Issues, 31,* (25–44). https://doi.org/10.1177/0193723506296824

Leong, E. (Director). (2013). *Linsanity* [Motion picture]. USA: 408 Films, Arowana Films, Defy Agency, Endgame Entertainment.

Leung, M. (2013). Jeremy Lin's model minority problem. *Contexts, 12*(3), 52–56. doi:10.1177/1536504213499879

Lewis, A. E. (2001). There is no "race" in the schoolyard: Color-blind ideology in an (almost) all-white school. *American Educational Research Journal, 38*(4), 781–811. https://doi.org/10.3102/00028312038004781

Library and Archives Canada. (2014, June 11). Thematic guides: Internment camps in Canada during the first and second world wars. Retrieved from http://www.bac-lac.gc .ca/eng/discover/politics-government/Pages/thematic-guides-internment-camps.aspx

Lieberman, R. (2011). *Breakaway*. Canada: Alliance.

Little, M. (2003). "Better than numbers . . ." A gentle critique of evidence-based medicine. *ANZ Journal of Surgery, 73*(4), 177–182. https://doi.org/10.1046/j.1445 -1433.2002.02563.x

Long, J., & Hylton, K. (2002). Shades of white: An examination of whiteness in sport. *Leisure Studies, 21,* 87–103. https://doi.org/doi:10.1080/02614360210152575

Lott, E. (2013). *Love and theft: Blackface minstrelsy and the American working class.* New York, NY: Oxford University Press.

Low, S. (2008). Behind the gates: Social splitting and the "other". In L. Weis (Ed.), *The way class works: Readings on school, family, and the economy* (pp. 44–59). New York, NY: Routledge.

Ludwig, M. (2016, December 15). Denman Arena, Canada's first artificial ice rink. *British Columbia Magazine*. Retrieved from https://www.bcmag.ca/denman-arena -canadas-first-artificial-ice-rink/

MacDonald, C. (2015, May 27). Gongshow Gear lifestyle hockey apparel and contradictory images of junior hockey players in Canada. *Hockey in Society*. Retrieved from https://hockeyinsociety.com/2015/05/27/gongshow-gear-lifestyle-hockey -apparel-and-contradictory-images-of-junior-hockey-players-in-canada/

———. (2016). *"Yo! You can't say that!": Understandings of gender and sexuality and attitudes towards homosexuality among male major midget AAA ice hockey players in Canada*. Concordia University, Montreal, QC. Retrieved from http://spectrum .library.concordia.ca/981103/1/MacDonald_PhD_S2016.pdf

MacDonald, C., Szto, C., & Edwards, J. (2017). The game that no one saw: Evaluating the cultural citizenship and legitimacy of women's professional hockey through the inaugural Women's Winter Classic. In A. Milner & J. H. Braddock II (Eds.), *Women in sports: Breaking barriers, facing obstacles* (pp. 101–121). Santa Barbara, CA: ABC-CLIO.

Mackey, E. (2002). *House of difference: Cultural politics and national identity in Canada*. Toronto, Canada: Routledge.

Margalit, A. (2002). *The ethics of memory*. Cambridge, MA: Harvard University Press.

Marsden, C. (2014, June 2). What Hockey Canada is doing to fight declining enrollment—Toronto. *Globalnews.ca*. Retrieved from http://globalnews.ca/news /1369788/why-cost-and-safety-concerns-may-keep-some-kids-from-playing-hockey/

Matsaganis, M. D., Katz, V. S., & Ball-Rokeach, S. (2011). *Understanding ethnic media: Producers, consumers, and societies.* Los Angeles, CA: SAGE.

Matsuda, M. (1993). We will not be used. *UCLA Asian American Pacific Islands Law Journal, 1,* 79–84.

McClearen, J. (2018). Don't be a do-nothing-bitch: Popular feminism and women's physical empowerment in the UFC. In K. Toffoletti, J. Francombe-Webb, & H. Thorpe (Eds.), *New sporting femininities: Embodied politics in postfeminist times* (pp. 43–62). Cham, Switzerland: Palgrave Macmillan.

McClintock, A. (1995). *Imperial leather: Race, gender, and sexuality in the colonial context.* New York, NY: Routledge.

McElroy, J. (2016, July 28). Suspect caught on camera vandalizing B.C. realtor's signs. *Globalnews.ca*. Retrieved from http://globalnews.ca/news/2855034/suspect-caught -on-camera-vandalizing-b-c-realtors-signs/

McGran, K. (2019, May 1). Defunct CWHL raises $90,000 through sales of trophies, jerseys to pay off debt. *Toronto Star.* Retrieved from https://www.thestar.com /sports/hockey/2019/05/01/defunct-cwhl-raises-90000-through-sales-of-trophies -jerseys-to-pay-off-debt.html

McKie, D. (2013, June 14). More people failing revamped citizenship tests. *CBC.* Retrieved from http://www.cbc.ca/news/politics/more-people-failing-revamped -citizenship-tests-1.1413674

McKinven, J. (2015, January 27). The art of chirping. *Glass and Out.* Retrieved from https://glassandout.com/2015/01/the-art-of-chirping/

Mendelsohn, P. (2019, April 22). Hockey's homophobia problems. *Daily Xtra.* Retrieved from https://www.dailyxtra.com/hockeys-homophobia-problem-153169 ?fbclid=IwAR07BoBwnBXNafSeFVmjbI13MkHogSArZUNaj5g _YS6F4DmpOCuvTsmtt2k

Milian, C. (2013). *Latining America: Black-brown passages and the coloring of Latino/a studies.* Athens: University of Georgia Press.

Miller, J. (2005). Who's telling the news: Racial representation among news gatherers in Canada's daily newsrooms. *International Journal of Diversity in Organisations, Communities and Nations, 5,* 1447–9583.

Minsky, A. (2017, June 13). Hate crimes against Muslims in Canada increase 253% over four years. *Globalnews.ca*. Retrieved from http://globalnews.ca/news/3523535/hate -crimes-canada-muslim/

Mirtle, J. (2013, November 8). The great offside: How Canadian hockey is becoming a game strictly for the rich. *Globe and Mail.* Retrieved from http://www .theglobeandmail.com/news/national/time-to-lead/the-great-offside-how -canadian-hockey-is-becoming-a-game-strictly-for-the-rich/article15349723/

Monkman, L. (2018, November 30). Peewee hockey game in Neepawa turns ugly as fans hurl racist taunts at First Nations team. *CBC News.* Retrieved from https://www.cbc .ca/news/indigenous/neepawa-waywayseecappo-peewee-hockey-game-1.4924967

Monzó, L. D. (2016). "They don't know anything!": Latinx immigrant students appropriating the oppressor's voice. *Anthropology & Education Quarterly, 47*(2), 148–166. https://doi.org/10.1111/aeq.12146

Mookerjea, S., Szeman, I., & Faurschou, G. (2009). *Canadian cultural studies: A reader.* Durham, NC: Duke University Press.

Morgan, P. B. C., Fletcher, D., & Sarkar, M. (2013). Defining and characterizing team resilience in elite sport. *Psychology of Sport and Exercise, 14*(4), 549–559. https://doi.org/10.1016/j.psychsport.2013.01.004

Morrison, T. (1985). A humanist view [speech]. Retrieved from https://www.mackenzian.com/wp-content/uploads/2014/07/Transcript_PortlandState_TMorrison.pdf

———. (1993). *Playing in the dark: Whiteness and the literary imagination.* Cambridge, MA: Harvard University Press.

Muñoz, J. E. (2007). "Chico, what does it feel like to be a problem?" The transmission of brownness. In J. Flores & R. Rosaldo (Eds.), *A companion to Latina/o studies* (pp. 441–451). Malden, MA: Blackwell.

Murray, C., Yu, S., & Ahadi, D. (2007). Cultural diversity and ethnic media in BC: A report to Canadian Heritage Western Regional Office. Retrieved from http://m.bcethnicmedia.ca/Research/cultural-diversity-report-oct-07.pdf

Nair, S. (2017, November 1). AFC comes down hard on racial slurs: Malaysia fined US$30,000. *The Independent.* Retrieved from http://www.theindependent.sg/afc-comes-down-hard-on-racial-slurs-malaysia-fined-us30000/

Nanayakkara, S. (2012). Crossing boundaries and changing identities: Empowering South Asian women through sport and physical activities. *The International Journal of the History of Sport, 29*(13), 1885–1906. https://doi.org/10.1080/09523367.2012.707649

Nayar, K. E. (2012). *The Punjabis in British Columbia: Location, labour, First Nations, and multiculturalism.* Montreal & Kingston, Canada: McGill-Queens University Press.

NCAA. (2014, January 27). Title IX frequently asked questions [Text]. Retrieved from http://www.ncaa.org/about/resources/inclusion/title-ix-frequently-asked-questions

Nebeker, K. C. (1998). Critical race theory: A white graduate student's struggle with this growing area of scholarship. *International Journal of Qualitative Studies in Education, 11*(1), 25–41. https://doi.org/10.1080/095183998236872

Nelson, D. (2017, January 16). Hockey Hall of Fame debates: Willie O'Ree. *The Hockey Writers.* Retrieved from http://thehockeywriters.com/hockey-hall-of-fame-willie-oree/

Netto, G., Bhopal, R., Lederle, N., Khatoon, J., & Jackson, A. (2010). How can health promotion interventions be adapted for minority ethnic communities? Five principles for guiding the development of behavioral interventions. *Health Promotion International, 25*(2), 248–257. https://doi.org/10.1093/heapro/daq012

NHL. (2011, September 23). Banana thrown at Flyers' Simmonds during NHL exhibition game in London. *NHL.* Retrieved from https://www.nhl.com/news/banana-thrown-at-flyers-simmonds-during-nhl-exhibition-game-in-london/c-589488

———. (2014). *National Hockey League official rules 2014–2015.* Retrieved from http://www.nhl.com/nhl/en/v3/ext/rules/2014-2015-rulebook.pdf

———. (2015, December 30). NHL partnering with RISE to combat racism. *NHL.* Retrieved from https://www.nhl.com/news/nhl-partnering-with-rise-to-combat-racism/c-795127

———. (2017). Hockey is for everyone. Retrieved from https://www.nhl.com/community/hockey-is-for-everyone

———. (2018). Policy brief: Shifting demographics and hockey's future. Retrieved from https://nhl.bamcontent.com/images/assets/binary/300993502/binary-file/file.pdf

Norman, M. (2012, July 5). The Hockey Hall of Fame and the politics of hockey legacy: How and why are certain players remembered? *Hockey in Society.* Retrieved from

https://hockeyinsociety.com/2012/07/05/the-hockey-hall-of-fame-and-the-politics
-of-hockey-legacy-how-and-why-are-certain-players-remembered/

———. (2014, June 26). On "NHL bloodlines" and social and cultural capital: Why do NHL fathers produce NHL sons? *Hockey in Society*. Retrieved from https://hockeyinsociety.com/2014/06/26/on-nhl-bloodlines-and-social-and-cultural-capital-why-do-nhl-fathers-produce-nhl-sons/

Norris, F. H., Stevens, S. P., Pfefferbaum, B., Wyche, K. F., & Pfefferbaum, R. L. (2008). Community resilience as a metaphor, theory, set of capacities, and strategy for disaster readiness. *American Journal of Community Psychology, 41*, 127–150. https://doi.org/10.1007/s10464-007-9156-6

O'Brien, E. (2008). *The racial middle: Latinos and Asian Americans living beyond the racial divide.* New York, NY & London, UK: New York University Press.

O'Connell, A. (2010). An exploration of redneck whiteness in multicultural Canada. *Social Politics, 17*(4), 536–563. https://doi.org/10.1093/sp/jxq019

Okihiro, G. (1994). *Margins and mainstreams: Asians in American history and culture.* Seattle: University of Washington Press.

Oliver, K., Lorenc, T., & Innvær, S. (2014). New directions in evidence-based policy research: A critical analysis of the literature. *Health Research Policy and Systems, 12*, 34. https://doi.org/10.1186/1478-4505-12-34

Omi, M., & Winant, H. (1986). *Racial formation in the United States.* New York, NY: Routledge.

Ong, A. (1999). *Flexible citizenship: The cultural logics of transnationality.* Durham, NC: Duke University Press.

Oswald, L. (1999). Culture swapping: Consumption and the ethnogenesis of middle-class Haitian immigrants. *Journal of Consumer Research, 25*, 303–318. https://doi.org/10.1086/209541

Oyedemi, T. (2016). Beauty as violence: "beautiful" hair and the cultural violence of identity erasure. *Journal for the Study of Race, Nation and Culture, 22*(5), 537–553. https://doi.org/10.1080/13504630.2016.1157465

Pandya, S. (2013). Situating Vijay Singh in (Asian) America. *South Asian Popular Culture, 11*(3), 219–230.

Paperny, A. M. (2016, April 13). Hate crimes against Muslim-Canadians more than doubled in 3 years. Retrieved from http://globalnews.ca/news/2634032/hate-crimes-against-muslim-canadians-more-than-doubled-in-3-years/

Paraschak, V. (1990). Organized sport for Native females on the Six Nations Reserve, Ontario from 1968–1980: A comparison of dominant and emergent sport systems. *Canadian Journal of History of Sport, 21*(2), 70–80. https://doi.org/10.1123/cjhs.21.2.70

Pardy, B., & Szto, C. (2019a, January 4). Renaissance women of the CWHL. *Hockey in Society*. Retrieved from https://hockeyinsociety.com/2019/01/04/renaissance-women-of-the-cwhl/.

———. (2019b, February 7). Renaissance women part 2: NWHL edition. *Hockey in Society*. Retrieved from https://hockeyinsociety.com/2019/02/07/renaissance-women-part-2-nwhl-edition/

Parsons, N. L., & Stern, M. J. (2012). There's no dying in baseball: Cultural valorization, collective memory, and induction into the Baseball Hall of Fame. *Sociology of Sport Journal, 29*(1), 62–88. https://doi.org/10.1123/ssj.29.1.62

Paterson, A. (2017, September 1). A look at the young women playing Canada's game. *Globe and Mail*. Retrieved from https://www.theglobeandmail.com/sports/hockey/womens-hockey-canada—disparity-history-present/article36147551/

Pecoskie, T. (2016, October 28). Pay to play: Odds stacked against many young hockey players. *The Hamilton Spectator*. Retrieved from http://www.thespec.com/news -story/6933956-pay-to-play-odds-stacked-against-many-young-hockey-players/

Pelak, C. F. (2002). Women's collective identity formation in sports: A case study from women's ice hockey. *Gender and Society, 16*(1), 93–114.

Penton, K. (2015, April 5). Vancouver's North Shore Winterhawks grab bantam championship. *Winnipeg Sun*. Retrieved from http://www.winnipegsun.com/2015 /04/05/vancouvers-north-shore-winterhawks-grab-bantam-championship?utm _source=facebook&utm_medium=recommend-button&utm_campaign =Vancouver's North Shore Winterhawks grab bantam championship

Perry, I. (2011). *More beautiful and more terrible: The embrace and transcendence of racial inequality in the United States*. New York, NY: NYU Press.

Pettersen, W. (1966, January 9). Success story, Japanese-American style. *New York Times*, p. 180.

Phillips, M. G. (2012). Introduction: Historians in sport museums. In *Representing the sporting past in museums and halls of fame* (pp. 1–26). New Haven, CT & London, UK: Routledge.

Pickering, M. (2008). *Blackface minstrelsy in Britain*. London, UK: Routledge.

Pierce, C. M., Carew, J. V., Pierce-Gonzalez, D., & Willis, D. (1977). An experiment in racism: TV commercials. *Education and Urban Society, 10*(1), 61–87.

Pierce, L. (2018, December 21). Referee with racist history makes high school wrestler cut dreadlocks. *Vice*. https://www.vice.com/en_ca/article/nepymm /racist-white-referee-alan-maloney-makes-high-school-wrestler-andrew-johnson -cut-dreadlocks

Pitter, R. (2006). Racialization and hockey in Canada: From personal troubles to a Canadian challenge. In D. Whitson & R. Gruneau (Eds.), *Artificial ice: Hockey, culture, and commerce*. Toronto, Canada: University of Toronto Press.

Pitts, M., & Smith, A. (2007). *Researching the margins: Strategies for ethical and rigorous research with marginalised communities*. Basingstoke, UK: Palgrave Macmillan.

Players Against Hate. (2019). 2019 NHL Award Announcement April 28, 2019. Retrieved from https://playersagainsthate.org

Poniatowski, K., & Whiteside, E. (2012). "Isn't he a good guy?": Constructions of whiteness in the 2006 Olympic hockey tournament. *The Howard Journal of Communications, 23*(1), 1–16. https://doi.org/10.1080/10646175.2012.641866

Prashad, V. (2000). *The karma of brown folk*. Minneapolis: University of Minnesota Press.

Puwar, N. (2004). *Space invaders: Race, gender and bodies out of place*. Oxford, UK & New York, NY: Berg.

———. (2006). Im/possible inhabitations. In N. Yuval-Davis, K. Kannabiran, & U. M. Vieten (Eds.), *The situated politics of belonging* (pp. 75–83). London, UK: Sage.

Ramsey, P. G. (1991). The salience of race in young children growing up in an all-white community. *Journal of Educational Psychology, 83*(1), 28–34. https://doi.org/10.1037 /0022-0663.83.1.28

Rana, S. (2015). Reading brownness: Richard Rodriguez, race, and form. *American Literary History, 27*(2), 285–304. https://doi.org/10.1093/alh/aju101

Raphael, R. (1988). *The men from the boys: Rites of passage in male America*. Lincoln: University of Nebraska Press.

Ratna, A. (2011). "Who wants to make aloo gobi when you can bend it like Beckham?" British Asian females and their racialized experiences of gender and identity in women's football. *Soccer & Society, 12*(3), 382–401. https://doi.org/10.1080 /14660970.2011.568105

———. (2014). "Who are ya?" The national identities and belongings of British Asian football fans. *Patterns of Prejudice, 48*(3), 286–308. https://doi.org/10.1080 /0031322X.2014.927603

———. (2018). Not just merely different Travelling theories, post-feminism and the racialized politics of women of color. *Sociology of Sport Journal, 35*, 197–206. https://doi.org/10.1123/ssj.2017-0192

Ratto, M., & Boler, M. (2014). *DIY citizenship: Critical making and social media.* Cambridge, MA: MIT Press.

Reading, A. (2011). Identity, memory and cosmopolitanism: The otherness of the past and a right to memory? *European Journal of Cultural Studies, 14*(4), 379–394. https://doi.org/10.1177/1367549411411607

Regalado, S. O. (1995). "Dodgers Béisbol is on the air": The development and impact of the Dodgers Spanish-language broadcasts, 1958–1994. *California History, 74*(3), 280–289. https://doi.org/10.2307/25177511

Reid, C., & Nash, R. (2004). Microliteracy and the discourse of Canadian multiculturalism. *Ethnologies, 26*(1), 35–60. https://doi.org/10.7202/013340ar

Reid, J. (2012). The disastrous and political debased subject of resilience. *Development Dialogue, 58*, 67–80.

———. (2013). Interrogating the neoliberal biopolitics of the sustainable development-resilience nexus. *International Political Sociology, 7*(4), 353–367. doi:10.1111/ ips.12028

Renan, E. (1992). What is a nation? In *Qu'est-ce qu'une nation?* Sorbonne, France: Presses-Pocket.

Richmond Minor Hockey Association. (n.d.). Rep hockey tryout tips. Retrieved from http://www.richmondminorhockey.com/default.aspx?p=rep%20hockey%20 tryout%20tips

Robidoux, M. A. (2001). *Men at play: A working understanding of professional hockey.* Montreal & Kingston, Canada: McGill-Queens University Press.

———. (2002). Imagining a Canadian identity through sport: A historical interpretation of lacrosse and hockey. *The Journal of American Folklore, 115*(456), 209–225. https://doi.org/https://doi.org/10.1353/jaf.2002.0021

———. (2012). *Stickhandling through the margins: First Nations hockey in Canada.* Toronto, Canada: University of Toronto Press.

———. (2018). Imagining a Canadian identity through sport: An historical interpretation of lacrosse and hockey. In J. Ellison & J. Anderson (Eds.), *Hockey: Challenging Canada's game* (pp. 61–76). Ottawa, ON: Canadian Museum of History and the University of Ottawa Press.

Rolen, E. (2019, January 13). Philadelphia Wings lacrosse apologizes after fans threaten to "scalp" Native player, announcer yells "snip that ponytail." *Philly Voice.* Retrieved from https://www.phillyvoice.com/philadelphia-wings-lacrosse -apologizes-after-fans-threaten-scalp-native-player-announcer-says-snip-pony-tail/

Rosaldo, R. (1993). *Culture & truth: The remaking of social analysis.* Boston, MA: Beacon.

Rutherford, K. (2019). What's right for the game. *Sportsnet.* Retrieved from https:// www.sportsnet.ca/hockey/nhl/inside-cwhl-nwhl-mess-big-read/

Said, E. (1978). *Orientalism* (1st ed.). New York, NY: Pantheon Books.

Samie, S. F. (2013). Hetero-sexy self/body work and basketball: The invisible sporting women of British Pakistani Muslim heritage. *South Asian Popular Culture, 11*(3), 257–270. doi:10.1080/14746689.2013

Samie, S. F., & Sehlikoglu, S. (2015). Strange, incompetent and out-of-place: Media, Muslim sportswomen and London 2012. *Feminist Media Studies, 15*(3), 363–381.

Sandberg, S. (2013). *Lean in: Women, work, and the will to lead*. New York, NY: Knopf Doubleday.

Sandhra, S. (2019, January 4). Save the date | "We are Hockey" exhibit at the Sikh Heritage Museum. *South Asian Studies Institute*. Retrieved from https://blogs.ufv.ca /sasi/2019/01/04/save-the-date-we-are-hockey-an-exhibit-at-the-sikh-heritage -museum/

Sando, M. (2016, July 19). Five signs NFL's Rooney rule isn't working. *ESPN*. Retrieved from http://www.espn.com/nfl/story/_/id/17103070

Sands, R. R. (2002). *Sport ethnography*. Philadelphia, PA: Open University Press.

Sarkar, M., & Fletcher, D. (2014). Psychological resilience in sport performers: A review of stressors and protective factors. *Journal of Sports Sciences, 32*(15), 1419–1434. https://doi.org/10.1080/02640414.2014.901551

Sax, D. (2013, April 26). A Punjabi show draws new hockey fans. *The New York Times*. Retrieved from https://www.nytimes.com/2013/04/28/sports/hockey/chak-de -goal-a-punjabi-show-draws-new-hockey-fans.html

Scherer, J., & Whitson, D. (2009). Public broadcasting, sport, and cultural citizenship: The future of sport on the Canadian Broadcasting Corporation? *International Review for the Sociology of Sport, 44*(2–3), 213–229. https://doi.org/10.1177 /1012690209104798

Schultz, J. (2005). Reading the catsuit: Serena Williams and the production of blackness at the 2002 U.S. Open. *Journal of Sport and Social Issues, 29*(3), 338–358. https://doi.org/10.1177/0193723505276230

Shah, J. (2019a). Episode 33: On Kendall Coyne-Schofield, white feminism in hockey and more. *Stick to Sports* [podcast]. Retrieved from https://soundcloud.com/stick-to -sports/episode-33-on-kendall-coyne-schofield-white-feminism-in-hockey-and-more

———. (2019b). Hockey East investigating racist remark. *College Hockey News*. Retrieved from https://www.collegehockeynews.com/news/2019/03/20_Hockey -East-Investigating.php

Shankar, S. (2015). *Advertising diversity: Ad agencies and the creation of Asian American consumers*. Durham, NC: Duke University Press.

———. (2016). Reflections on sport spectatorship and immigrant life. In S. I. Thangaraj, C. R. Arnaldo Jr., & C. B. Chin (Eds.), *Asian American sports cultures* (pp. 53–74). New York, NY and London, UK: New York University Press.

Sharma, N. T. (2010). *Hip hop desis*. Durham, NC & London, UK: Duke University Press.

Shek, Y. L. (2006). Asian American masculinity: A review of the literature. *The Journal of Men's Studies, 14*(3), 379–391. https://doi.org/10.3149/jms.1403.379

Shoalts, D. (2014, October 10). Hockey Night in Canada: How CBC lost it all. *Globe and Mail*. Retrieved from http://www.theglobeandmail.com/sports/hockey /hockey-night-in-canada-how-cbc-lost-it-all/article21072643/

Sidhu, N. (2012, May 16). CICS collaborates with Abbotsford Heat for hockey game for Vasakhi. Retrieved from http://blogs.ufv.ca/indocanadianstudies/2012/05/16 /cics-collaborates-with-abbotsford-heat-for-hockey-game-for-vasakhi/

Singh, S. (2016, May 10). "@HkyNightPunjabi may have altered my dream to become a sports journalist to becoming a punjabi sports journalist" [Twitter Post]. Retrieved from https://twitter.com/SatbirSingh_/status/730207592933298177

Slade, B. (2002). "Not just 'little ladies' in hockey gear": Hockey experiences in a small town. *Canadian Woman Studies; Downsview, 21*(3), 155–156.

Slotkin, R. (1973). *Regeneration through violence: The mythology of the American frontier, 1600–1860.* Middletown, CT: Wesleyan University Press.

Smith, E. (2007). *Race, sport, and the American dream.* Durham, NC: Carolina Academic Press.

Solnit, R. (2014). *Men explain things to me.* Chicago, IL: Haymarket Books.

Spencer, D. (2019, March 31). CWHL ceasing operations due to "economically unsustainable" business model. *CBC Sports.* Retrieved from https://www.cbc.ca /sports/hockey/cwhl-ceasing-operations-unsustainable-finance-1.5078834

Spivak, G. (1988). Can the subaltern speak? In C. Nelson & L. Grossberg (Eds.), *Marxism and the interpretation of culture* (pp. 271–313). Basingstoke, UK: Macmillan Education.

Sportak, R. (2014, January 23). Calgary Flames first NHL squad to offer coverage in Punjabi. *Calgary Sun.* Retrieved from http://www.calgarysun.com/2014/01/23 /calgary-flames-first-nhl-squad-to-offer-coverage-in-punjabi?utm_source =facebook&utm_medium=recommend-button&utm_campaign=Calgary Flames first NHL squad to offer coverage in Punjabi

Sportsnet. (2019, March 14). Sportsnet, APTN team up for first Cree-language NHL broadcast. Retrieved from https://www.sportsnet.ca/hockey/nhl/sportsnet-aptn -team-first-cree-language-nhl-broadcast/

Statistics Canada. (2006). *British Columbia's farm population: Changes over a lifetime.* Retrieved from https://www.statcan.gc.ca/ca-ra2006/agpop/bc-cb-eng.htm

———. (2007). The South Asian community in Canada. Retrieved from http://www .statcan.gc.ca/pub/89-621-x/89-621-x2007006-eng.htm#11

———. (2012). Surrey, British Columbia (Code 5915004) and Greater Vancouver, British Columbia (Code 5915). Retrieved from http://www12.statcan.gc.ca /census-recensement/2011/dp-pd/prof/details/page.cfm?Lang=E&Geo1 =CSD&Code1=5915004&Geo2=CD&Code2=5915&Data =Count&SearchText=surrey&SearchType=Begins&SearchPR=01&B1 =All&Custom=&TABID=1

———. (2013). Surrey, CY, British Columbia (Code 5915004) (table). National household survey profile. Retrieved from http://www12.statcan.gc.ca/nhs-enm/2011/dp-pd /prof/details/page.cfm?Lang=E&Geo1=CSD&Code1=5915004&Data=Count &SearchText=surrey&SearchType=Begins&SearchPR=01&A1=All&B1=All &Custom=&TABID=1

———. (2016a). Census Profile, 2016 census. Retrieved from https://www12.statcan.gc .ca/census-recensement/2016/dp-pd/prof/details/page.cfm?Lang=E&Geo1=ER &Code1=5920&Geo2=PR&Code2=59&Data=Count&SearchText=Lower%20 Mainland—Southwest&SearchType=Begins&SearchPR=01&B1=All&GeoLevel =PR&GeoCode=5920&TABID=1

———. (2016b). Immigration and ethnocultural diversity in Canada. Retrieved from http://www12.statcan.gc.ca/nhs-enm/2011/as-sa/99-010-x/99-010-x2011001-eng .cfm

Stayman, D., & Deshpande, R. (1989). Situational ethnicity and consumer behavior. *Journal of Consumer Research, 16,* 361–371. https://doi.org/10.1086/209222

Stein, J. G. (2007). Searching for equality. In J. G. Stein, D. R. Cameron, J. Ibbitson, W. Kymlicka, J. Meisel, H. Siddiqui, & M. Valpy, *Uneasy partners: Multiculturalism and rights in Canada* (pp. 1–22). Waterloo, ON: Wilfrid Laurier University Press.

Stevens, J., & Adams, C. (2013). "Together we can make it better": Collective action and governance in a girls' ice hockey association. *International Review for the Sociology of Sport, 48*(6), 658–672. https://doi.org/10.1177/1012690212454466

Stewart, K. F. (2012). *"Mahriaa shot, keeta goal": A critical discourse analysis of media stories about Hockey Night in Canada - Punjabi Edition*. Victoria, Canada: Royal Roads University.

St. Louis, B. (2011). On "the necessity and the 'impossibility' of identities": The politics and ethics of "new ethnicities." In C. Alexander (Ed.), *Stuart Hall and "race"* (pp. 103–126). New York, NY: Routledge.

Sue, D. W. (2010). *Microaggressions in everyday life: Race, gender, and sexual orientation*. Hoboken, NJ: John Wiley and Sons.

Sundstrom, R. (2003). Race and place: Social space in the production of human kinds. *Philosophy and Geography, 6*(1), 83–95. https://doi.org/10.1080/10903770032000063333

Szto, C. (2016). #LOL at multiculturalism: Reactions to *Hockey Night in Canada Punjabi* from the twitterverse. *Sociology of Sport Journal, 33*(3), 208–218. https://doi.org/10.1123/ssj.2015-0160

———. (2018, October 19). The time for women's hockey is now. *Hockey in Society*. Retrieved from https://hockeyinsociety.com/2018/10/19/the-time-for-womens-hockey-is-now/

———. (2019, April 13). Roundtable on racism in hockey—Video. *Hockey in Society*. Retrieved from https://hockeyinsociety.com/2019/04/13/roundtable-on-racism-in-hockey-video/.

Szto, C., & Gruneau, R. (2018). The Hockey Night in Punjabi broadcast: A case study in ethnic sports media. In J. Ellison & J. Anderson (Eds.), *Hockey: Challenging Canada's game* (pp. 199–216). Ottawa, Canada: University of Ottawa Press.

Takagi, A. (2019, January 21). White nationalist group Students for Western Civilization advocates against "multiculturalism" in poster campaign. *The Varsity*. Retrieved from https://thevarsity.ca/2019/01/21/white-nationalist-posters-found-around-utsg/

Takeuchi, C. (2014, June 27). Hate crimes in Canada: Most violent against gays, black people most targeted racial group. *Georgia Straight*. Retrieved from http://www.straight.com/news/675221/hate-crimes-canada-most-violent-against-gays-black-people-most-targeted-racial-group

Tapias, M. (2016). Re-assessing the silent treatment: Emotional expression, preventive health, and the care of others and the self. In V. Broch-Due & B. E. Bertelsen (Eds.), *Violent reverberations: Global modalities of trauma* (pp. 173–191). Cham, CH: Palgrave Macmillan.

Teelucksingh, C. (2006). *Claiming space: Racialization in Canadian cities*. Waterloo, Canada: Wilfrid Laurier University Press. Retrieved from http://site.ebrary.com/lib/alltitles/docDetail.action?docID=10125987

Thangaraj, S. (2013). Competing masculinities: South Asian American identity formation in Asian American basketball leagues. *South Asian Popular Culture, 11*(3), 243–255. https://doi.org/10.1080/14746689.2013.820482

Thangaraj, S. I. (2015). *Desi hoop dreams: Pickup basketball and the making of Asian American masculinity.* New York, NY: NYU Press.

Theberge, N. (1989). Women's athletics and the myth of female frailty. In J. Freeman (Ed.), *Women: A feminist perspective* (4th ed.). Mountain View, CA: Mayfield.

———. (1997). "It's part of the game": Physicality and the production of gender in women's hockey. *Gender & Society, 11*(1), 69–87. https://doi.org/10.1177 /08912439701100105

———. (2000). *Higher goals: Women's ice hockey and the politics of gender.* Albany, NY: State University of New York.

———. (2003). "No fear comes": Adolescent girls, ice hockey, and embodiment of gender. *Youth & Society, 34*(4), 497–516. https://doi.org/10.1177 /0044118X03034004005

Thobani, S. (2007). *Exalted subjects: Studies in the making of race and nation in Canada.* Toronto, Canada: University of Toronto Press.

Thompson, D. (2009). Racial ideas and gendered intimacies: The regulation of interracial relationships in North America. *Social & Legal Studies, 18*(3), 353–371. https://doi.org/10.1177/0964663909339087

Tierney, K. (2015). Resilience and the neoliberal project: Discourses, critiques, practices—and Katrina. *American Behavioral Scientist, 59*(10), 1327–1342. https:// doi.org/10.1177/0002764215591187

Todd, D. (2014, March 28). *Vancouver is the most "Asian" city outside of Asia.* Retrieved from https://passport2017.ca/widget/

———. (2017, September 1). Douglas Todd: Immigrants could prosper in Canada's small towns. *Vancouver Sun.* Retrieved from http://vancouversun.com/opinion /columnists/douglas-todd-immigrants-could-prosper-in-canadas-small-towns

Tootoo, J. (2014). *All the way: My life on ice.* Toronto, Canada: Penguin.

Toronto Police Service. (2015). *Toronto Police Service 2015 annual hate/bias crime statistical report.* Retrieved from https://www.torontopolice.on.ca/publications /files/reports/2015hatecrimereport.pdf

Truth and Reconciliation Commission of Canada (2015a). *The Survivors Speak.* Retrieved from http://trc.ca/assets/pdf/Survivors_Speak_English_Web.pdf

———. (2015b). *Truth and Reconciliation Commission of Canada: Calls to action.* Retrieved from http://www.trc.ca/websites/trcinstitution/File/2015/Findings /Calls_to_Action_English2.pdf

Tyakoff, A. (n.d.). South Asian-based group crime in British Columbia: (1993–2003) Focus Groups Report: Review of findings. *Department of Canadian Heritage.* Retrieved from http://epe.lac-bac.gc.ca/100/200/301/pwgsc-tpsgc/por-ef/canadian _heritage/2002/2002-529-e.pdf

United Nations. (2004, November 5). Universal language of sport brings people together, teaches teamwork, tolerance, secretary-general says at launch of international year. Retrieved from http://www.un.org/press/en/2004/sgsm9579.doc.htm

United Sikhs. (n.d.). About Sikhs. Retrieved from http://www.unitedsikhs.org /aboutsikhs.php

Vaidhyanathan, S. (2000). Inside a "model minority": The complicated identity of South Asians. *Chronicle of Higher Education, 46*(42), B4–B7.

Valentine, J. (2012). New racism and old stereotypes in the National Hockey League: The "stacking" of Aboriginal players into the role of enforcer. In J. Joseph, S.

Darnell, & Y. Nakamura (Eds.), *Race and Sport in Canada* (pp. 107–135). Toronto, Canada: Canadian Scholars' Press.

Varma-Joshi, M., Baker, C., & Tanaka, C. (2004). Names will never hurt me? *Harvard Educational Review, 74*(2), 175–208. https://doi.org/10.17763/haer.74.2 .p077712755767067

Vega, J., & Boele van Hensbroek, P. (Eds.). (2012). *Cultural citizenship in political theory.* London, UK: Routledge.

Ventresca, M. (2016). *Mo bros: Masculinity, irony and the rise of Movember.* (Doctoral dissertation, Queen's University).

Vesselinov, E. (2008). Members only: Gated communities and residential segregation in the metropolitan United States. *Sociological Form, 23*(3), 536–555. https://doi.org /10.1111/j.1573-7861.2008.00075.x

Walton-Roberts, M. (2003). Transnational geographies: Indian immigration to Canada. *Canadian Geographer / Le Géographe Canadien, 47*(3), 235–250. https:// doi.org/10.1111/1541-0064.00020

Walton-Roberts, M., & Pratt, G. (2005). Mobile modernities: A South Asian family negotiates immigration, gender and class in Canada. *Gender, Place & Culture, 12*(2), 173–195. https://doi.org/10.1080/09663690500094823

Weiler, A. M., Dennis, J. E., & Wittman, H. (2014). *Growing good agricultural jobs in British Columbia* (p. 25). Retrieved from https://www.policyalternatives.ca/sites /default/files/uploads/publications/WorkingPaper_WeilerDennisWittman _GoodJobsConf.pdf

Wendell, S. (1996). *The rejected body: Feminist philosophical reflections on disability.* New York, NY: Routledge.

Whitson, D., & Gruneau, R. S. (Eds.). (2006). *Artificial ice: hockey, culture, and commerce.* Peterborough, Canada: Garamond Press.

WHL. (2015). *Western Hockey League official rules 2015–2016.* Retrieved from http:// whl.uploads.s3.amazonaws.com/chl_whl/2015/11/30/2015-2016_Rulebook.pdf

Williams, M. (1995). Women's hockey: Heating up the equity debate. *Canadian Woman Studies; Downsview, 15*(4), 78–81.

Williams, R. (1958/2011). Culture is Ordinary. In I. Szeman & T. Kaopsy (Eds.), *Cultural Theory: An anthology* (pp. 53–59). Malden, MA: Wiley-Blackwell.

Wolpe, H. (1972). Capitalism and cheap labour-power in South Africa: From segregation to apartheid. *Economy and Society, 1*(4), 425–456. https://doi.org/10 .1080/03085147200000023

Wong, L. L. (1993). Immigration as capital accumulation: The impact of business immigration to Canada. *International Migration, 31*(1), 171–190. https://doi.org/10 .1111/j.1468-2435.1993.tb00723.x

Worthington, P. (2011, September 6). CBC's tax dollars cost Canadians too much. Retrieved from http://www.huffingtonpost.ca/peter-worthington/cbc-tax-dollars _b_950656.html

Wortley, S., & Tanner, J. (2006). Immigration, situation défavorisée sur le plan social et bandes de jeunes dans les villes: Résultats d'un sondage mené dans la région de Toronto. *Canadian Journal of Urban Research, 15*(2), 21–45. https://www.jstor.org /stable/26192512

Yep, K. S. (2012). Linsanity and centering sport in Asian American Studies and Pacific Islander Studies. *Amerasia Journal, 38*(3), 133–137. doi:10.17953/ amer.38.3.c6423501kt300ljp

Yu, S. (2016). Instrumentalization of ethnic media. *Canadian Journal of Communication, 41*(2), 334–352. https://doi.org/10.22230/cjc.2016v41n2a3019

Yu, S. S., & Murray, C. A. (2007). Ethnic media under a multicultural policy: The case of the Korean media in British Columbia. *Canadian Ethnic Studies; Calgary, 39*(3), 99–124. doi:10.1353/ces.0.0054

Yuval-Davis, N. (2011). *The politics of belonging: Intersectional contestations*. London, UK: Sage.

Zuurbier, P. (2016). Cultivating distinction through hockey as commodity. In D. Taras & C. Waddell (eds.), *How Canadians communicate V: Sports* (pp. 247–266). Edmonton, AB: Athabasca Press.

Index

Figures are indicated by page numbers in italics

About the Author

COURTNEY SZTO is an assistant professor in the School of Kinesiology and Health Studies at Queen's University in Kingston, Ontario, Canada. Her research focuses on intersections of injustice as they pertain to sports and physical activity. She is the senior editor for the blog *Hockey in Society*. You can find her at the rink, in the gym, or on a mountain.